Praise for *The Rise and Fall of the Department for International Development*

"For 20 years, DFID transformed Britain's position in the world and changed for the better the lives of millions of the world's poorest people. Reaching for a time the global goal of 0.7 percent of GDP on aid, Britain led the world on global health, education, and climate change. The story not just of this unique period but of the continuing relevance of the path-breaking thinking that lay behind it is told with precision, eloquence and passion by leaders in this journey, Mark Lowcock and Ranil Dissanayake."
—*Gordon Brown*

"DFID was widely admired globally, and its demise much lamented. The story of its life and its distinctive contribution to improving the lives of many of the world's poorest people—which Mark Lowcock and Ranil Dissanayake have set out in a dispassionate, insightful and convincing way—provides important inspiration to the new British government as they consider their role now in dealing with the world's urgent problems."
—*Helen Clark*

"DFID was an important partner to the Gates Foundation. It is also a vital part of the UK's great history as a global leader in international development, not just being generous with aid but also making sure it goes where it will have the most impact. This book serves as an important reminder that the world has made incredible progress improving lives of the poorest people—and can do so again."
—*Bill Gates*

"DFID was one of New Labour's proudest achievements. Its destruction was an act of wanton vandalism. If we want to hold our heads high in the world again, it (or something very similar) will need to be rebuilt."
—*Chris Mullin*

"We talk quite a lot about Britain's soft power and should recognise that one of the best examples of this over the years has been the Overseas Development Programme. It was very good news when this programme became the responsibility of an independent ministry—DFID—and was able to combine its highly professional development goals with a growing budget. When this budget was cut and the ministry was closed and rolled into the existing Foreign Office, Britain lost a huge international asset. All those who read this book will, I am sure, be convinced that it would be an excellent idea for the new Labour government to re-establish the independent Department which was so admired around the world."
—*Chris Patten*

"Over two decades of working closely with DFID colleagues, I watched in admiration as the Department grew into a major component of British soft power, a globally respected thought leader on development policy and a driving force for poverty reduction. DFID also pioneered partnerships with Britain's armed forces and diplomats in tackling the conflicts and poor governance which were often at the root of poverty. This is a powerful and deeply researched account of a noble and sustained effort to treat international development not just as a national interest, but a moral responsibility. It deserves to be read by anyone with an interest in the making of public policy and the scope for governments to be a force for good in the world."
—*Peter Ricketts*

"This is much more than an excellent history of DFID. It is a story of how the thinking and practice of development evolved over the most impactful period of poverty reduction in history. Read it and you will feel inspired at what the combination of political leadership, clarity of vision, and good management can achieve."
—*Minouche Shafik*

THE RISE AND FALL OF THE DEPARTMENT FOR INTERNATIONAL DEVELOPMENT

The Rise and Fall of the Department for International Development

Mark Lowcock
Ranil Dissanayake

CGD CENTER FOR GLOBAL DEVELOPMENT

Copyright © 2024
CENTER FOR GLOBAL DEVELOPMENT
Washington, DC and London
www.cgdev.org

All rights reserved. No part of this publication may be reproduced or transmitted in any form or by any means without permission in writing from the Center for Global Development.

British Library Cataloguing in Publication Data.
A catalogue record for this book is available from the British Library.

Library of Congress Control Number: 2024937102
ISBN 978-1-944691-13-4
ISBN 978-1-944691-14-1 (ebook)
ISBN 978-1-944691-15-8 (paperback)

CONTENTS

List of Figures and Tables	vii
Introduction	1

PART I
SETTING THE COMPASS: 1997-2003

1	Why Labour Created DFID	7
2	Policy, Money, and Organisation	26
3	Whitehall and the International System	56
4	"Clare's New World"? The Verdict on the Short Years	82

PART II
DELIVERING ON THE JOB: 2003-10

5	The Policy Evolves, the Budget Grows, and DFID's Reputation Blossoms	95
6	Crises and Summits	119
7	Lives Getting Better: How DFID Made a Difference	130

CONTENTS

PART III
HEADWINDS SLOW PROGRESS: 2010-16

8 The Problem Gets Harder   159
9 Old Wine, New Bottles   170
10 Better Lives: Reprise   187

PART IV
FALL: 2016-20 AND BEYOND

11 The Last Gasp   213
12 "The Writing Is on the Wall"   225
13 Aftermath   235
14 Eliminating World Poverty?   251

Acknowledgements   263

Appendix A. Secretaries of State and Permanent Secretaries 1997–2020   265

Appendix B. Trends in Global Development Indicators   267

Appendix C. UK ODA and DFID Spending 1997–2020   271

Abbreviations   279

Notes   281

Bibliography   317

Index   333

FIGURES AND TABLES

Figures

Figure 1.1. Timeline of overseas development arrangements, 1964–79   10

Figure 2.1. Inflation and GDP per capita growth, sub-Saharan Africa 1980–2000   28

Figure 3.1. Deaths in state-based conflicts by world region: Direct deaths of both military personal and civilians, attributed to world regions according to location of the conflict   59

Figure 3.2. Net ODA from DAC countries 1980–2005   73

Figure 4.1. Inflation and GDP per capita growth, sub-Saharan Africa 1980–2015   83

Figure 4.2. Human Development Index 1997–2003   85

Figure 6.1. Net ODA from DAC countries 2000–2010   125

Figure 7.1. Human Development Index 2003–2010   152

Figure A.1. GNI per capita (current US$) for focus countries, 2000–20   267

Figure A.2. Life expectancy at birth for focus countries, 2000–20   268

FIGURES AND TABLES

Figure A.3. Mortality rate, under five (per 1,000 live births) for focus countries, 2000–20 — 269

Figure A.4. Human Development Index 1997–2020 — 270

Tables

Table 1.1. DAC Development Goals — 19

Table 2.1. Extracts from DFID Public Service Agreements 1999–2006: Performance measures — 36

Table 2.2. DFID budget and UK ODA 1997/98 and 2002/03 — 42

Table 5.1. DFID budget and UK ODA 2003/04 and 2009/10 — 101

Table 5.2. Cumulative growth in DFID aid in focus countries — 103

Table 9.1. DFID budget and UK ODA 2010/11–2015/16 — 182

Table 10.1. How DFID's spending power increased between 1997–2002 and 2010–16 — 188

Table 11.1. DFID budget and UK ODA 2016–20 — 221

Table A.1. UK ODA and DFID spending 1997/98–2002/03 — 271

Table A.2. UK ODA and DFID spending 2003/04–2009/10 — 272

Table A.3. UK ODA and DFID spending 2010/11–2016/17 — 274

Table A.4. UK ODA and DFID spending 2017/18–2020/21 — 276

Introduction

THE CLUE is in the name. When the Blair government created the Department for International Development – DFID (note the capital F) – they were sending a message. This was a government that was *for* international development. They believed that helping poorer countries was a moral responsibility. More than that, though, they thought that if these countries developed, the result would be a world that was better for everyone else too – richer, fairer, and safer for all.

It was not ever thus. DFID's history, from its establishment in 1997 to its abolition in 2020, is book-ended by governments that did not entirely share that view. The Thatcher and Major governments from 1979 to 1997 included some people who thought international development was, at least on balance, desirable. But there were others who were more sceptical, who feared the loss of influence that might follow for the UK, and who worried that some of these newly prosperous countries might harbour ambitions or opinions injurious to Britain. Most of the leading voices in these governments were willing to support progress in countries they thought might remain or become allies, or who shared a similar world view – democracies, with market-based economies, and a commitment to the rule of law and fundamental human freedoms as set out in the UN Charter. They thought a modest overseas aid programme could help with that, as well as being useful for lubricating Britain's commercial and political interests. They recognised, too, that their citizens – like those of their key international allies – believed rich countries had a moral responsibility to help relieve extreme suffering elsewhere, especially in the case of famines, floods, or other humanitarian catastrophes. A limited aid programme was needed for that purpose too. But all this was an optional extra, not a core governing objective.

And at the other end of the story, the most influential voices in the government led by Boris Johnson from 2019, hailing from the right of the Conservative Party, believed like their predecessors of the 1980s and 1990s that immediate British national interests should determine how the nation engaged with the rest of the world. They set themselves up in opposition to others – most notoriously the European Union (EU) and its member states – and believed the UK was more influential, respected, and listened to than it was. They liked to talk about international leadership and Global Britain. Their hubris made the UK a laughingstock on the world stage. One thing they knew was that they did not want a Department for International Development. So they abolished it.

The most important fact about DFID, however, under both Conservative- and Labour-led governments, was not that it was charged with supporting international development broadly or as a general principle. DFID had the more precise mandate to make poverty history: to work to eliminate the most severe, life-long human suffering across the planet.

Such extreme poverty is the condition in which people have exceptionally low incomes, are frequently hungry, live lives decades shorter than others, commonly watch their children die in infancy, often do not survive pregnancy and childbirth, drink dirty water, do not have access to modern sanitation, cannot see their children through a decent basic education, and generally exercise few rights or freedoms. These features have characterised the lives of most people across the world throughout human history. As late as 1960, the majority of the world's population still lived in such poverty.

From the 1990s the extreme poverty line was defined by the World Bank as an income of no more than a dollar a day.[1] In 1998, 1,870 million people, 31 per cent of the global population, were below that poverty line. Current estimates suggest that in 2023 it was

INTRODUCTION

690 million, or 9 per cent of the population.[2] Or to put that another way, in 1998 about 4 billion people in the world were not living in extreme poverty, but by 2023 that number had grown to about 7 billion. And they were living longer. There were major gains in life expectancy over this period, and by 2023 the parents of newborns in poor countries could realistically expect that their babies would probably live full lives, into their sixties and beyond. In no other quarter century of human history has life improved so much for so many. This book explains DFID's role in that improvement.

Part I (Setting the Compass) recaps the history of Britain's previous institutional arrangements, explains how Labour came to create DFID and how the department then set about its task up to 2003, when Clare Short, who had been the secretary of state since 1997, left her role.

Part II (Delivering on the Job) covers the period from 2003 to 2010, when DFID entered its heyday, during which its contribution to the goals it was mandated to pursue started to peak. Between 2003 and 2013, the proportion of the global population in extreme poverty fell by 14 percentage points, which is probably more than in any other ten-year period. We detail what DFID did in those years to contribute to that result. This period also saw the emergence for the first time of a cross-party political consensus in the UK that Britain should seek to play a leading role in international development and the elimination of poverty.

Part III (Headwinds Slow Progress) covers the years of David Cameron's Conservative-led premiership from 2010 to 2016. Much of DFID's previous contribution was sustained in these years, but growing conflict in many of the poorest countries and heightened geopolitical tensions meant it was gradually more difficult to sustain the previous rate of progress. Meanwhile, domestic criticism of the priority the government was attaching to international development became louder and more insistent.

Part IV (Fall) deals with DFID's decline, its abolition, and the immediate aftermath, and considers what might happen next. From

INTRODUCTION

2013 to 2023 the international development juggernaut slowed: the global poverty rate is estimated to have fallen by only 3 percentage points in that whole decade. At the end of the period, in the wake of COVID-19, the Ukraine war, and deepening economic problems, poverty in some countries was increasing, with earlier gains unravelling.

Daunting challenges now lie ahead. The new government, which is still in the early stages of developing its plans after the election in July 2024, has important decisions to make over the role they want Britain to play internationally and the institutional arrangements they put in place. We have set out some proposals in the final chapter in the hope of helping those responsible to make good choices.

PART ONE

Setting the Compass

1997–2003

ONE

Why Labour Created DFID

IN THE early hours of 2 May 1997, the vote count in the Birmingham, Ladywood constituency confirmed what everyone knew: Clare Short would be returned to Parliament with a massive majority.[1] But before long, fuelled by a story in *The Sun*, rumours were swirling about whether or not she would be included in the new prime minister Tony Blair's first Cabinet. In order to avoid calls from journalists, Short turned off her phone. She went back to London, attending a birthday party for her brother in the evening.[2]

The Sun was wrong: later that night, phone back on, Short saw missed calls from 10 Downing Street. Calling back, she was asked to come in the next morning, a Saturday. On the way, she spoke to John Vereker, then permanent secretary for the Overseas Development Administration, the aid wing of the Foreign Office. His advice was simple: don't leave the room without agreement to a new department covering international development. At the end of the meeting – attended by Blair, Short, and Blair's chief of staff, Jonathan Powell, and media chief, Alastair Campbell – Short climbed into a government car for the short journey to meet her new senior officials in their Victoria Street offices. Meanwhile, Vereker took a call from Number 10: "It's a separate department, but everything else is a bit of a muddle." Vereker and Richard Calvert, Short's new principal private secretary, were tasked with resolving the details with Number 10. That included agreeing a name. Campbell wanted to avoid the media headaches a department abbreviated or pronounced as "DID"

CHAPTER 1

(Department of International Development) or "DIED" (Department of International Economic Development) would present. Vereker's concern was that "DFID" would be pronounced "Diffid", like the Welsh region (Dyfed) – not, as he put it, the sound of a serious arm of government.[3] Campbell won that argument, and DFID was born. The name was the least of its early worries. Facing hostility from the Foreign Office, the new department needed quickly to set out its stall – its purpose and role in the Whitehall machinery. It made a claim for important government functions, fighting the Treasury for the right to provide the UK's executive director to the World Bank, and soon secured agreement to publish a White Paper setting government policy.[4]

Labour governments since the 1960s had usually created development departments and there was a commitment from mid-1996 onwards that they would do so again. But the fight to make sure it happened, and the work to turn the "bit of a muddle" which was agreed in that meeting in Number 10 into a functioning department, was critical in setting up what was to become one of the world's most important development actors over the next two decades. Creating a department for international development with the form and function it eventually developed was not remotely inevitable – the Overseas Development Administration, which it replaced, was, though very small, with only around 1,600 staff, generally considered effective;[5] and there were no immediate plans to increase its budget beyond the £2 billion (roughly 0.2 per cent of gross national income (GNI)) it inherited. The effort to create an effective and powerful development organisation was intentional, and hard won. And much of that itself stemmed from why and how the Labour Party came to the decision to establish a standalone department, headed by Clare Short as a Cabinet minister reporting directly to the prime minister, from day one of their time in power.

Previous accounts addressing this question have tended to focus on the history: Labour governments, going back to 1964, typically elevated the priority given to international development, while Conservative administrations had consistently subjugated it. Labour in 1997 was indeed conscious of the history. But they were acutely aware that the responsibilities, form, and structure of what would become DFID needed to be decided, and a wide range of outcomes was possible. Three other considerations, beyond what previous Labour governments had done, were germane: the signal Labour wanted to send by creating the new department; the politics around its creation and Clare Short's appointment; and the goals the key players in DFID's creation wanted to pursue. This last issue was the biggest factor: Clare Short had a thought-through strategy, the successful pursuit of which she judged much more likely if she could lead it from a position inside the Cabinet while running her own department. Much of what became DFID followed from this; indeed, as we will see in later chapters, Short's initial vision influenced how DFID worked (and its challenges) well beyond her tenure or even the Labour Party's time in government.

This chapter considers each of these four factors (history, signal, politics, and strategy) in turn, and how they each shaped the creation of DFID and the UK's role in international development.

The institutional history

Looking back on the run up to the creation of DFID in 1997, those involved tend now to tell two stories: first that it was simply "in Labour's DNA" to uplift development and give it a separate voice in government, and second that the creation of DFID was very much about the circumstances of the moment. Both are true, and less of a contradiction than appears at first sight.

In the 50 years from the early 1960s, Labour governments tended to have independent development departments, while Conservative governments consistently made development subsidiary to foreign policy, answerable to, or part of, the Foreign Office. However, there is more nuance to this story than a pendulum swinging between binary points of "independent" and "not" (See Figure 1.1). Both Labour

CHAPTER 1

Figure 1.1. Timeline of overseas development arrangements, 1964–79

Separate Department, Ministers in Cabinet	Separate Department, Ministers Outside Cabinet	No Separate Department, Ministers Outside Cabinet	Separate Department, Ministerial Status Varied
Barbara Castle (1964–65)	Reginald Prentice (1967–69)	Richard Wood (1970–74)	Judith Hart (1974–75, outside)
Anthony Greenwood (1965–66)	Judith Hart (1969–70)		Reginald Prentice (1975–76, in Cabinet)
Arthur Bottomley (1966–67)			Frank Judd (1976–77, outside)
			Judith Hart (1977–79, outside)

1964 — 1967 — 1970 — 1974 — 1979

Source: Barder 2005 and Ireton 2013.

and Conservative governments appointed ministers responsible for international development; variation was found in the specific institutional form development work was organised in, and the specific standing of the ministers responsible.[6]

Under Labour, the first three ministers of Overseas Development in the 1960s – Barbara Castle, Anthony Greenwood, and Arthur Bottomley – were all part of the Cabinet (and it is worth noting that the then prime minister, Harold Wilson, had in the 1950s written a number of pieces on world poverty and international aid, about which he was well informed and passionate).[7] But none was long in post. The first served for less than a year and the last just over two years; none was particularly influential in the role.[8] Subsequent Labour ministers up to 1970 were not in the Cabinet (though the Overseas Development Ministry remained a separate government department). With a Conservative government in 1970 came the further demotion of the role: Richard Wood, holding the post of minister for International Development for four years, did not attend Cabinet and the development function of government was once again brought under the Foreign Office.

With the return of Labour to power, a separate department was again created in 1974.[9] Four different ministers headed it over the next five years: but only one, Reg Prentice, sat in the Cabinet. In

1975, the development department was again made answerable to the Foreign and Commonwealth Office (FCO): Prentice sat in the Cabinet as minister *for* Overseas Development, but the foreign secretary was minister *of* Overseas Development and hence exercised the parliamentary powers of that office.

Frank Judd, minister for Overseas Development briefly from December 1976 to February 1977, reported through the foreign secretary. His successor, Judith Hart, served three different terms as minister for Overseas Development but never, in that role, in the Cabinet. Described as a "firebrand",[10] she was charismatic and driven. She tried (unsuccessfully) to get the government to implement the new United Nations (UN) target of 0.7 per cent of national income going to foreign aid. She ensured that it was mentioned in the Labour election manifesto and won a limited budget increase in 1974 against strong Treasury resistance. She championed more help for the poorest (on which, as noted below, a White Paper incorporating many of her words was published in 1975 while she was in another role). Less positively, she established the Aid and Trade Provision, a ring-fenced fund linking aid to UK exports.[11] She also was regarded by some as a security risk; and she had a tendency to antagonise her colleagues (for example, by visiting Mozambique to establish an aid programme there and telling the foreign secretary only after she returned).[12]

It is also important to recognise that the impact of the Labour government on global development in the mid-1970s was inevitably affected by the domestic situation. Acute economic and fiscal pressures affected Britain's international role and reputation, most visibly when in 1976 a balance of payments crisis forced the country to seek assistance from the International Monetary Fund (IMF).

Margaret Thatcher's election in 1979 saw the establishment of the Overseas Development Administration, again answerable to the Foreign Office and led by a minister outside of Cabinet. From 1979 to 1997 Britain's contribution to global development was progressively eroded, both through years of real-terms budget cuts but also through the choices made over what to use the limited remaining budget for.[13]

CHAPTER 1

In short, the Conservatives consistently demoted international development institutionally; though Labour usually gave it greater standing, what "greater standing" actually meant varied considerably. Critically, it was historically rather rare (before 1997) that the UK's development arrangements benefitted from both a separate institution, with specific development objectives and expertise, and being headed by a secretary of state in the Cabinet (or even a minister of state attending Cabinet). In the UK system the precise status of a minister has particular importance in the setting of broader policy: a secretary of state in the Cabinet can effectively advocate for their portfolio and can be overruled only by the prime minister. A minister of state (whether they attend Cabinet or not, and whether or not they notionally run their own institution) must typically first make representations to a secretary of state (in this case, the foreign secretary).

In his personal reflections on the history of the UK's international development efforts, John Vereker points out that while Labour's early efforts signalled a seriousness to its work on international development in the form of an independent department under Castle, Greenwood, and Bottomley it was really more a vestige of the old Colonial Office, with the attitudes and paternalistic approach that suggests:[14]

My first boss had been a District Officer in Kenya. My first Permanent Secretary had spent the previous five years governing Uganda. And the already minuscule budget was under constant threat, thanks to the UK's recurrent economic crises of the 60s and 70s. So the Department developed a touching faith in the effectiveness of dreaming up in London a range of small interventions regardless of the wider economic and political circumstances of the recipient. At the top of the office there was a strong sense that London knew best, that self-determination would probably prove disastrous, and that while we could help countries develop, there really wasn't much we could do about poverty ... Aid was almost invariably tied to the purchase of British goods and services. Sometimes this descended into farce. I recall being instructed to use my budget to supply British instruments for a brass band in Guayaquil so they could perform during Princess Anne's honeymoon in Ecuador, on her way to the Galapagos. No one could pretend that this was a model form of development aid.

The arrangements were less clearly delineated between Labour and Conservative governments than is commonly supposed; and it is clear that much was imperfect throughout the 1964–97 period. An equally mixed picture emerges when we look at the ethos and strategic approach of the government with respect to development. A great deal of effort and ink was used in establishing the intellectual and political foundations of the UK approach to aid and development.[15] The policy direction under Conservative governments tended to focus on UK interests and the economic development of developing countries (which was seen as an economic and commercial opportunity for the UK, and not restricted to the poorest places). In 1960, before the establishment of a separate department, a Treasury White Paper was published arguing that economic development in poor countries was the best way of lifting people out of poverty; a 1963 White Paper argued that aid was both a good thing in and of itself and would help the UK increase its global trade. After 1979, in the Thatcher years, no White Paper was published, but the policy direction – stated in Parliament – was for a stronger focus on UK interests, greater use of the Aid and Trade Provision,[16] and the pursuit of UK commercial interests. That government contained people who even questioned whether it was in Britain's interests for poorer countries to develop, for fear that their doing so could undermine the UK's global influence, or that they may form views potentially harmful to the UK.

By contrast, under Labour, a 1965 White Paper argued that aid was a moral necessity and in the long-term UK interest. And in 1975, a new White Paper argued for a focus on the poorest places, where aid would have the greatest impact on alleviating poverty – a genuinely new commitment to poverty reduction and how effectiveness should be judged.[17]

The historical argument that Labour was bound to create DFID is thus too simple; 1997 was effectively the first time the UK had a separate government department for development, headed by a secretary of state in the Cabinet, with a clearly stated focus on reducing global poverty. Even if it was to be expected that Labour would change the Thatcherite arrangements that had stood since 1979, history provided no clear guide as to what the new arrangements would look like.

Signalling Labour's approach would be different

Labour wanted, in the run up to the 1997 election, to use its stance on development to send a signal. By 1995, most observers thought they would form the next government. The polls predicted a landslide victory; senior officials of that era suggest that Lynda Chalker – the minister with responsibility for international development from 1989 to 1997 – herself expected a Labour government.[18] Some of Labour's attention shifted in the year before the election to how they might govern, and how they would distinguish themselves from the unpopular administration they were hoping to replace.

By 1997, the Conservatives faced three severe political problems. The first was the fallout from Black Wednesday in 1992, when the UK crashed out of the European Exchange Rate Mechanism following a run on sterling. That cratered the Conservatives' reputation as the 'safe stewards' of the economy, making economic management genuinely contested political ground for the first time in a generation. (Labour's claim that it was now the party of sound economic management meant bending over backwards to avoid being painted as spendthrift. As part of this, Gordon Brown, the shadow chancellor, committed to maintaining for the first few years of any Labour government the very low planned levels of public spending that the Conservatives had laid out in 1997.)[19]

Secondly, John Major, the Conservative prime minister, was fighting an internal battle in his party. The Conservatives were riven by political divisions, most obviously on European issues. He was battling the Eurosceptic wing of his party, specifically over the Maastricht treaty and the UK's response to it.

Thirdly, the Conservatives were dogged by questions about their probity and fitness for public office. This happened on a personal level, as when Neil Hamilton, a prominent Conservative MP and former minister, was found to have accepted bribes in exchange for asking questions in Parliament.[20] But these concerns touched on formal government policy, too, and in ways that were particularly pertinent for foreign and development policy. The Scott Inquiry into the sale of arms to Iraq – sales that breached government guidelines with knowledge of these contraventions running to the top of government – began in 1992, concluding in 1996. Its report was a damning indictment of the government's mode of operation: secretive, incompetent, and willing to bend or break rules in support of short-term commercial or political gain. It did not stand in isolation, either. The government had already lost a hugely damaging and embarrassing court case in 1994: the Pergau dam case.[21]

Pergau dam remains the most notorious use of aid in UK history.[22] The Overseas Development Administration, answering to then foreign secretary Douglas Hurd,[23] used £234 million of aid money to fund a hydroelectric dam on the Pergau river in Malaysia. It was not considered an economically viable enterprise, and the money was linked to, and alleged to be a sweetener for, a £1 billion sale of arms from the UK to the Malaysian government – something that a number of ministers and officials objected to at the time.[24] When the World Development Movement brought a case against the government, Hurd was found to have acted unlawfully in approving the project. Officials recalling this period have different views on precisely why it was unlawful: whether because the project was not economically viable and therefore not "developmental"; or because it was approved not on its development merits, as required by the 1980 Overseas Development and Co-operation Act, but because of the link to arms sales. Nevertheless, the key point is that there was apprehension about the project at the time, and the government's increasingly desperate attempts to extricate itself from the political and legal difficulties it created made for a terrible press and the strong sense that the aid budget was being badly misused.[25]

In the run up to 1997, Labour was therefore doing all it could to present the party as a clean alternative to the Conservatives: a party that could be trusted with the economy; a party united, with agreement on the biggest issues; and a party of probity, who would run the government effectively and in good faith. That all played a role in shaping the form that DFID would eventually take.

Some people have suggested that Labour's attempt to distinguish themselves from the scandal-hit Conservatives directly affected the nature of the development department it proposed. Certainly Robin Cook, Labour's foreign affairs spokesman, was forensic and persistent in Parliament in criticising the government for presiding over scandals and pledging that Labour would be different, and, as we will come on to, he played a significant role in the creation of DFID. Similarly, David Miliband[26] recalls that "we ran a lot harder on 'no more Pergaus' than on ending world poverty", suggesting that one of the reasons behind the creation of an independent, development-focused DFID with a strong professionalised approach to its work was to draw a line under the murky past of British foreign aid.[27]

All of this meant that Labour was trying to signal clear differences with the Tory party it was seeking to replace as government. The form, content, and leadership of its development arrangements might be seen as a direct part of this signalling operation.[28]

Labour's internal politics

There were other political considerations reflecting internal party dynamics too. As the 1997 election neared, Labour wanted to signal a unity of purpose, and efforts to this end were important for the creation of DFID. In 1996, they established a process through which to iron out their approach to international affairs – foreign policy, defence and security, and development. A policy review was undertaken, chaired by Robin Cook as the shadow foreign secretary. The product was a published report, *Britain in the World*.

The report committed Labour to "transform the Overseas Development Administration (ODA) into the Department of International Development (DID), to be headed by a Cabinet minister".[29] A wide range of additional, in some cases quite detailed, policy commitments were set out giving flesh to the intent to ensure a stronger focus on poverty reduction, many of which were later taken up by the Blair and Brown governments. Some of the key policy proposals then found their way into Labour's manifesto for the 1997 election. The manifesto reiterated the commitment to spending more on poverty and in the poorest places. It said Labour "affirm the UK's commitment to the 0.7 percent UN aid target" and would "in government start to reverse the decline in UK aid spending".[30]

This amounts to a completely different approach to that of the government. The prioritisation of poverty was a call-back to the pre-Thatcher years, but this time paired with a Cabinet minister with their own department. An emphasis on effectiveness implied that the primary consideration for aid programmes will be how good they are at reducing poverty, not the political, economic, or commercial return to the UK. And the aid budget would in time grow, reversing many years of Conservative cuts. All this chimed with long-standing Labour values.

As always, personalities also played an important role. Between 1992 and 1997, Labour had four different shadow ministers for international development: Michael Meacher, Tom Clarke, Joan Lestor, and Clare Short.[31] In July 1996, Joan Lestor, a charismatic and popular figure on the left of the party, who had been in the Shadow Cabinet for three years and in the development brief for two, announced that she would not be standing at the next general election, and left the Shadow Cabinet.[32] That created a vacancy. Tony Blair asked Clare Short, who had first been elected to the Shadow Cabinet the previous year and was initially appointed to the transport brief, to move across. Her initial reaction was negative. She was enjoying transport and thought she was being asked to move because the leadership were unhappy about some of her public statements (on legalising drugs, the desirability of wealthier people paying more tax, and tensions over whether to renationalise the railways).[33] But on reflection, she decided had she been offered international development over transport earlier, she would have taken it, so accepted the switch.[34]

This proved momentous. Short was a darling of the party membership (partly because she took positions popular with them but less on-message with the centrist stance Blair and Brown were staking out for electoral reasons). She was also popular with Labour MPs. In the 1996 Shadow Cabinet elections she came third, ahead of many of the heavyweights, including Brown and Cook.[35] She was exceptionally bright, with a strategic, inquiring mind, determined to pursue a strategy when she had decided upon it, and more than happy to fight her corner against all-comers. What's more, with Blair and Brown keen to demonstrate that Labour was a party united (unlike the Conservatives), putting Short in the development brief made a watering down of the commitments in the 1996 policy review more difficult: alienating her would make conflict between the left and centre of the party much more likely.

Short decides

Clare Short had followed foreign affairs since being elected to Parliament in 1983, and attended meetings on the review which led to the publication of *Britain in the World*.[36] She rapidly immersed herself in her new role, reading and consulting widely. She quickly became passionate and knowledgeable. And she soon decided what she wanted to do. She read a new report by the Development Assistance Committee (DAC) of the Organisation for Economic Co-operation and Development (OECD), "Shaping the 21st Century",[37] and decided to make achieving its proposals the focus of her efforts.

The DAC report took as its starting point agreements reached in UN conferences since 1990 ("the great UN conferences of the 1990s").[38] They covered education (Jomtien, 1990), children (New York, 1990), the environment (Rio de Janeiro, 1992), human rights (Vienna, 1993), population (Cairo, 1994), poverty and social development (Copenhagen, 1995), and women (Beijing, 1995). Each adopted goals and targets for global progress. The fact that the DAC started with UN agreements was important to Short: the UN provided legitimacy and universality and the goals reflected "broad agreement in the international community, arrived at with the active participation of developing countries".[39]

She also liked the fact that the DAC had boiled down the agenda in a highly specific and precise way, focused on the extreme poverty of the poorest people.[40] The DAC proposed a first, overarching goal should be to reduce by at least one-half the proportion of people living in extreme poverty in developing countries by 2015. Similar precise quantitative targets were included on primary education, gender equality in education, infant and maternal mortality, and reproductive health services (see Table 1.1).

The DAC was also clear that developing countries themselves held the main responsibility for their own development. International sup-

Table 1.1. DAC Development Goals

Economic well-being	Reduction by one-half in the proportion of people living in extreme poverty by 2015.
Education	Universal primary education in all countries by 2015.
Education	Eliminating gender disparity in primary and secondary education by 2005.
Infant mortality	Reduction by two-thirds in the mortality rates for infants and children under age 5 by 2015.
Maternal mortality	Reduction by three-quarters in maternal mortality by 2015.
Reproductive health	Access to reproductive health services for all individuals of appropriate ages as soon as possible and no later than the year 2015.
Environmental sustainability	Implementation of national strategies for sustainable development in all countries by 2005.

Source: OECD, 1996. The base year against which progress was proposed was 1990.

CHAPTER 1

port was important, but this was not merely – or even mostly – a matter of aid (which nevertheless needed to be more generous and more effective): wider policies needed to be improved to support and facilitate poverty reduction in the poorest countries. All this resonated with Short and became central to her approach.

In summary, what appealed to Short about the DAC approach was that it was legitimate in its origin, precise in its focus, comprehensive in how to achieve it, and balanced in who was responsible for doing so – but also that it was ambitious. It:

> *suggested that a great advance was possible if we focused on the systematic reduction of poverty, built on past successes and drew the international system together to work in partnership to deliver clear targets in each country. . . . I decided that I would work to make this the framework for our development efforts.*[41]

There were echoes in Short's thinking of the philosophical approach developed in the Fabian Society in the early 1960s. In early 1964, the Fabian Society started work on a blueprint for the new ministry Labour leader Harold Wilson had announced he would create, stressing a minister of Cabinet rank and sufficient independence to resist pressures from other ministries to arrange its programme according to nondevelopment criteria. The ministry should not be about aid but about development, independent of foreign policy, or trade or the economy. The recipients must believe that the Labour government was entering into a partnership and not dispensing charity.[42] In February 1964, speaking in Parliament after a visit to Africa, Barbara Castle, who later that year would enter the Cabinet as the minister for the new department, landed the point in language redolent of the view Short herself came to more than 30 years later:

> *Every country is giving its dollops of help for motives which have nothing to do with the prime purpose of securing the economic development of the recipient countries of the world. They are giv-*

ing help for reasons of national prestige, or for political motives to sustain certain régimes as against others, or for reasons of rivalry in the cold war, or for reasons of their own internal economic self-interest. Because the motives are wrong, the help bears no relationship to the results in terms of maximum economic development.[43]

In the period running up to a general election in the UK, it is the convention for the prime minister to authorise the civil service to hold private discussions with the leading members of the opposition parties to help both sides prepare for the possibility of the opposition taking office. An election had to be held by the spring of 1997. Short was therefore soon able to meet John Vereker, who had been the Overseas Development Administration permanent secretary since 1994. Their backgrounds were different: Vereker was from an establishment family, had been educated at a famous public school, and had worked closely with Margaret Thatcher at 10 Downing Street.[44] It was not obvious that they would hit it off, and Short was therefore "delighted"[45] to find that Vereker had been a key author of the DAC proposals and was a strong advocate for them.

Having established the strategic and policy goal Short wanted to focus on, their discussions also covered the institutional structures best suited to implement them – not just the establishment of the new department, but its form. From the outset, Short and Vereker discussed the key features of the Department of International Development Labour had said it would establish. Short was "determined to make my new ministry an exemplary player and to use UK influence to drive the international system forward".[46] Three major conclusions followed from this.

First, the new department would need to organise its staff and financial resources very explicitly on poverty reduction and the other DAC targets. The Overseas Development Administration, while small and lacking influence, did have committed, well-trained staff who were keen to justify each proposed project in terms of its developmental benefit.[47] A senior projects committee reviewed all major proposals before they were signed off. The permanent secretary was responsible directly to Parliament as the accounting officer, charged with ensuring the quality and propriety of spending, and that it followed the requirements of the law. The Overseas Development Administration also had a reasonably well-developed overseas network and strong technical specialists in the economics, governance, social sectors, and natural resources of developing countries. And the UK aid programme, even if modest in size, did at least focus more on the poorest countries than was common across the DAC as a whole. However, the approach was transactional: to the extent that the Overseas Development Administration internally had a strategic approach to its resource allocation in the years up to 1997, it did not have a serious focus on reducing poverty, as opposed to broader, more nebulous concepts of "development" (under which pretty much any project that was economically viable and well designed, and did not cross governance or human rights red lines, could be justified).[48] Moreover, its experience of the years between 1979 and 1997 was of struggling, not always successfully, to see off pressures from the Foreign Office, the Department of Trade and Industry, and others to use the aid budget, modest as it became through those years, not just for a broadly understood concept of development but also to lubricate relationships in the pursuit of other diplomatic or commercial objectives.[49] Every year a Joint Aid Policy Committee of Whitehall mandarins debated how to allocate the available resources: these pressures were constantly exposed, and aid officials were perpetually in a defensive crouch trying to see them off.[50] Lip service was paid to poverty, but it was far from the driving focus and determinant of how resources were allocated. A new department with its own Cabinet minister would be much better able to resist outside pressure and allocate money based solely on how it would reduce poverty.

Second, a new department could engage differently with the rest of government on non-aid policies – from the rules on arms sales, to the EU's trade policy, to international discussions on debt and a host of other issues – which affected the development prospects of poorer countries. Short and Vereker were alive to this from the outset. The DAC focus on outcomes for the extreme poor meant they were interested in development overall, not just aid. A development department with its own seat at the table in wider Whitehall discussions contrasted sharply with the Overseas Development Administration's experience: its staff had learned that they might be welcome in Whitehall meetings where others thought their money could be of use, but ignored (or simply not invited) in broader discussions of the implications for developing countries of non-aid policy choices the UK might make.[51] They might brief their more powerful Foreign Office counterparts to speak to these issues, but were under no illusions about the difference that would make. The Foreign Office was responsible for weighing the gamut of external policy objectives, of which development was just one, before deciding what line it would take in Whitehall debates.

Third, Short understood from the outset that Britain on its own was not going to move the dial on global poverty. Hence her wish to "use UK influence to drive the international system". The UK economy by the mid-1990s was significantly stronger than 20 years earlier. That and Britain's status as a nuclear power, in the G7, as a permanent member of the UN security council, a holder of its own seat on the boards of the IMF and World Bank, and at the head of the Commonwealth, meant that it could credibly claim, in Douglas Hurd's phrase, to punch above its weight – a view held across party lines. As a Cabinet member with her own ministry, Short would be the UK's representative in a wide range of international negotiations affecting development. She thought she could use that to get others on board to advance the DAC agenda.

A last-minute wobble?

Notwithstanding what Labour had said in *Britain in the World*, it was not guaranteed when Short took up her new role that an incoming Blair government would in fact create the new department. In the autumn of 1996, Blair asked Short to consider whether it was right

CHAPTER 1

that the commitment in the policy document should be retained. Short "agreed to survey examples in other countries and consult the permanent secretary at the Overseas Development Administration and get back to him".[52] Vereker was "adamant that the department needed its independence to fulfil the commitment laid out in Labour's policy document" and to maximise its contribution to the agenda Short wanted to pursue.[53] Short wrote back to Blair accordingly.

Not everyone bought into her conclusion. Short wrote in 2004 that

I am pretty certain that, when Robin Cook consulted the Foreign Office in the six months before the election, they suggested he had made a major mistake in giving away his control over the policy and budget of the Development Department.[54]

In 2003, not long after Short had resigned from the government over the Iraq War, John Kampfner similarly wrote that Blair came under pressure to water down the commitment in *Britain in the World* from Robin Cook, Jonathan Powell (Blair's chief of staff, and a former diplomat), and Foreign Office diplomats.[55] Likewise, John Vereker recalls the Foreign Office being "pretty vigorously opposed to the proposal"; his permanent secretary counterpart there, Sir John Coles, told him, "I don't know why you are worrying about this, John. It's not going to happen."[56] It has also been suggested that Short threatened to resign unless the commitment was honoured.[57] Several people we interviewed who were close to Blair, however, cast doubt on this interpretation. Robin Cook (who had, after all, chaired the *Britain in the World* process) did not seek to backtrack; if Foreign Office officials were running a campaign, they omitted to convey that to those close to Blair who were advising him on this issue; and while it is true that Blair did not finalise the decision to create DFID and appoint Short until after the election, that was the case for all Cabinet appointments.[58] Nor should the story in *The Sun* immediately after the election that Short would not be included in the Cabinet be seen as part of these machinations. *The Sun* had been engaged in a war of words with Short for many years for entirely different reasons.[59] When Labour published its manifesto on 2 April 1997, the commitment that a Cabinet minister would lead a new department of international development was included. At that point it was effectively locked in.

DFID was brought into existence by a confluence of political circumstance, which meant that Labour wanted to draw a clear line on competence and effectiveness of international spending (as well as fiscal responsibility), the fact that it was Clare Short specifically – who may never have had the portfolio had Joan Lestor been in better health – who was "demoted" into the role, and the fact that she had an unusually clear idea about what she wanted to achieve and got good help before taking office in developing a plan to deliver it. No other British development minister has assumed the role with such a strong grounding and clear vision.[60]

Day one of DFID

Early on 5 May journalists gathered at the door of 94 Victoria Street to report on Clare Short's arrival.[61] Among them was Peter Gill, with a BBC documentary crew in tow. He was barred from entry by the security guards. He replied that he had been invited in by Clare Short, to make a TV documentary – *Clare's New World*.[62] A stand-off ensued, with the department's head of media relations eventually summoned to the front door. Rattled, he retreated to ring Number 10 for advice. Alastair Campbell, unsurprisingly, was not happy to hear about a documentary he had no control over. But DFID officials let the camera crew and Peter Gill in anyway, and they filmed Short addressing staff on their first day in the new department.[63]

This was an early symbol of what was to follow: Short had the intellectual self-confidence and authority to get her way and was willing to fight battles small and large in pursuit of her agenda. Over the following six years that sometimes landed her in hot water, but, as we shall see next, it meant she and DFID played a disproportionate role in the fight against world poverty.

TWO

Policy, Money, and Organisation

CLARE SHORT'S resignation from government in May 2003 was a long, agonised, and drawn-out affair. She had been at odds with Tony Blair over Iraq for the best part of a year, with tempers repeatedly fraying on all sides.[1] The moment of her departure was the nadir of their relationship, making what he said in his immediate response to her resignation letter all the more interesting:

> *I believe you have done an excellent job in the department [DFID], which has the deserved reputation as one of the best such departments anywhere in the world. That is in no small measure down to you. Our record on aid and development is one of the Government's proudest achievements.*

No one would have forecast that in May 1997 when the government took office.

Other than Gordon Brown as chancellor of the exchequer, no other Cabinet minister under Blair served continuously in the same role for as long as Short (1997–2003). She was a dominant force and a powerful personality, and her leadership, sustained as it was over a significant period, made an important contribution to what DFID became, not just while she was there but for long after. She was supported by a department which grew significantly in size and became more effective, energetic, and confident. Crucially, DFID also benefitted from increasing personal engagement from Blair on humanitarian crises and Africa from 1999 onward, as well as growing financial and policy support from Brown. The fact that both the government's dominant figures were enthusiastic proponents of the development agenda was important in ensuring that Short's traumatic departure did not torpedo the department.

Earlier assessments of DFID in this period are full of plaudits. The head of the Canadian International Development Agency wrote in a government report in 2005 that

> *ten years ago, DFID was considered a middle-of-the-pack development agency. Today it is generally considered to be the best in the world.*

The Economist said it was "a model for other rich countries". Oxfam described it as "the best bilateral development agency".[2]

The foundations for what the department achieved were the promulgation of its policy goals, the budget it was given, and its organisational arrangements and staffing. That is what we are looking at in this chapter. From that platform, everything else followed.

The economic backdrop

It is important to start with some contextual points. As the 1990s drew to a close, Britain was beginning to recover from the recession of the early part of the decade.[3] The UK economy had contracted by 1.7 per cent in 1991, and its performance relative to other G7 economies was sluggish for the five years between 1988 and 1993. By 1997 the tide had turned: not only had the UK returned to steady growth, but it was beginning to catch up (in terms of real GDP per capita) with its G7 peers.

The situation was also improving in most low-income and lower-middle-income countries. Figure 2.1 shows the average, and range, of inflation and GDP per capita growth for sub-Saharan Africa from 1980 to 2000.

CHAPTER 2

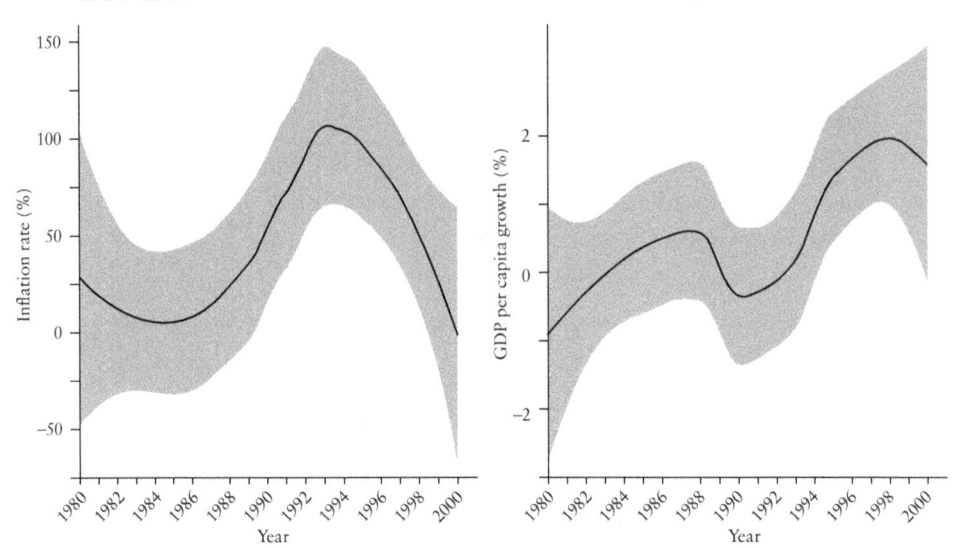

Figure 2.1. Inflation and GDP per capita growth, sub-Saharan Africa 1980–2000

Note: The central line is a local regression showing how inflation and GDP per capita growth changed over time. The grey shaded areas give the 95 per cent confidence intervals for this relationship.

Source: World Bank World Development Indicators, accessed through the R package "WDI".

Double-digit inflation had been the norm in much of Africa. Growth veered from boom to bust, and there was on average little improvement in per capita incomes. Indeed, most of Africa experienced negative per capita growth for the first part of the 1980s, and some parts of the continent did in the following decade too.[4]

Most African countries were still burdened by extremely high debt levels, accumulated in the 1970s and 1980s. The painstaking process of agreeing and then executing debt relief packages was barely underway in 1997; the Heavily Indebted Poor Countries (HIPC) framework, which promised debt relief from a number of official creditors on the achievement of a set of pre-specified macroeconomic and policy conditions, was agreed in 1996.[5] No country had achieved HIPC "Completion Point" (the point at which debt was finally written off) by 1997.

What did "poverty" mean?

These were not ideal conditions for development, and it showed. Using the World Bank's new "dollar a day" metric, estimates suggested close to 40 per cent of the world, amounting to around 2 billion people, were in extreme poverty. That included more than half the population of sub-Saharan Africa and around half the population of South Asia.[6]

The standard of living at such low levels of consumption was very low indeed, and insufficient for the maintenance of a healthy life. When so much of the world lived below the extreme poverty line, it was a no-brainer than development policy should make that the priority. Increases in income that accrue to those living at the very bottom of the scale have a larger impact on their welfare than those that accrue to people even slightly better off, as it helps them satisfy their most basic needs.[7]

And of course, material poverty is not the only metric by which to judge the lives of the poor. By almost any other indicator one cares to choose – life expectancy, child mortality, maternal mortality, schooling – conditions in both Africa and South Asia were abysmal. In India in 1990, for example, 12 per cent of children would be expected to die before the age of five; in Nigeria, the figure was 20 per cent, and in Sierra Leone fully one in four children could expect such a fate. In the same year, the equivalent figure in the UK was less than 1 per cent.[8]

People living in extreme poverty, in other words, were chronically malnourished, hungry most of the time, frequently sick, rarely completed basic education, and typically died much younger than better-off people. There is a further point that might seem obvious but should be stated clearly, and has been reinforced by our experience talking to thousands of extremely poor people across dozens of countries over nearly forty years: the most deprived people have exactly the same human hopes, fears, anxieties, and aspirations as everyone else – but their life experience is dramatically worse.

CHAPTER 2

And while chronic poverty is a slow-burn horror, acute disaster was in this era also common. Famine in Ethiopia and conflict in the Democratic Republic of Congo killed millions in the 1980s and 1990s; the genocide in Rwanda in 1994 was still fresh in the world's memory, with more than half a million people slaughtered in just three months. Many people working on global development believed that such events might be a feature of the landscape into the future.

Setting out the stall

Given the state of the world in May 1997, there were plenty of options for how precisely the new department would focus and organise its work. The first task was to clarify what it was going to do.

In the UK system, White Papers are presented to Parliament to promulgate major planks of government policy. They sometimes then get embedded in legislation. There had been no White Paper on development since 1975, because it was not a political priority. Within weeks of the establishment of DFID, Short received approval from Number 10 to publish a White Paper covering what the government (not just DFID) intended to do on international development. While she was personally focused on making the main task of her new department the reduction of global poverty, through the achievement of the DAC goals, Labour's election manifesto had been less specific. She wanted the White Paper to nail down the agenda.

There was an initial tussle over who should lead the process: Foreign Office officials tried to argue that as the lead department on foreign affairs and with a key role on the non-aid issues that Short wanted the White Paper to address (trade, investment, human rights, etc.), they should be in charge. They got no serious backing from Robin Cook, the foreign secretary, who had other priorities; and Number 10 promptly agreed to DFID leading the work, consulting other departments in areas of their responsibility and interest.[9]

Myles Wickstead, a long-standing senior Overseas Development Administration civil servant who had recently been based in Nairobi with responsibility for the organisation's work in East Africa, headed a small team preparing the White Paper. But Short was intimately involved throughout, chairing countless meetings and delving deep into the policy detail.[10] She saw the White Paper as a key vehicle both for setting the agenda for the government and as a vehicle for mobilising global action.

The focus was unambiguous. It was stated in the title: *Eliminating World Poverty: A Challenge for the 21st Century*. The inside front cover included a scene-setting quote from Tony Blair, selected from what he had said during the election campaign in April 1997.[11] Short's foreword summarised the message in two pithy sentences:

This White Paper sets out the Government's policies to achieve the sustainable development of this planet. It is first, and most importantly, about the single greatest challenge which the world faces – eliminating poverty.

The summary set out 12 "strands", including support for the DAC goals, a commitment to partnerships between poorer countries and donors, pledges to reverse the decline in UK aid[12] and focus resources on reducing poverty, and an emphasis on development rather than aid.[13]

The White Paper had a strong analytical base. Short was intellectually curious but also believed that facts and analysis would bring others, inside and beyond DFID, along with her vision. The document also had a clear philosophical stance (consistent with the broad ideology of the Blair government). It dismissed both the "dominant state" and the "minimalist state with unregulated markets" models of development: both states and markets "are good servants and bad masters". Instead, a synthesis was proposed, of the "virtuous state" which encouraged human development, stimulated enterprise, and created an environment to mobilise domestic resources and attract foreign direct investment. Some people were surprised that the White Paper was as clear as it was about the instrumental role of the private sector, but Short saw economic growth, trade, investment, job creation, and increasing the incomes of the poor as being at the heart of development.

The White Paper contained directional statements which proved totemic and were repeatedly reinforced and built upon in the years that followed. But it also included a number of more specific commitments. One was that the government would consider the case for a new International Development Act, the prevailing 1980 legislation having fallen into disrepute as a result of the Pergau dam scandal. Another was the commitment that resources would be rigorously redirected towards achieving the DAC goals in the poorest countries. At the G7 summit in Denver in the summer of 1997, Blair announced, at Short's instigation, that DFID would "raise by 50 per cent our bilateral support for basic health, basic education and clean water in Africa". There was no new money: the existing budget was redirected to finance that pledge. The Aid and Trade Provision was closed to new applications and the scheme wound up, releasing resources for Short's priorities. A new approach was announced for the Commonwealth Development Corporation[14] (a company fully owned by the government which invested in businesses in poorer countries with a view to promoting development). It would be transformed into a private-public partnership seeking to attract private capital to scale up its activities, with a commitment that the government's share of the proceeds of successful investments "will be ploughed back into the development programme". The focus on partnerships with developing countries would involve low-income countries committed to poverty elimination being offered more money, longer-term commitments, and greater flexibility in the use of resources. The stated intent was to concentrate resources where the needs were greatest but the scope for achieving results was also the highest: in other words, those low-income countries prioritising improvements for their poorest citizens.

In another theme that would become a sustained preoccupation for DFID over the following 20 years, the White Paper was ambitious and unambiguous in setting out an intent to use the UK's position to influence the multilateral development system: "Our first priority is to encourage all the multilateral development institutions to strengthen their commitment to poverty elimination." The emphasis was on reform, effectiveness, and efficiency, and the intent was to mobilise the international development system as a whole behind the DAC goals.

Strikingly, the section of the White Paper analysing and making new policy commitments on how the UK's non-aid policies could support developing countries, which Short and DFID could seek to influence but did not control in the way they did DFID's own budget, was just as detailed as the section dealing with aid.[15] The scope was comprehensive: it covered trade, market access and standards, debt, investment and other private sector financial flows, agricultural and environmental policies (including on climate change), migration (including the possibility of brain drain, with skilled people leaving poorer countries), labour standards, intellectual property, human rights, illegal narcotics, arms control, money laundering, conflict prevention and resolution, and the quality of governance (including tackling bribery and corruption). No previous major policy statement by a British government on relations with developing countries had ranged so widely.

The preparation of White Papers in the UK system often sees tense and time-consuming inter-departmental wrangles to resolve contentious issues, frequently requiring arbitration from the Cabinet Office or the prime minister's team. Short got drawn into a brief (and from her point of view successful) argument with the Department of Trade and Industry over the abolition of the Aid and Trade Provision, but otherwise there were few rows. (A separate early tussle with the Treasury over responsibilities for Britain's policy on the World Bank was resolved outside the White Paper process, with Short accepting that she would, like her predecessors, be the UK Governor of the World Bank but that the Treasury would retain the bigger prize of selecting the official who would act as the UK's representative on the Bank's board of directors.)[16] So the whole White Paper process was completed in little more than six months.

It was launched in Parliament in November 1997. The response of the opposition Conservative spokesman was lukewarm, comprising two dozen questions effectively restating the previous government's views. The Liberal Democrats, on the other hand, were more positive, their main concern being not the content of the proposals but whether they would be implemented. Bowen Wells, the (Conservative) chair of the new cross-party parliamentary development committee, was effusive, saying that he was "delighted" by the abolition of the Aid and Trade Provision.[17] The committee conducted a brief enquiry, issuing a positive report welcoming the creation of DFID, its role in Whitehall discussions and the fact that, for the first time since the 1970s, there was now a high-level government-wide statement of policy on development.[18]

The wider reaction was also broadly positive. The DAC, in conducting one of its periodic reviews of the UK in 1998, welcomed "this new foundation for Britain's development policies".[19] Others thought that it signified that "the UK now aspired to global leadership on international development issues".[20] The White Paper "put on the public record clear statements of the government's approach" which "had a considerable impact".[21] The Journal of International Development devoted the whole of a special issue in March 1998 to reviews by researchers, NGOs, opposition politicians, and others: most were largely welcoming, with caveats, including that what mattered was implementation not just policy intention, and that poverty was more complicated than implied by the DAC goals.[22]

Short and her senior civil servants wanted to make sure that staff across DFID understood that the White Paper comprised the marching orders for everything they were doing. Hence it included a statement of purpose, which began: "DFID's aim is the elimination of poverty in poorer countries." The purpose statement set clear, detailed objectives for the department linked to the goals.[23]

While the core work of preparing the White Paper was done mostly by a small team working closely with Short, many other staff in the new department contributed analysis and ideas and attended meetings to hammer out detailed content. The buy-in of staff across all grades and disciplines in DFID was unusually high: they believed in the ideas being developed and were enthused by the chance to work on them. The process of producing the document and its promulgation excited and energised them: on the launch day, Short addressed a staff meeting packed to the rafters in the basement of DFID's London headquarters.[24] This was the start of a sustained effort to ensure that the drive to eliminate poverty and achieve the goals became deeply ingrained in DFID's organisational culture. As John Vereker wrote in 2002, the

clarity of purpose, rapidly transmitted through the organisation has been a powerful motivating, unifying and guiding force over the last five years.

By then, it was embedded for the long term.[25]

The import of the White Paper was not primarily in the detailed policy commitments it contained (many of which were successfully implemented, but some of which eventually ran into the sand). Rather it was in the establishment of a clear vision and long-term goals which the government as a whole was signing up to, and which, updated, reinforced and built upon, in fact turned out, as we will see in later chapters, to be the central driving focus of Britain's development efforts and the mobilising endeavour for DFID for the following 20 years.

The 1997 White Paper was, because it set an ambitious agenda which proved to be robust over time, the most consequential statement of British government policy on international development of the last 60 years.[26]

Marching orders

Vereker and his senior colleagues at the top of the DFID hierarchy were alive to the need to ensure that the policy focus of the White Paper was given life in the day-to-day work of the new department. That meant integrating it into DFID's planning and management systems.

CHAPTER 2

They were assisted in this by a new system Brown introduced at the Treasury, in which budget allocations to each government department were linked to formal published statements ("Public Service Agreements") on the outcomes that would be pursued with the money provided. In this period, three consecutive Public Service Agreements were agreed between the Treasury and DFID, as part of the spending reviews in 1998, 2000, and 2002 which set rolling three-year budgets for the period ahead. The intent (and effect) of this was to link the Treasury's assessment of DFID performance (and hence, to some degree, future budget allocations) to the contribution the department was aiming to make to achieving the DAC goals both globally and in a core group of countries in which much of the budget was spent. The outcomes DFID agreed with the Treasury for its Public Service Agreements were therefore focused explicitly on progress with the goals (Table 2.1).

Table 2.1. Extracts from DFID Public Service Agreements 1999–2006: Performance measures

1999–2002	2001–03	2003–06
At least 75 per cent of bilateral country resources to low-income countries (LICs) by 2002.	Increase in proportion of DFID bilateral (non-humanitarian) resources to LICs from 71 per cent in 1998/99 to 80 per cent by 2002/03.	Increase in proportion of DFID bilateral programme to LICS from 78 to 90 per cent.
Annual increase in GDP/capita of 1.5 per cent in top 30 recipients.		Sustainable reduction in proportion of people in poverty in sub-Saharan Africa from 48 per cent.
		Sustainable reduction in proportion of people in poverty in South Asia from 40 to 32 per cent.

Table 2.1. (continued)

1999–2002	2001–03	2003–06
Decrease in under-five mortality from 74 to 70 per 1,000 live births in top 30 recipients.	Decrease in under-five mortality from 132–100 per 1,000 live births in top 10 recipients of health assistance 2000–04.	Decrease in under-five mortality from 158–139 per 1,000 live births in 16 key sub-Saharan Africa countries.
		Decrease in under-five mortality from 92 to 68 per 1,000 live births in four key Asian countries.
Increase in primary school enrolment from 81 to 91 per cent in top 30 recipients.	Average increase in primary school enrolment in top 10 recipients of education assistance from 75 to 81 per cent from 2000 to 2004.	In 16 key African countries, increase in primary school enrolment from 58–72 per cent.

Note: The full published PSAs, and data on progress against the performance measures they contain, are in the 2001 and 2003 DFID Departmental Reports Cm 5111, 23–24 and Cm 5914, 134–40. The point being illustrated is that the PSAs were closely linked to the OECD's International Development Goals and the MDGs, and the performance framework was consistent over time.

Both DFID and the Treasury recognised that it was unrealistic to quantify precisely how far progress on the goals could be directly attributed to DFID's activities. But they deliberately opted where possible for a focus on outcome targets in preference to input or output measures, over which DFID might have more control, because they believed that would reduce the risk of distortions. What they cared about was the outcome: so they decided to concentrate attention on that. They did so in the full understanding that DFID's direct activities may not be the largest factor (or even, sometimes, anything but a relatively small one) in determining whether the outcome was achieved.[27]

The DFID-wide Public Service Agreement was then linked to the budgets set for organisational units across the department.[28] The Africa Division, for example, was allocated resources to pursue the development goals in a subset of countries in which it had significant programmes. Senior staff identified other strengths of this approach too. The fact that budgets were set for three years in advance provided more predictability. Staff were given scope to tailor what they did in pursuit of the goals to local circumstances, so strengthening trust and partnerships with the national authorities.[29] The performance framework was cascaded into personal objectives for senior staff and further down to their teams. The intent was to enable everyone in the department to see how what they were doing linked with DFID's overall vision.

From 1998 onwards DFID also published a series of "Target Strategy Papers" proposing in detail what would need to be done to achieve each of the DAC goals. Their preparation, generally led by the relevant senior subject-matter specialist (the chief health adviser for the infant mortality goal, for example) drew in hundreds of people across the department. Short again was closely involved throughout. The amount of staff time being devoted to this created some internal debate, but the effect was to further reinforce the centrality of the goals in DFID's work.[30]

Doubling down

A second White Paper was published in 2000. The strap line was the same ("Eliminating World Poverty"), but the focus was on globalisation and how it could be made to work for the poorest countries. The origin was partly the failure of the World Trade Organization negotiations in Seattle in 1999, a failure which Short feared would end up hurting poorer countries; she therefore wanted to make the case for integrating them better into the global economy as a means of helping grow their economies and reduce poverty. She argued that "the wealth and potential of globalisation could be shaped to bring benefits to the poor".[31]

This time there was a foreword (not just a quote) by Tony Blair, an indicator of his growing interest in DFID's work. The coverage of the document was again extremely broad, but the detailed commitments this time were more granular and refined, reflecting the fact that (as described below) the department had substantially strengthened its intellectual heft and analytical capacity and wanted to profile new insights it had generated.

Perhaps the most important thing about the 2000 White Paper, though, was what it did not do. It did not change DFID's fundamental purpose: the reduction of poverty and the mobilisation of the international system to meet the DAC goals. As Short put it at the very beginning of her own foreword:

> *We have spent the last three years working to achieve these objectives. We now have unprecedented consensus – across the UN system, the IMF and World Bank, most regional development banks, leaders of developing countries and the OECD – that the achievement of the Targets should be the focus of our joint endeavours.*[32]

Short never veered from this laser-like focus. She understood the tendency of development agencies to be diverted by new ideas, fads, and global events. She recognised the importance of repeating the poverty reduction and development goals mantra everywhere and all the time. She appeared never to tire of doing that.[33] The first substantive section of the 2000 White Paper was, accordingly, titled "Reaffirming the International Development Targets". While there follows a wealth of new analysis and policy detail, it is all vested in that vision.

The 2000 White Paper was admired in some surprising quarters. Jim Wolfensohn, president of the World Bank, asked his staff why they had not produced something as clear, compelling, and well argued on the topic.[34] *The Economist* described it as "full of good sense and some courageous policy", saying it made "a strong intellectual case for global capitalism . . . as the solution to global poverty rather than the cause of it".[35] The usual suspects liked it too: the DAC said that, as with the 1997 White Paper, it provided a

> *solid basis for the UK's development policy and cooperation, consistent with current good practice in development thinking but ahead of many other donors*

and that it was "a timely and impressive document".[36]

In summary, there is no question that the department achieved an unusual degree of clarity in what it was trying to do in its early years. As the DAC put it in its 2001 peer review of the UK, "DFID has an ambitious and well-articulated policy framework, primarily focused on the achievement of the international development targets."[37] The mission was well understood and energetically acted on across the department.

Follow the money

It is unhappily common in public organisations to see a gap between the stated objectives and how money and staff are actually deployed. In the first two years of Labour's tenure, the budgets of government departments remained as announced in the plans of the previous Conservative administration. This was a strategic decision taken by Gordon Brown to ensure market and popular confidence in him as a prudent steward of the public purse. Short complained about this, to no avail. But by the 2001/02 spending review, the situation had changed. Continued economic growth and a stronger fiscal position, reflected in the fact that government debt was declining between 1997 and the early 2000s, created scope for increasing spending.[38] As Short put it:

> *The relationship with Gordon Brown and his senior officials had consolidated and we achieved the commitment to increase our*

spend from the £2.2 billion we inherited in 1997 to £4.6 billion by 2005/06. This was a rise from 0.26 per cent of GNP to 0.4 per cent.[39]

The aid budget was then growing at a faster rate than that of most other departments: the DFID share of (rapidly growing) total public spending increased from 0.6 per cent to 0.76 per cent.

Short and her senior officials adopted and sustained a determined approach to setting priorities within the available budget. They wound down programmes which were considered marginal for the achievement of the DAC goals (for example in a range of better-off developing countries in the Pacific, the Caribbean, eastern Europe, and elsewhere, where the goals had already been achieved). Short turned down a number of proposals which had been developed under the previous government but not yet approved, including a tertiary education project in Ghana and an electricity interconnector in India, again because she did not think they were central to the development goals. (Working through her red box of ministerial papers at night and during the weekends, she would sometimes scribble "what's this got to do with poverty?" on documents she found unpersuasive. This quickly had a powerful demonstration effect across the department: the secretary of state really meant what she said.) Following the decision announced in the 1997 White Paper to close the Aid and Trade Provision, the resources freed up (amounting to around 10 per cent of the bilateral programme) were reallocated. Vereker persuaded Short that DFID should no longer share financing of the British Council's government grant with the Foreign Office, so they transferred £30 million a year to them to cover that. They also divested DFID of the Chevening Scholarship programme, under which foreign students were awarded scholarships to British universities, again transferring money to the Foreign Office.[40]

Some things could not be changed: nearly 30 per cent of the total DFID budget was absorbed by obligatory contributions to EU development programmes as a result of multi-year decisions made by the previous government.[41] The department had long found that

Table 2.2. DFID budget and UK ODA 1997/98 and 2002/03

£m (current prices)	1997/98	2002/03
Total DFID	1,979	3,240
Of which regional programmes	736	1,335
Of which focus countries (a)	357	850
Share (b)	49%	64%
Total UK ODA	2,332	3,847
Of which: bilateral	1,609	2,365
multilateral	723	1,482
DFID share of UK ODA (c)	85%	84%

Source: DFID Annual Reports.
(a) Afghanistan, Bangladesh, Democratic Republic of Congo, Ethiopia, Ghana, India, Kenya, Malawi, Mozambique, Nepal, Nigeria, Pakistan, Rwanda, Sierra Leone, Tanzania, Uganda, Zambia, Zimbabwe. These countries were all low income in 1997 and were prioritised as recipients of DFID development resources (as opposed to humanitarian aid during crises) for most (in many cases all) of DFID's existence. See Appendix C for details for the 1997–2020 period.
(b) The proportion of regional programme resources allocated to focus countries.
(c) The remaining UK ODA (official development assistance) was in most years related to debt relief (which involved no new financial transfer, just an ODA accounting credit at the moment of write-off), Treasury support for the IMF, and modest expenditure by other government departments.

frustrating, believing that the EU spent too much in the wrong places and did not even do that well enough; with its new status and help from other EU member states, it pursued an energetic and ultimately successful campaign to improve the quality of EU spending and get more of the money channelled to low-income countries. On the multilateral side, support to the World Bank's soft lending arm, the International Development Association, which focused on low-income countries, was also given priority, which may have helped increase the UK voice in the bank.

Within what DFID could control, a high priority was given to increasing funding direct to developing countries particularly important for the achievement of the OECD goals. In particular there was a focus on 18 countries which between them housed the majority of the global population living below the dollar-a-day line. Those 18 countries (listed in Table 2.2) were all in Africa and South Asia. In most, the UK had provided development assistance for many years. With many, there had also been a long-standing colonial relationship, though there were some, including Afghanistan, the Democratic Republic of Congo, Ethiopia, and Rwanda, where that was not the case. DFID's directly managed programmes in the 18 countries more than doubled in the Short years, with their share of the total country programmes growing from less than half to nearly two-thirds. This was a clear, practical manifestation of the department putting its money where its mouth was. (It is a striking feature of DFID's 23-year life that the focus on these 18 countries was always sustained. We will in subsequent chapters describe their progress and how the department contributed to it.)

Backing partner countries

The approach was, however, selective: the department wanted particularly to support those countries where they judged there was a high degree of commitment to reducing poverty. The 1997 White Paper had set this out in plain terms:

Partnerships are needed . . . if poverty is to be addressed . . . and will require political commitment to poverty elimination on both sides.

Where low-income countries are committed to the elimination of poverty and pursuing sensible policies to bring that about, the Government will be ready to enter a deeper, longer-term partnership and to provide . . . a longer-term commitment, an enhanced level of resources and a greater flexibility in the use of resources.

It is right to concentrate our bilateral programmes on priority areas where the needs are greatest and we can achieve results.

CHAPTER 2

There will be some circumstances under which a government to government partnership is impossible, because the government concerned is not committed to the elimination of poverty, is not pursuing sound economic policies or is embroiled in conflict.[42]

In those circumstances, help would be offered through alternative channels and "tightly focused on the victims of neglect and oppression".

DFID used the best available evidence to assess whether the policies of recipient countries were conducive to reducing poverty, and developed its own resource allocation model based on recent academic evidence to inform its decisions on how to divide the resources between countries. This approach reversed the trend of the 1990s, which had seen an increasing proportion of global aid going to richer countries at the expense of the poorer (low-income) ones.[43]

DFID received strong support from the Treasury in all this. They liked the fact that it was evidence based. Gordon Brown was particularly seized of DFID's proposal in one spending review that 90 per cent of bilateral resources should go to low-income countries.[44]

DFID, like the Overseas Development Administration before it, was a commissioning organisation. It did not directly hire teachers or health workers in developing countries, or have its own staff procure and then distribute textbooks or drugs. It designed projects and programmes in cooperation with implementing partners, and signed agreements to pay for them. It then monitored progress while they were being implemented, and after that evaluated the outcome.

There were four main categories of implementing partners: developing country governments; multilateral agencies; NGOs (or quasi-independent UK bodies, like university researchers); and private contractors.

DFID was an important and growing source of finance for multilateral agencies, and had to accept whatever priorities their management and members set. But within its bilateral programmes, the department was in control and it was integral to the partnership philosophy that it wanted wherever possible, and more frequently than previously, to work through governments.[45]

Short had a clear-eyed view that in order to achieve the development goals and become self-sufficient, low-income countries needed national institutions to deliver public services, develop infrastructure, uphold the rule of law, and manage the economy in a way that created jobs, incomes, and a growing tax base. She was willing to take risks in helping with all that in a way that none of her predecessors had been. That meant both that more of the available resources would be channelled government to government, and that there were changes in how those resources were delivered.

For much of the previous 30 years, aid money provided directly to governments mostly financed discrete one-off projects: a road here, a hospital there, and a power station somewhere else. The Overseas Development Administration had developed high-class skills in designing and executing such projects.[46] Alan Coverdale, briefly the department's chief economist in the 1990s, described the prevailing Overseas Development Administration culture as one which sought the perfect project in an imperfect world.[47] One flaw in this approach was that once the project was completed, the partner government frequently struggled to find the money to maintain and run it. That got worse with the oil shocks, higher interest rates, and reduced commodity prices in the era from the late 1970s, which saw many developing countries build up unmanageable levels of debt and fall into fiscal crisis.

Richer countries reacted by promoting financial assistance from the IMF, World Bank, and bilateral donors to help with the move away from state control to more market-based economic systems. They provided foreign currency to help adjust and stabilise the economy, in exchange for reform. The foreign exchange was paid to central banks, and facilitated expansion of the national budget. That opened up the question of what those budget increases were spent on.[48] Although it was not initially a particularly large financier, the Overseas Development Administration and then DFID was from the second half of the 1990s at the heart of that debate in African countries.

The issue was then supercharged by the focus on poverty and the development goals. As Mick Foster, a senior economist in the department in the 1980s and 1990s, put it:

The poor are distributed across the whole country in small communities. They depend on thousands of primary schools and primary health facilities, each with a tiny budget. Most of the spending of these facilities is on recurrent inputs such as salaries and drugs, much of it procured locally. Traditional donor project aid is good at financing large infrastructure investments. It is ill suited to financing a health or education system, and attempts to use a project approach tended to result in tiny islands of excellence in a sea of neglect, with small scale donor projects having negligible impact on the system as a whole, and often collapsing once support ended.

Much of the growing DFID budget in the African countries it focused most on from the late 1990s went into national budgets to finance a dramatic expansion of services, especially in health and education, to achieve the development goals.[49]

The department was also trying to address two other issues in doing this. First was the goal of increasing partner governments' ownership. Short and her senior officials had heard legion stories, not apocryphal, of how finance ministers in poor countries were spending a lot of their time negotiating aid agreements with large numbers of donors, each bringing their own conditions and preoccupations. (The World Bank was particularly notorious for being very demanding.) Over a period of years, DFID pursued a campaign to streamline, simplify, and harmonise donor procedures and reduce the burden on counterparts.[50] Second, many donors had also traditionally wanted visible credit for what they were doing, often in the form of their national flags flying over projects they had helped pay for. DFID thought that undermined the accountability link between governments and their citizens, and so was inimical to self-sufficiency and effective development.

DFID was alive to the risks inherent in the greater use of budget support. As Richard Manning, in these years one of John Vereker's deputies, commented to us, it meant that DFID ministers were "associated with all spending decisions of recipient governments".[51] But this forced donors to stop shutting their eyes to the lamentable state of public sector financial management and related risks. Corruption and leakage were prominent among them. Annual reviews of spending were conducted by governments and donors, with donors rolling forward their support into future years on the basis of progress being made. Innovative safeguards were developed – for example local publication in newspapers of budgets sent to schools, and hotlines people could contact if they did not appear. There was an expansion in technical support to strengthen the capacity of finance ministries, audit offices, and parliamentary accountability systems.[52]

According to one calculation, DFID bilateral financial aid increased about three-fold to nearly £2 billion a year between 2000 and 2005. The share of financial aid going as budget support rather than as individual projects (or a group of projects supporting a broad sector, such as health) increased from an average of 30 per cent from 1985–95 to 55 per cent from 2000–10.[53] Moreover, other important donors to Africa, especially the World Bank and the European Commission, did the same thing. For a brief period, DFID was providing around 5 per cent of the total national budget in some countries, and donors as a whole sometimes 50 per cent.[54] This approach made a huge difference to the financing of the MDGs, especially in their early years. Over time, of course, the idea was that poorer countries would grow their economies and tax base, and finance the bulk of their budgets themselves.

Policy becomes law

When DFID was created, its budget was voted annually by Parliament under the 1980 Overseas Development and Cooperation Act.[55] Short teased officials that something had to be done about that, given that they had not realised that funding the Pergau dam was illegal. What she most wanted to do, though, was to embed the poverty focus in legislation. It took a while for time to be found in the parliamentary calendar (and the passage of the first bill was incomplete when the 2001 election was called, so the process had to start again when the new Parliament convened).

The International Development Act became law in early 2002. It is tightly drawn.[56] There are two key provisions. First, Section 1(1) of the act stipulates that the minister (or, in practice, the department acting for them) may provide development assistance as long as they are "satisfied that the provision of the assistance is likely to contribute to a reduction in poverty".[57] Section 1(2) then defines development assistance as assistance provided "for the purpose of furthering sustainable development . . . or improving the welfare of the population" in developing countries.

In (slightly crude) summary, the purpose must be development, and the effect must be less poverty.

Most attention at the time and subsequently, in the department and elsewhere, was on the poverty focus. In practice, however, it was the purpose test that provided the bite. During the parliamentary passage of the bill, ministers explained that tied aid would be unlawful under the new legislation. Tied aid could in fact help reduce poverty (there's nothing wrong with British-made vaccines, for example). But it would not be plausible to argue that the purpose of tying was to further development or improve the welfare of recipient populations.[58]

The new legislation was quickly stress tested. In mid-2002, the Home Office and some Downing Street advisers proposed that aid to some developing countries should be made conditional on accepting the return of asylum seekers. The context was heightened concern in the UK and the EU over the growing number of asylum seekers from Africa and the Middle East. Short rejected that on principle, describing it as "blackmail".[59] Some of her colleagues, however, were less prissy. The issue became sufficiently charged that the attorney general was asked for a ruling. He confirmed that the proposed conditional-

POLICY, MONEY, AND ORGANISATION

ity was illegal under the 2002 Act, because it could not be claimed that the purpose was furthering development.

We will say more in later chapters about other aspects of DFID's approach to resource allocation. That will include more detailed analysis of money for multilateral agencies, funding for NGOs (where, under Short, DFID revamped its approach, introducing a number of new schemes in an attempt to make funding more strategic and less opportunistic), and investment in research and technology for development. We will also delve deeper into some of the sectors in which concentrated activity was needed to support the development goals (including health and education).

For now, however, we have established that DFID was true to its word in concentrating its resources on its espoused priorities, in terms of (a) the countries in which it focused its effort, (b) the way it supported them, and (c) the legal framework put in place to sustain the policy into the future.

Political direction and creating an organisation fit for purpose

Clare Short was supported by a sequence of four junior ministers.[60] The ministerial workload was not the same as in some other departments: DFID did not have the same volume of new or continuing legislation for which ministerial time was needed in Parliament; the burden of engagement with the UK public was lower than in departments responsible for public services at home; and there were fewer other countries and international fora to engage with than was the case with the Foreign Office, because DFID's effort was in 30 or 40 countries, compared with nearly 200 for the Foreign Office. While other departments had several junior ministers, the Blair government (rightly) thought one was enough for DFID.

It was clear to all of Short's deputies[61] that their role was to support and reinforce her agenda, and they were broadly happy to do that. George Foulkes was a particularly good foil for her: avuncular, popular, and placatory. Chris Mullin, too, fitted in very well, bringing an international outlook and experience that endeared him to many civil servants. He wrote in his best-selling diaries of his admiration for what Short had done.[62] As Hilary Benn put it:

> *Clare didn't really need a deputy. She was on top of everything. What we did was in her footsteps, and we 'snucked in'.*

Benn was loyal, hardworking, easy to work with, and very well liked by staff, all of which stood him in good stead when he returned to DFID in 2003.[63] In later phases of DFID's life, the ministerial cohort grew, the individuals were sometimes less collegiate, and more difficulties arose, but in this period there was an impressive degree of political coherence inside the department.

John Vereker had been the Overseas Development Administration's permanent secretary for three years by 1997. He was supported by two director generals as deputies, and a management structure amounting to some 60 senior civil servants below that. He retained essentially the same structure when the Overseas Development Administration became DFID until shortly before he left in 2002. (His successor, Suma Chakrabarti, then changed it.[64]) There were, however, important innovations in the DFID operating model over these years.

First, Short and Vereker agreed, consistent with their vision of more effective partnerships with recipient governments, that decision making should be decentralised, with more authority delegated to DFID staff working in developing countries. The Overseas Development Administration had previously had regional offices, each servicing several countries. Following successful experience with a dedicated country office in India, the model was extended. The two largest regional offices covering Africa were restructured into seven country teams, each based in the local capital so as to be close to national decision makers.[65] Over time, some 40 major country offices were established. Country offices were required to seek approval from ministers and senior officials in London for their overall strategies and for spending commitments greater than £7.5 million, but they otherwise had high levels of delegated powers. (Senior officials in London at this time had delegated authority up to £20 million; commitments greater than that had to go to ministers through the permanent secretary.)[66]

The department embraced Blair's government-wide public sector reform agenda, especially in a deliberate effort to improve performance management. As the DAC put it in its 2001 review,

the current government's objective of improving the delivery of the UK's public services has reinforced DFID's attention to the development impact of its activities.[67]

Conveniently, Short's focus on the development goals sat well with the wider government approach. She was eager to track progress herself, which ensured her officials did so too. She knew setting the target was the easy bit, commenting in 2004:

Obviously the setting of agreed targets does not of itself deliver progress but it did help galvanise the world and provide a clearer focus for development efforts in each country and at a global level. The world is currently on track to achieve the target of halving income poverty . . . Progress is being made against other targets, but not fast enough.[68]

But there was also an external imperative, in the form of scrutiny from the Treasury, Parliament and the National Audit Office (NAO). The decision makers in DFID well understood that performing well against the targets was essential to sustain support. They gained confidence from what independent judges found. In April 2002 Sir John Bourn, head of the NAO, published a report which found that:

performance management in the Department had a number of strengths. There was a strong focus on poverty reduction, explicitly addressed in Departmental performance targets. And planning and review arrangements provided a good, if largely qualitative, view of poverty reduction prospects in developing countries. The Department had met, or were on track to meet, most of their performance targets.[69]

At the project and programme level, independent assessment of the results of DFID projects also confirm a positive story. A 2001 review of more than 1,400 projects from the 1990s onwards concluded that, in the year 2000, about 85 per cent of projects by value had been successful. That compared with 65–70 per cent earlier in the 1990s. A follow-up report in 2004 found that the 2000 success rates had been sustained.[70]

This was also corroborated by sector studies: an analysis in 2001 of health projects found that the bulk of projects were technically well designed and effective, and that they achieved their immediate objectives.[71]

With a government-wide programme of greater transparency introduced early in Blair's tenure, it became even more important to demonstrate that resources were being used successfully to achieve outcomes that were viewed publicly and politically as worthwhile. That required that development policy become more open and transparent. Country assistance plans, setting out how DFID aimed to help each of its major partner countries over the following three years, were for the first time published.[72] Institutional strategies covering major multilateral agencies were written and published too. The resultant scrutiny itself fuelled a greater focus on performance. As DFID's reputation grew, interest in its published strategies broadened too, which made them more influential.

More and better staff

The size of the department grew dramatically between 1997 and 2003, partly to create capacity to handle issues not previously covered by the Overseas Development Administration (in particular, non-aid issues like trade and investment) but also to ensure the growing budget could be spent well. Total staff numbers increased from around 1,500 to some 2,800.[73]

Most importantly there was a major expansion in the networks of sector specialists – the advisory cadres, as they were known internally. For decades, the Overseas Development Administration had a significant cohort of professional economists, who exerted substantial influence on policy issues. These economists also wielded influence in conducting cost benefit analysis of projects under appraisal to judge whether they provided good value for money.[74] There were also long-standing (if small) groups with expertise in, for example, natural resources, infrastructure, health, and education, as well as a few individuals with a background in various dimensions of governance (such as policing). From the mid-1980s, under the influence of a determined and capable social anthropologist, Ros Eyben, a network of social development advisers was established.[75]

By 2003 the advisory cadres included more than a hundred economists, many of them based in the overseas offices. But they were no longer the largest group: that was now the governance network, a broad school (later split up), with expertise ranging from public finance to institutional management to conflict and the rule of law. A private sector group grew from three to 30 by 2003; social development roughly doubled from 40 to 80; and there were corresponding increases in health, education, and the range of other specialisations. Each profession was headed by a chief adviser, who had responsibilities both for policy development in their area and for ensuring and sustaining high standards in the professional calibre of their groups. (Some chief advisers also gained access to substantial programme budgets.) Sector specialists were typically mid-career professionals with postgraduate qualifications in their discipline and several years' experience working in developing countries. Most of them were posted to the growing network of country offices. DFID was unusual among development agencies in the breadth and depth of its professional expertise, bettered probably only by the World Bank and (in their discrete individual areas) UN agencies like the World Health Organization. Sometimes described as the "jewel in the crown" of the organisation, the advisory cadres were an important source of DFID's international influence.

The opening of larger numbers of DFID overseas offices brought with it an expansion of locally hired staff. (To the extent that the Overseas Development Administration had had local staff, they were formally employees of the British Embassy or High Commission.) This grouping, however, extended beyond the traditional diplomatic model of support staff: DFID started hiring local professionals, some in senior decision-making roles and in some cases supervising colleagues on postings from the UK. The DAC commended what it described as a "thoughtful and strategic approach to employing local staff", noting the rationale was "achieving a more effective policy dialogue with partner countries".[76]

The workforce was diverse in professional background and nationality. But not in other ways. Like other government departments at the time, the senior echelons of DFID remained mainly white and male: just 8 per cent of staff in the senior civil service grades in 2002 were from an ethnic minority, and only 16 per cent were women. At the mid-levels the gender ratios were better; the ethnic mix (among the UK-based staff) was not. This was a growing concern; by 2001, the department had adopted an action plan setting targets for greater diversity at senior levels by 2005.[77]

Significant efforts were made to improve staff management so that the workforce was as productive as possible. DFID achieved accreditation under the "Investor in People" benchmark in 2000, which at the time was in vogue as a way for organisations to test how effectively they were managing their employees. The department became the most popular choice for applicants under the civil service fast stream recruitment programme, attracting many of the most capable young graduates. Senior managers observed the high calibre of new entrants at every level. They believed that the overall quality of staff was increasing as the department grew.[78]

Consolidating a high-performance mindset

The department's culture evolved in a number of notable ways. First, as we observed earlier, there was a very high degree of commitment to the poverty reduction goals: staff were motivated by DFID's ambition. Second, expertise and knowledge were prized, generating a commitment to innovation and research. These features also incentivised competition, not all of it productive. Health advisers argued they needed more resources; education staff did the same; and likewise across the professional groups.[79] Third, the strong value-for-money gene inherited from the Overseas Development Administration and reflecting the prominent role of the department's economists, together with the government's commitment to greater transparency, ensured that the performance culture was strengthened. It is not uncommon in public services for the availability of more money to allow marginal activities to be pursued or the agenda to dissipate. DFID's senior staff worked hard to avoid that.

Short did not ostensibly play a prominent role in organisational issues. She was suspicious of management fads (especially when they came out of Number 10 and associated bodies at the centre of government). Before becoming an MP, she had been a civil servant, and had a respect for its systems and integrity. She relied on senior civil servants to deliver her agenda. Many staff saw her regularly face to face; she insisted junior staff speak in meetings and her drive and determination conveyed itself to everyone.[80]

In the years that followed, more formal tools were developed to assess DFID's capability as an organisation. But it was already clear by 2003 that DFID had thrown off what John Vereker has described as the defensive crouch which characterised the Overseas Development Administration in the mid-1990s. It was a self-confident organisation (a DAC peer review even warned of the danger of arrogance). The organisational culture developed a virtuous circle: as the opportunity to do meaningful work grew and DFID's reputation improved, abler people applied for jobs; they contributed to further improving performance; and that attracted still more capable people.

THREE

Whitehall and the International System

CLARE SHORT was determined to influence everything the government did which had an effect on developing countries. The department's levers here were inevitably weaker than those over decisions she could take herself, and there were clearer trade-offs with the UK's own national interests. She was equally determined to shape the international system – those organisations and groupings which could make a difference on global poverty – in the direction of the DAC goals. There, too, she had a voice but also needed to get others on board.

Short had a reputation, gleefully reinforced by the right-wing press (who were sometimes egged on anonymously by her political colleagues), as a combative politician who actively enjoyed fighting her corner. John Vereker, too, had sharpened his elbows over decades as a Whitehall warrior. DFID in this period has sometimes been portrayed as uncollegiate and unpopular with other government departments, with strained relations with the Foreign Office in particular.[1] There may be something in that, but it can be overstated. Arguments inside departments are often more vigorous than between them. And there were plenty of issues and occasions on which DFID found common cause with other departments. As Owen Barder concluded:

The task of changing attitudes and policies across Whitehall ... proved easier than expected: other government departments increasingly saw the need to build support among developing countries and civil society organisations for their own policies with an international dimension and regarded DFID as a potentially useful ally.[2]

Christopher Hill, reviewing the overall track record of the Blair government up to 2001 on foreign policy, reached a similar view, saying that

tensions . . . have not yet shown up too obviously in policy making. . . . There have been turf wars but these have mostly arisen from problems of coordination during crises.[3]

All that said, ultimately what matters is less whether the conversations between departments were conducted nicely, but more what they produced. The record is somewhat patchy. Here we will look first at trade policy, conflict prevention and resolution, the UK's approach to arms exports, environmental policy, and asylum and migration. We will then move on to DFID's international influence.

Trade

Because the UK was part of the European Union, some of its non-aid policy was not determined in Whitehall. Trade policy was set in Brussels and adopted on an EU-wide basis. As such, DFID's influence on trade policy was doubly indirect: it needed to influence the UK policy position, which in turn needed to influence the EU's negotiating stance. DFID's role in the government's inter-departmental trade group grew steadily from 1998, and by the time of a review completed in 2003, it was a "major source of expertise" for the group, particularly due to its ability to commission and undertake research to inform and support policy positions.[4] The EU's own position was mixed. It adopted the "Everything But Arms" (EBA) scheme, which removed tariffs and quotas for the imports of all goods coming into the EU from the least developed countries, provided the goods satisfied the EU's rules of origin.[5] DFID advocated strongly for this scheme and certainly influenced

UK policy, and with it added momentum and support to the EBA. EBA is a generous scheme, but faced criticisms for providing preferential access to too many countries, and thus being insufficiently focused on the poor.[6] What's more, even though DFID put some effort into building the capacity of poorer countries to access the EU market, results were modest; though tariffs and quotas were eliminated, various standards and bureaucratic requirements that remained were cumbersome and expensive for poor countries to meet.

Even so, the achievement of EBA was more impressive than anything achieved on trade on the global stage in this period. The Doha Development Round, negotiations launched by the World Trade Organization in 2001, sought to broker agreements to lower global trade barriers, putting the needs of developing countries first; it was a failure. After multiple rounds, talks broke down (largely) over the issue of agricultural subsidies, specifically those of the US and the EU, which – according to many developing countries – constituted a trade barrier. DFID put a considerable effort into the Doha Round, especially in highlighting the need for the least developed countries to see some improvement in their trading conditions, but ultimately it was a small player in a larger set of disputes.

Conflict and humanitarian response

The Overseas Development Administration had earned a creditable reputation as a quick and reliable provider of humanitarian assistance in disasters and emergencies, including in the (belated) international response to the Ethiopia famine in the 1980s and the Balkan wars of the early 1990s.[7] Humanitarian response had generally accounted for 2 per cent of the Overseas Development Administration's budget in the 1980s (though it reached 5 per cent in 1985 as a result of the Ethiopia famine). It increased slightly, as the overall budget was constrained, to 5–9 per cent in the early and mid-1990s, and remained around the same proportion up to 2003. That was not, as Figure 3.1 reveals, because there were more crises. In fact, the decade from the

Figure 3.1. Deaths in state-based conflicts by world region: Direct deaths of both military personal and civilians, attributed to world regions according to location of the conflict. Deaths from disease or famine are not included

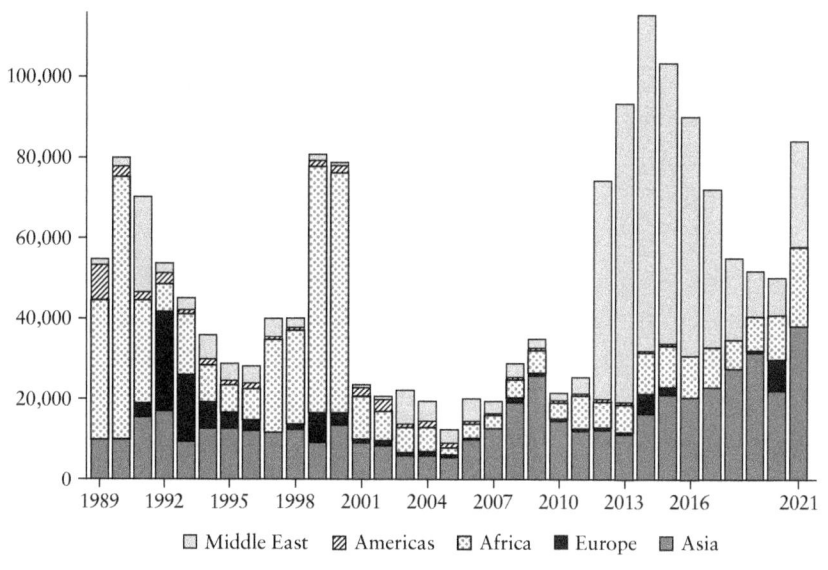

Source: Our World in Data (OurWorldInData.org//war-and-peace.)

late 1990s saw reductions in conflicts on most measures. Rather, there was a growing international tendency to intervene in civil wars to provide assistance to civilians, so that events that had previously been essentially ignored now attracted a response.[8]

We will in later chapters look at the department's engagement in conflict situations in more detail. For now, there are two points particularly worth drawing out. First, for much of the UK population who were not greatly engaged in the issues, their consciousness of what the government was doing on international development was fullest when disasters struck. Tragedies, from volcanic eruptions to cyclones to wars, made headlines, which created public expectations for a response. Being perceived to respond quickly and effectively was reputationally important. DFID did not always get that right. In August 1997 it hit the headlines for the wrong reasons when its response to a volcanic eruption on the Caribbean island of Montserrat (which was a UK-dependent territory) attracted criticism from the local population for being too mean. That irritated Short. She gave an infamous interview to the political editor of *The Observer* complaining that the islanders would want "golden elephants" next. That inflamed the situation, and the government had rapidly to backtrack. Had this minor debacle not occurred in mid-summer when most of the government was on holiday, the consequences could have been more serious.[9] The mistake was not repeated.

Second, Short was in her early years as secretary of state exposed to a series of case studies of the impact of conflict on development, including in Kosovo, Sierra Leone, and Timor Leste. She took the view (partly from observing ethnic cleansing in the Balkans in the early 1990s) that there was in some cases a respectable argument for international intervention, not least to protect local populations.[10] Blair reached the same conclusion, especially as a result of the Kosovo crisis in 1999. He gave an influential speech in Chicago later that year on the international community's "responsibility to protect" civilian populations, which contributed to the adoption of a UN Security Council resolution justifying intervention.[11]

Short proposed that as part of the 2001 spending review a new allocation be created to permit more strategic collaboration between the Ministry of Defence, the Foreign Office, DFID, and other relevant parts of government to reduce and resolve conflict. In fact, two allocations were created, a Global Conflict Prevention Pool, coordinated by the Foreign Office, and an Africa Conflict Prevention Pool, led by DFID. Initially, the two pools had a budget of £200 million a year. Some of their activities were classified as official development assistance (ODA); some were not. Initiatives included programmes for disarming and demobilising armed groups, tackling the trade in small arms, training for the police and army in countries recovering from conflict, and strengthening civilian oversight of the security sector to improve respect for human rights.[12] The approach was novel and attracted interest from other Western countries. It made a significant contribution to strengthening collaboration between arms of government that needed each other to succeed in their roles but had often struggled to join up. Relations between DFID, the Ministry of Defence, and other parts of the UK's national security system notably improved. It is, however, also the case that apparent success in dealing with relatively small problems in places like Kosovo and Sierra Leone may have spawned hubris. The Iraq experience from 2003 speaks to that.

Arms exports

However, successes on conflict did not give DFID an equivalent voice on UK policy on arms sales, an area which combined commercial, military, and political sensitivity. The establishment of an independent department did provide the opportunity to elaborate institutional safeguards; indeed, DFID played a direct role in the government's export control system, which oversaw arms exports. As the department itself wrote to a parliamentary committee (in 2007):

> *As a major exporter of conventional weapons, and a significant provider of development assistance, the UK has a particular responsibility to ensure that its arms exports do not undermine development. DFID works closely with other government departments to do this. The department leads on the assessment of licence applications under Criterion 8, which deals with the impact of the proposed export on sustainable development and the recipient country's economy. DFID also contributes to assessments against the other criteria, particularly when the proposed export might increase the risk of human rights abuses or violent conflict.*[13]

Yet, despite this formal role, the department's actual influence appears to have been small; indeed, the committee to which this evidence was submitted was investigating, among other things, why Criterion 8 was so rarely used to reject the case for arms sales. While there is an obvious case for getting this system right on human rights grounds, there are also strong development reasons to be careful about approving arms sales where the cost to the purchasing country is large in relation to the value of the development work foregone.[14]

These concerns, and DFID's weakness in combatting them, were laid bare by the Tanzanian air traffic control scandal.[15] In 2002, BAE Systems, a British company, won a bid to provide two radar systems to the government of Tanzania to monitor its airspace. The contract was worth £28 million. Even on cursory examination, the deal was dubious: the BAE systems were military and unsuited to the (legitimate) civil purposes they were being bought for. Tanzania was a low-income country with pressing human development problems and an extreme poverty rate most recently measured (in 2000) at 84 per cent of the population, yet it was paying what was even at the time remarked to be an abnormally high price – not far from 10 times the cost of a typical civil aviation system.[16] DFID was, accordingly, against the deal. Short, as secretary of state, expressed her opposition in Cabinet; according to various accounts she was supported by both Gordon Brown as chancellor and Robin Cook as foreign secretary.[17] Short, in her typically direct style, said that BAE was "ripping off" developing countries and that the deal "stank" of corruption. These objections were overruled, in Short's account by Tony Blair directly.[18] BAE was a significant British firm; in December 2002 it issued a shock profit warning, suggesting it was on somewhat shaky footing at the time. Clearly, DFID's principled objections were no match for commercial and political factors.

In time, Short, Cook, and Brown's reservations would be vindicated. Over the following decade it emerged, thanks to an investigation by the UK's Serious Fraud Office, that more than one-third of the extraordinary bill for the systems was funnelled back to Tanzanian politicians and policymakers in bribes to ensure the deal was approved. The Serious Fraud Office recommended that BAE be prosecuted over the deal. Eventually the company pled guilty to false accounting and making misleading statements in relation to allegations of corruption, and agreed to make global payments of around £300 million, including a £30 million payment for the benefit of the people of Tanzania (which was eventually used to fund the expansion of its primary education system).[19] Though BAE never formally admitted to the charge of bribery (doing so would have resulted in a blacklisting from all future international contracts), it was clear that the deal was deeply unsavoury. If a case like this, apparent in real time to be inappropriate and shrouded in an air of malfeasance, against which technical and political representations were made at the highest levels, could nevertheless be approved, one must question the effectiveness of DFID's role in policing arms exports.

Asylum and migration

As with arms, so with asylum and immigration, where domestic political salience trumped development concerns. By 2002, it was clear that migration was an important driver of development. The parliamentary development committee held a session in 2003/04 on the role of migration in development and how it could best be managed to maximise development gains. They drew on expert evidence and testimony to paint a picture of a policy area where substantial improvements could be made to existing practice.[20] Quoting DFID's own evidence, the report suggested that

> *the debate on migration and development is at the stage where the debate on trade and development was ten years ago; people are beginning to say there is a development dimension to migration, but there is a lack of joined-up thinking at national or international levels, and some resistance to connecting the issues.*

Yet DFID's own (nascent) work on migration in these years was almost totally divorced from UK policy on immigration and asylum. The development committee's report proposed closer working with other Whitehall departments,[21] but DFID's work seemed to have little effect on Home Office policy.

Immigration had not been a major issue in 1997 – just 3 per cent of the respondents to a survey that year rated it as the most pressing issue facing the country, less than a tenth of the figure who would say so in 2010 – and as a consequence, Labour had little in the way of a concrete policy when it came to power.[22] That changed under David Blunkett, who became home secretary from 2001. Labour's rhetoric around immigration shifted towards emphasising the limits to migration that the government was imposing, and "protecting" communities from too large an inflow of migrants. Later, looking back at his time as home secretary, Blunkett recalled that

> *unlike the Conservatives in the 1950s – who appealed to those from the Caribbean to come to work in our public services – the Labour government did not go out to encourage people to come to the UK.*[23]

Asylum numbers, increasing since the late 1990s, began to fall, and in this period we see the roots of the current discourse about "genuine" versus "undeserving" asylum seekers.

Nevertheless, despite coming under pressure, DFID did succeed in defending development policy from becoming a tool for migration objectives. First, it was able to resist Home Office proposals that aid should be made conditional on any asylum or migration objectives; to this end, the 2002 International Development Act was particularly valuable, as noted in our earlier discussion of DFID's legal framework. Second, DFID's influence ensured that the UK took the principled position that resources put towards the sustenance of asylum seekers and refugees in donor countries should not be counted as aid. This was made explicit in a 2000 review of how refugee costs should be reported as ODA undertaken by the OECD's DAC:

> *The UK has always upheld the principle that the sustenance of refugees and asylum seekers in donor countries should NOT be considered as humanitarian aid ... The UK is strongly against extending the 12-month limit for reporting expenditures for sustenance. It would on the contrary welcome efforts to reduce the time limit.*[24]

Climate and environment

DFID's role on climate and environment policy in the early years, both internally and across Whitehall, was modest. Thanks in part to its strong scientific and agricultural advisory groups, the department's leadership was acutely aware of the negative effects of environmental pressures on developing countries. But that did not at this stage translate very far into policy changes or large-scale spending. Parliament's Environmental Audit Committee from the mid-2000s took a critical view of DFID's performance to that point.[25] The department was, however, often an active participant in international fora, like the World Summit on Sustainable Development in 2002, which helped establish a stronger focus on adaptation to climate change (rather than just slowing emissions growth). As climate change in particular took on greater policy significance in the following decade, the department would step up its efforts.

One take on DFID's overall impact on non-aid policies affecting developing countries was offered by the Center for Global Development, which in 2003 published its first "commitment to development" index assessing the performance of a large number of developed countries. The UK was decidedly middle-of-the-road on non-aid issues; it scored below average on migration and peacekeeping[26] and was just about average on almost every other non-aid dimension. The contrast between the UK's aid and non-aid scores in the index would continue to grow in future years, reflecting DFID's success in aid policy as well as its failure to persuade the rest of government to adopt policies more favourable to developing countries.

Influencing the international development system: The Millennium Development Goals

As we said in Chapter 1, one of the reasons Clare Short wanted DFID established as a department of state reporting direct to the prime minister was to maximise her ability to influence the goals, operations, and priorities of the rest of the international development system. Here the scorecard is notably better than it was on the UK's non-aid policies.

In the 1997 White Paper, Short was clear she wanted other major donors and multilateral organisations to make the achievement of the DAC goals the central focus of their work. She understood the UK on its own could not change things dramatically. But if she could get others on board, that would make a real difference.

The process by which the DAC goals became, with minor changes, the Millennium Development Goals (MDGs) has been well described elsewhere.[27] The strengths, weaknesses, and impact of the MDG framework has also been hotly debated, and we will come back to that later. Here, we consider the particular role Short and DFID played in the international negotiations over the four years from mid-1997 which culminated in the authoritative promulgation of the MDGs.

DFID lobbied for the goals all the time, and everywhere.[28] But there were a number of key moments where its advocacy was decisive.

First, the MDGs would not have been adopted without the acquiescence of the US, the world's only superpower then near the height of its international prominence, which had (and often used) the power to veto any UN agreement. The US was in 1997 and 1998 lukewarm about the goal of halving world poverty. The then head of the US Agency for International Development, Brian Atwood, had gone along with it in the DAC discussions. But he ran into opposition from the State Department and US Treasury when, in the preparations for the 1998 G8 summit to be held in Birmingham (where Short was from), the UK made clear that it wanted the summit to endorse the goals as a whole. Short was well regarded in Washington as a capable minister on top of her brief and a formidable operator, and she enjoyed the respect of her American counterparts.[29] Her advocacy, and the fact that the US decided they did not want to offend the UK in Short's home city, was instrumental in the agreement of the language in the G8 communiqué: "We commit ourselves . . . to reach the internationally agreed goals for economic and social development, as set out in the OECD's 21st Century Strategy."[30]

Second, if the OECD goals were to be pursued in a meaningful way, they had to be taken seriously by the leading international financial institutions, led by the World Bank and the IMF. From 1998, Short developed strong relationships with the Dutch, German, and Norwegian women who were the development ministers for their countries and represented them in the World Bank.[31] For several years the four, known as the Utstein group (after the Norwegian abbey where they held their first joint meeting), were a powerful force, especially in the World Bank, the OECD, and the EU.[32] In February 1999, Short and Gordon Brown wrote together to Michel Camdessus (managing director of the IMF) and Jim Wolfensohn (president of the World Bank) calling for a fundamental review to look at the link between debt relief and the DAC goals. Then, at the 1999 Spring Meeting of the governors of the World Bank in its Development Committee, the four European ministers coordinated their interventions to push the bank to make poverty reduction the overarching objective of all its programmes. Others on the Development Committee were irritated, especially when the four ministers broke established protocol by refusing to sign off the pre-prepared communiqué, which they thought did not adequately do justice to their proposals, and forced a continuation of the discussion over lunch. In the end, they had on this occasion to back off, but they had established themselves as a coalition to be accommodated in future.[33]

By the time of the World Bank and IMF annual meetings a few months later, the management of the institutions had got the message: Camdessus was actively handing out little cards with what he called the seven pledges (the DAC goals) to everyone. The Development Committee endorsed a paper prepared by the staff of the World Bank and the IMF analysing the goals and how they could be operationalised, noting particularly the advantages of outcome targets compared to input or spending commitments, while also calling for indicators to be developed which could serve as proxies for

CHAPTER 3

the measurement of interim progress before the end date of 2015. The Development Committee's endorsement effectively marked the adoption of the goals by the Bretton Woods institutions. The German minister Heidemarie Wieczorek-Zeul later wrote of Short's determination and persistence in leading the promotion of the goals in the international financial institutions.[34]

Third, there was the process through which the DAC goals were translated into the MDGs and adopted by the UN General Assembly. Short attached importance to that, reflecting her respect for the legitimacy and universality of the UN. She liked and admired UN Secretary-General Kofi Annan (who reciprocated her feelings). From mid-1998, he was thinking about how the UN would mark the coming millennium, and considering what goals could be adopted for global action in the first years of the 2000s. Work was then already underway between the OECD Secretariat, the World Bank, and the UN to develop indicators of development progress related to the seven DAC goals. An agreed set of 21 indicators was presented to the DAC ministerial meeting in April 1998. Short, with Gus Speth, then head of the UN Development Programme, proposed that the DAC Secretariat should "take the work to the UN".

In March 2000, Annan published proposals for a Millennium Declaration including a range of time-bound, specific development goals, some of which were from the DAC goals. In the summer of 2000, egged on by Short, her Utstein colleagues, and others, the heads of the UN, OECD, World Bank, and IMF put their joint names to a document launched at the UN in Geneva entitled "A Better World for All". That marked an important joining together of the UN and Bretton Woods systems, which was essential for Short's goal of getting the international development system as a whole on the same page.[35] The Millennium Declaration was adopted by the world's heads of government at their annual UN summit in New York in late 2000. It largely validated the DAC goals (though the goal relating to reproductive health was relegated, under opposition from the Vatican, conservative Islamic states, and US evangelical organ-

68

isations, and replaced with one on HIV/AIDS). And over the following year what became the final version of the MDGs, comprising eight goals and 18 targets, was developed, and then published in late 2001 by the UN.[36]

The UN negotiations were complex (as they always are) with many interests to be accommodated. Short and DFID officials followed them closely. She credited the UK's Ambassador to the UN, Jeremy Greenstock, for playing "a very helpful role" in the New York machinations.[37] Mark Malloch Brown, who as head of the UN Development Programme from July 1999 was the most influential UN official in the negotiations, has said that "the British role was critical".[38]

Short had achieved her objective of the widest possible adoption and endorsement of the DAC goals. Attempts to add new targets and cover all the different interest groups, which are ubiquitous in UN negotiations, led to some dilution of the framework. But the tight, prioritised, time-bound, and quantified focus of the goals at the forefront of the framework was retained. As Richard Manning summarised it, of the eight MDGs:

In essence, Goals 1–5 and Goal 7 were based closely on the International Development Goals, Goal 6 (HIV/AIDS) replaced the reproductive health goal, and Goal 8 [which proposed a global partnership for development, with commitments from developed countries] was entirely new. . . . The key achievement was agreement on a paradigm that had near universal acceptance and covered a large part of the development and poverty agenda.[39]

Why was the adoption of the MDGs important? They were different from all previous and subsequent internationally adopted frameworks for global development because they were (a) almost universally accepted, (b) sufficiently comprehensive to represent overall progress but also sufficiently prioritised to be tractable and actionable, and (c) supported by concerted and sustained efforts after their adoption to finance, implement, and monitor them.

Overall, then, how influential were Short and DFID during the process? David Hulme concluded that it

> *is probably accurate to say that Short did more than any other individual, and more than many DAC member countries, to promote the international development goals as a central component in the fight against world poverty.*[40]

Certainly, it is hard to think of anyone who can claim to have done more.

Debt relief

Indebtedness, especially among the poorest countries, had been a growing concern for several years when DFID was established. Most of the debt was owed to the World Bank, the IMF, and richer countries (including their aid agencies). Much of it was not being serviced, which prevented new lending. Earlier initiatives, including by the previous UK government led by John Major, had made limited impact, notwithstanding the adoption in 1996 of the new framework for heavily indebted poor countries. There were two main problems. First, the conditions for gaining relief were prohibitively restrictive, so few countries qualified. And second, it proved difficult to agree how, if the debt owed to multilateral institutions was written off, they would be compensated so that the effect was not simply to cut the resources they had to support future development.

Most of the international discussions on the debt issue took place among finance ministers, often in and around World Bank and IMF meetings. From 1998 onwards, however, Short and her Utstein colleagues invited themselves to play a prominent role in the debate, especially in the World Bank. And they brought one crucial new perspective with them. Many NGO campaigners, who were increasingly getting a hearing from finance ministries and had been successful in engaging public interest in Western countries, were seeking unconditional debt cancellation. Short did not agree with that: she thought it mattered what happened to resources freed up by reducing debt.

She and her European allies therefore proposed that debt relief should be extended but should be offered on the

> *condition that poor countries drew up poverty reduction strategies for better economic management, a crackdown on corruption, improved management of the public finances and the delivery of basic health care and education for all.*[41]

Debt relief, in other words, should be a tool for the achievement of the DAC goals.

With substantial help from Gordon Brown, who as the chair of the IMF's ministerial governing body from 1999 to 2007 was in an influential position, the Utstein group were able to get the Bretton Woods bodies to change their approach. Camdessus redesigned the IMF's main funding vehicle for the poorest countries, the Enhanced Structural Adjustment Facility, and renamed it the Poverty Reduction and Growth Facility. A decision to offer debt relief now depended on the adoption of a national poverty reduction strategy that met criteria developed by the IMF and World Bank; and the final debt write-offs depended on (normally) several years of adequate performance in implementing it.

How to pay for the new deal remained a point of contention. Incremental progress was made over a period of years, and the issue was regularly on the agenda of G8 summits. Short and her Dutch and German Utstein colleagues were instrumental in securing EU agreement by 2001 to provide 1 billion euros of unspent balances from previous European Commission aid commitments, most of which went to compensate the Bretton Woods institutions and thus underpin their future lending. Short was also happy to allocate part of her now growing budget to debt relief. She provided money both for the World Bank and IMF, and to pay for additional, unilateral steps the UK took to write off debt owed to it.[42]

CHAPTER 3

In September 2000, just 10 poor countries had reached the "decision point" (and were therefore starting to benefit from relief), but none had reached completion point, with the totality of their debts irrevocably cancelled. (Uganda was the first to get to that point, later in 2000.) By the time of Short's resignation in 2003, 26 had reached decision point, and eight completion. The package was by then worth $60 billion, though the annual savings which countries could use to increase their social spending and reduce poverty was only $2 billion.[43] The benefitting countries were also now able to access significant new funding for their development and poverty reduction goals.

Greater progress was made on debt relief subsequently. But many former DFID staff see this as one of the main achievements of the department's first years.[44] They also, however, give substantial credit to Gordon Brown and his Treasury officials for that. DFID's key contribution was in helping establish the link between debt relief and poverty reduction, which proved of lasting importance.

Financing for development

We covered earlier the significant increase in DFID's budget between 1997 and 2003. A growing DFID budget was a major asset, not least in negotiations with other countries, in what objectively was the bigger prize: increases in global levels of development assistance.

Aid levels had stagnated globally in the decades up to 2000 (Figure 3.2).[45] Part of the deal reached at the Millennium Summit was that richer countries would now provide more money to support the achievement of the MDGs. It was agreed that a major conference on financing for development would take place in Monterrey, Mexico, in March 2002. President George W. Bush decided he would go; and he wanted to help his Mexican counterpart enjoy a successful event, which meant that the US took a notably less restrictive approach than it had in the past.

That had the helpful effect of putting pressure in particular on the EU to step up. The Utstein group[46] worked closely together to coordinate positions in EU meetings with their counterparts from other

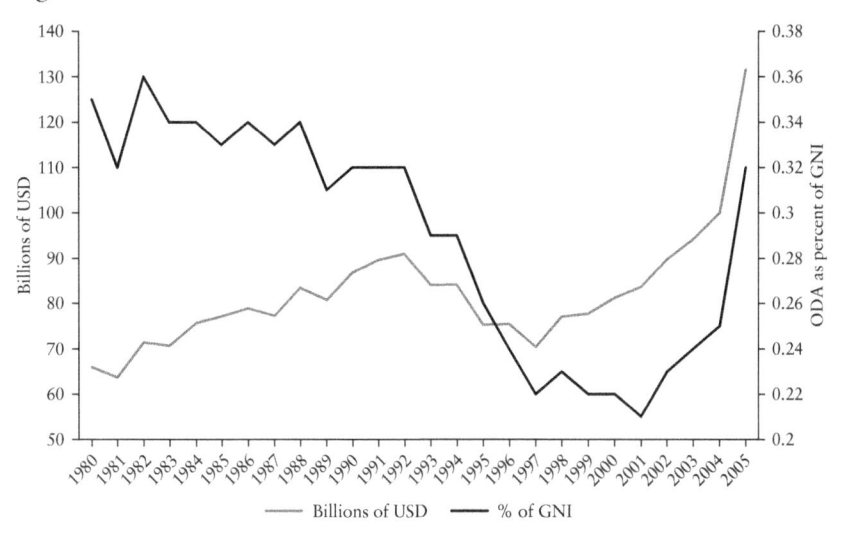

Figure 3.2. Net ODA from DAC countries

Source: OECD Creditor Reporting System (2023) (Constant 2021 prices).

member states in late 2001 and early 2002, though in fact the UK and Germany were constrained on what they could agree. Those EU countries, including the Netherlands, who had already reached the UN 0.7 per cent target, pushed for a collective EU agreement to make faster progress towards it. Short was sympathetic to that. But Brown had already set her budget up to 2004; he was marketing a different initiative to increase aid levels, and he was reluctant at that stage to set a timetable for the UK reaching the 0.7 per cent target.[47] Short and Wieczorek-Zeul nevertheless helped their Dutch colleague Eveline Herfkens and others, against opposition from Southern members states, to punt the decision on the EU's offer in Monterrey up to a meeting of EU heads of government in March 2002. There, a communiqué was agreed committing the EU to reach a collective level of 0.39 per cent by 2006, with each country aiming for a minimum of 0.33 per cent.

The upshot of the Monterrey conference was pledges that implied that development assistance would increase from $55 billion globally in 2003 to at least $67 billion by 2006.[48] The promises were kept. Aid levels did indeed increase significantly (Figure 3.2), though the headline figures are inflated by the impact of debt relief (where write-offs are credited as aid even though they do not involve new flows). Despite the caveats, Michalopoulos concludes that:

> There is little doubt that the four [Utstein] ministers made a considerable difference in pushing for and attaining concrete commitments to raise the volume of assistance ... several major donors did increase both their commitments and their actual assistance levels.[49]

Untying

For decades, aid resources from most countries were largely tied to procurement of goods and services from the donor country. The rationale was that this would make foreign assistance more tolerable to the donors' taxpayers.

The result of this approach was to reduce the effectiveness of aid. Countless studies confirmed that, as did a summary review by the OECD in the early 1990s, which found that aid tying inflated its cost to recipients by 15–30 per cent. One estimate of the scale of the wasted money put it at more than $7 billion a year.[50]

British development officials, many of them trained in economics and committed to promoting value for money, resented tying. They had also observed over the years that the commercial benefits appeared minimal. Major scandals like the Pergau dam were the tip of the iceberg. But they had never previously worked for a minister willing to create a stink over the issue. They were now keen to test out the scope for reform, and believed that it would be much better to promote a collective international agreement in which everyone would clean up their act than for the UK to go it alone. The 1997 White Paper therefore made a commitment to "pursue energetically the scope for multilateral untying of development assistance".

A saga ensued.[51] In April 1998 the ministerial meeting of the DAC tasked the secretariat to come up with a proposal for untying assistance to the least developed countries. This was thought less likely to be blocked by the traditional opponents of untying, led by France, Japan, Denmark, and, sometimes, the US. It was also judged that the least developed countries were worse affected by tying than better-off developing countries. But the proposal, when it arrived on DAC ministers' desks for their meeting the following year, was again stymied, again by France, Japan, and Denmark.

Short was irritated by the failure to progress what she thought should have been a straightforward issue. But she had to watch her back: there was a risk that British businesses might seek to join the opponents of untying. She characteristically decided to take the bull by the horns. In December 1999 she made a speech at the Adam Smith Institute, the London bastion of free market economics. The title was "Protectionism in Aid Procurement: Disposing of a Dinosaur". The first sentence set the scene: tying "wastes money, distorts objectives and makes it increasingly difficult to increase effectiveness in international development". She continued in a similar vein: "aid remains stuck in the mercantilist past, against which Adam Smith was complaining over two centuries ago"; aid tying "encourages corruption, inappropriate technology and a supplier driven mentality"; "no competitive firm has anything to fear [from untying] . . . and if you are not competitive you should not get the job".[52]

Some months later, while working on her new White Paper, Short decided to try to get cross-government agreement for it to include a commitment to full unilateral untying. She asked her officials to talk to the business lobby group, the Confederation of British Industry. They tested the water with their members and came back with a message: "no one cares". The Department of Trade and Industry were told that, and they decided not to object to Short's proposal.[53]

When the DAC ministerial gathering in June 2000 again saw progress blocked by the same opponents of untying, the UK announced that it was going to put the subject on the agenda of the G8 meeting in Japan the following month. Senior DFID officials already had the backing of Number 10 for that; and the UK team at the summit were ultimately successful in getting supportive language in the communiqué.[54]

CHAPTER 3

Then in December the White Paper was published, including the commitment to "end UK tied aid and work for multilateral untying". And finally, in 2001 the DAC agreed a package to untie aid to least developed countries, which came into force the following year. The ratio of untied to total aid to least developed countries increased from 53 per cent in 1999–2001 to 70 per cent by 2003.[55] However, multilateral untying was not extended to aid for the majority of developing countries who were not classified as least developed. Data published by the DAC in 2006 shows that only 42 per cent of total aid to all recipients was reported as untied.[56]

The results of a substantial effort were therefore ultimately disappointing. The UK's aid remains untied, but there has been no appetite for more international reform.[57]

Aid effectiveness

Other attempts were, however, made to improve the quality and effectiveness of aid. Short was keen to see some of the reforms she had agreed in the management of DFID's bilateral programme[58] taken up more widely, and this was another area in which she found common cause with her Utstein colleagues. A DAC task force on aid effectiveness was established in 2000. The outcome of the Monterrey financing for development conference in 2002 had included commitments for donors to work to reduce transactions costs, harmonise their efforts, and enhance recipient country ownership. It was followed up by a declaration agreed at a meeting of 28 recipient countries and more than 40 ministers and agency heads from development organisations in Rome in February 2003. The focus was on aligning development assistance with recipient priorities and strategies, reducing the burden donors placed on weak developing country systems, and channelling more resources through developing country budgets and institutions, rather than operating entirely outside them (as was common). The Utstein ministers characterised these reforms as "lowering the flag".

Short's interest in aid effectiveness extended to the role of multilateral agencies. She wanted to create greater incentives for multilateral agencies to improve their performance. A number of initiatives followed.[59]

From 1998 onwards, DFID published institutional strategy papers assessing the individual performance of the major agencies (including the EU's development programmes and the World Bank) and their contribution to the development goals, and setting out proposals for improvement. DFID used these strategies in its dialogue with the agencies and tracked progress. This was novel, especially because the strategies were published and widely commented upon.[60] And there was an edge to the process: Short told her senior staff that she wanted to use the evidence in determining future funding decisions for each agency.

This process was conducted purely between each institution and DFID. It did not lend itself to the construction of league tables, other comparisons, or the drawing of generic lessons. But in a related initiative, attempts were also made to produce a comparative analysis of all the major institutions, based on published data. The first iterations lacked depth and rigour, and duly attracted a lot of negative feedback especially from those being criticised. But they became more sophisticated. DFID created a multilateral effectiveness framework (MEFF) from 2003. A report commissioned by the Danish government offered an assessment:

DFID established the MEFF for assessing the organisational effectiveness of multilaterals . . . to provide information for public accountability, and as an input to policy and financing decisions . . . Among bilateral donor methodologies the MEFF comes closest to a comprehensive measurement approach and has been considered by other donors a good starting point.[61]

In parallel, DFID was interested in whether, rather than conducting such exercises on its own, a collective approach involving other donors could be set up. It promoted the establishment from 2002 of the first collective donor system: the Multilateral Organisation Performance Assessment Network. With around 20 countries now among its members, the network has conducted dozens of reviews on major agencies: the UN Development Programme has been reviewed four times.

All these innovations have flaws and limitations. They are, though, better than the lacuna they replaced. The aid effectiveness agenda, including multilateral reform, was built up further in subsequent years, with DFID consistently playing a leading role. Valuable foundations were established in this period.

New international organisations on global health

Some of today's most important aid institutions, in particular the Global Fund to Fight Aids, Tuberculosis and Malaria and the Global Alliance on Vaccines and Immunization (Gavi), the vaccine alliance, were created in the years after DFID's establishment. They were a response to a growing swell of concern that new health technologies – including vaccines, drugs to combat HIV/AIDS, and insecticide-treated bed nets to protect people against malaria – were taking too long to reach enough people in the poorest countries.

A new initiative promoted by the Bill and Melinda Gates Foundation to encourage manufacturers to reduce prices for vaccines for the poorest countries in return for long-term, large-scale, and predictable demand from those countries was given public life in 2000 through the establishment of Gavi. DFID staff recall persuading Clare Short to host one of its early board meetings. Broadening access to immunisation had a strong appeal for the hardheaded, economically literate senior officials of DFID. For a cheap, one-time investment which was relatively easy to implement even in countries with weak administrative capacity, babies and young children could be given lifetime protection against a variety of diseases that still took millions of lives a year in poorer countries.[62] It was not a hard sell.

Similar ideas to tackle HIV/AIDS and tuberculosis were initially more controversial. There were discussions at the G8 summits in Japan and Italy in 2000 and 2001 about establishing a new global health fund, but disagreements about how far its mandate should extend. The main push was for something to make new drugs for people with HIV/AIDS more widely available. Some DFID staff worried that the new drugs were still expensive, and that recipients would need to take them continuously for the rest of their lives. They feared that the effect of switching aid resources into this potentially at the expense of other health problems (like maternal mortality and malaria) might paradoxically be higher loss of life.[63] Nevertheless, global concern, not least in the US, grew, and the Global Fund to Fight AIDS, Tuberculosis and Malaria was established with DFID's involvement in 2002.

Public-private partnerships on investment and infrastructure[64]

Clare Short thought private enterprise had a crucial role in increasing incomes. But she was aware that markets often worked badly for poor people and their enterprises, and she was interested in how that might be addressed.

She quickly focused on the potential role of the Commonwealth Development Corporation (CDC), for which DFID was the 100 per cent shareholder. Established in 1948, CDC lent money and took equity stakes in businesses. In 1997 it was investing around £250 million a year, financed by proceeds from earlier investments. (The government had not put in new money for decades.) Advised by Barrie Ireton, one of DFID's director generals, Short wanted to find ways to expand its impact; directly, through mobilising capital from others, and indirectly by demonstrating that it was possible to make commercial returns in poorer countries. (In 1997 developing countries received $185 billion in foreign direct investment, but the bulk went to better-off countries, with the least developed attracting less than $4 billion.) The DFID budget was too constrained to afford new capital; and the Treasury refused to allow CDC to borrow on the markets.

So a plan was hatched – and announced by Tony Blair in October 1997 – to allow private investors to buy shares in CDC, with the government retaining a controlling interest to preserve CDC's developmental purpose. The hope was that this would both bring in more capital and demonstrate that private money could be used successfully in the poorer countries. Legislation was passed in 1999; new management was brought into CDC; and a new investment policy and higher ethical, environmental, and social standards were adopted. Reality then intervened: stock market downturns in 2001 and worries over whether the government would stick to its new policy cooled investor interest. The plan was quietly dropped.

Instead, CDC was restructured into a model common in the private equity industry: an asset holder with a few dozen staff was created (keeping the name CDC), and the bulk of the business and staff were spun out into a management company, Actis. CDC and Actis were encouraged to bring in more third-party private capital; Actis were incentivised to manage it as profitably as possible in line with CDC's investment policy and principles. This all took time, and the new arrangements only went live in 2004.

In a related initiative, struck by the massive inadequacy of basic public infrastructure (transport, water distribution and sewage plants, power stations, etc.), Short asked her officials to explore the scope for new public-private partnerships there too. The most important concrete result was the creation in 2002 of a Private Infrastructure Development Group, which created an Emerging Africa Infrastructure Fund. DFID provided $100 million in equity; Standard Bank, Barclays, and others provided $205 million in loans. DFID quickly sold on half its investment, by bringing in government bodies in the Netherlands, Sweden, and Switzerland. The Emerging Africa Infrastructure Fund has subsequently mobilised more than $27 billion for profitable infrastructure investments benefitting more than 150 million people in Africa, mostly from private sources.[65] It was another example of DFID's early impact and influence over others which later bore rich fruit.

One more among the wide range of new international public-private partnerships is particularly deserving of mention. The 2000 White Paper had been up-front on the toxic effect of corruption in holding back developing countries. The government undertook to bring UK law into line with the OECD Convention on the Bribery of Foreign Public Officials (i.e., to make it a crime in the UK to pay a bribe to an official overseas). Corruption was widely known to be a particular scourge in the hydrocarbons and minerals sector. In 2003, following years of preparatory work,[66] DFID, alongside other governments, leading companies, and civil society groups, launched the Extractive Industries Transparency Initiative. Its mandate was to promote greater transparency in what foreign investors pay to host governments – and what governments receive in revenues – from the mineral sector. Years after leaving office, Clare Short chaired its board from 2011 to 2016.

FOUR

"Clare's New World"? The Verdict on the Short Years

WE HAVE explained why Labour created DFID, how it set out its stall, how it worked as part of the wider government and how Britain in these years sought to influence what the rest of the world was doing to reduce extreme poverty.[1] But what was the ultimate effect of all this activity, especially on the lives of those it was intended to help? Here we discuss, first, how the policies, money, and activities we have analysed translated into progress on the MDGs, identifying DFID's particular role in that; and, second, how well positioned the department was by 2003 for the period that lay ahead.

The big picture

The available data is clear that between 1997 and 2003, life was getting better for billions of people in developing countries, including in sub-Saharan Africa and South Asia where extreme poverty was concentrated. Partly, this was due to better macroeconomic conditions in these parts of the world. Figure 4.1 extends the data on inflation and growth we presented earlier to cover the 2000s. The improved performance is unmistakeable. Inflation fell from a double-digit norm, with a wide range, to being manageable almost everywhere; per capita growth went from negative to moderately positive and consistent.

Three key factors contributed to this economic improvement. First, there was positive impact from the economic situation in the rest of the world. The East Asian "miracle" economies crashed in 1997 but

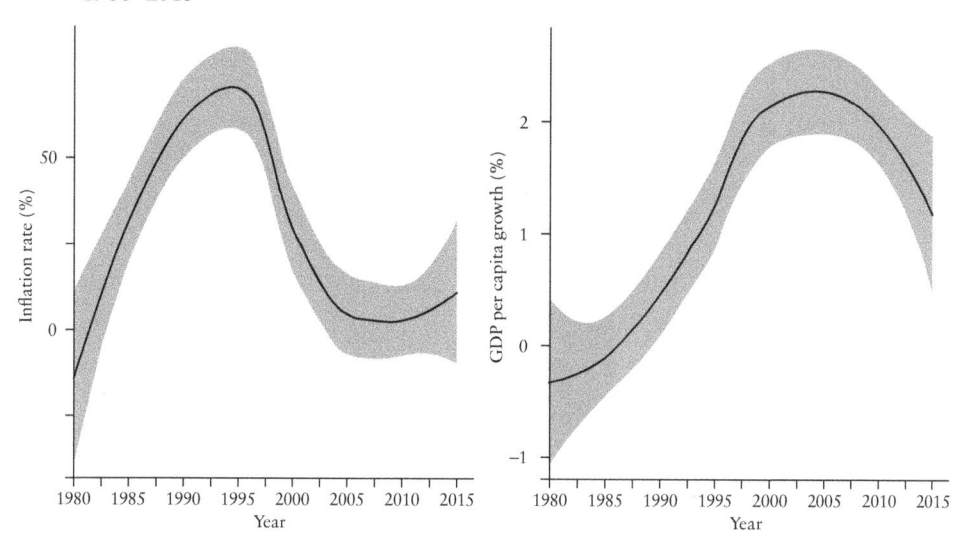

Figure 4.1. Inflation and GDP per capita growth, sub-Saharan Africa 1980–2015

Source: World Bank World Development Indicators, accessed through the R Package "WDI".
Note: The central line is a local regression showing how inflation and GDP per capita growth changed over time. The grey shaded areas give the 95 per cent confidence intervals for this relationship.

recovered quickly and spent most of the 2000s in steady, relatively high growth. China was at this point still a recipient of grant aid from the UK and a significant borrower from the World Bank, and not, as it would become, a major source of development finance for poorer countries. Nevertheless, it did play a role in the economic recovery in Africa. It was just entering its extraordinary period of sustained high economic growth, and its rapid industrialisation pushed global commodity prices up, with proceeds flowing to many African commodity exporters. The US and EU grew more slowly, but without any serious blips. Fiscal policy was steady in the advanced economies, and interest rates in the US and UK began to decline in the beginning of the 1990s, reaching what were then historically low levels for much of the late 1990s and 2000s. Oil prices rose steadily from the early 1990s, peaking in 2008, a boon to poor but resource-rich countries

CHAPTER 4

like Nigeria, home to a large share of the world's poor.[2] The late 1990s and 2000s were, until the crash of 2008, as benign and serene a period of global economic progress as we have ever witnessed.

Second, painful as it was, the structural adjustment policies forced on most developing countries as they struggled with unsustainable debt burdens and unmanageable fiscal deficits moved them into broadly sound macroeconomic management. The evidence is clear in the inflation graph in Figure 4.1: economic mismanagement was certainly not a thing of the past, but some of its worst and most destructive aspects had been at least temporarily tamed.

And third, as discussed earlier, the 2000s was a period of reduced conflict in most developing countries. It is extremely hard to grow the economy steadily in the midst of bloody violence; relative peace was the necessary basis on which a decade of increasing prosperity was founded.

Economic stability was necessary for progress on the MDGs; and economic growth contributes towards their achievement.[3] But to accelerate progress, directed and focused action was also needed. Progress shows up clearly in the data. The Human Development Index (HDI), a composite measure bringing together life expectancy, access to education, and average incomes, saw notable increases in the regions of greatest poverty, and also in the 18 countries in which DFID focused much of its direct effort. Data on progress on the MDGs in these regions and the 18 focus countries tells the same story. Progress was gradual but noticeable.[4] Figure 4.2 shows progress on the HDI over this period. Three points are worth noting. First, this was a period of general improvement – the HDI was improving globally and in each region. Second, the 18 countries which by 2003 accounted for roughly two-thirds of DFID's aid had particularly low scores on the HDI (i.e., they were particularly needy – that of course was why the department was making most of its effort in those countries). And third, their rate of improvement was slightly faster than the global average and the average for sub-Saharan Africa or South Asia. These last two points are particularly important; as we said in Chapter 2,

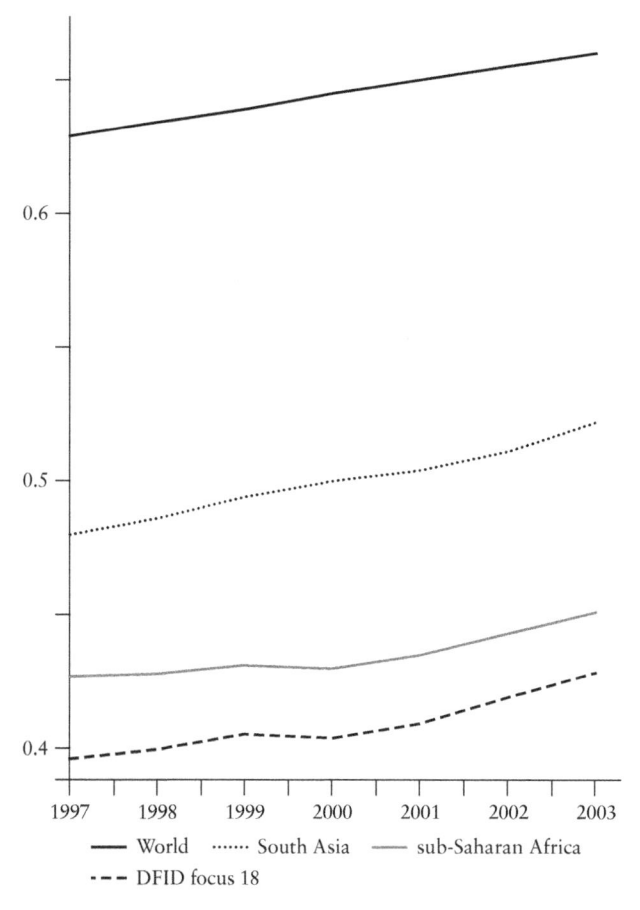

Figure 4.2. Human Development Index 1997–2003

——— World ······· South Asia ——— sub-Saharan Africa
--- DFID focus 18

Source: World Bank World Development Indicators, accessed through the R Package "WDI".

the first steps out of extreme deprivation have the largest effect on welfare. It is also worth noting that the improvement is not an artefact of the aggregation of multiple countries or indicators into a single index: the figures in Appendix B show that improvements are clear and visible in under-five mortality, life expectancy at birth, and GNI per capita in all of the 18 countries except Zimbabwe (which was in the midst of some truly remarkable economic mismanagement).

CHAPTER 4

What was DFID's contribution?

How far progress on the development goals can be ascribed to DFID is a more difficult question to answer. Any country's fate and progress are determined primarily internally, by the actions of its own leaders, citizens, businesses, and the state and other institutions. The global economy was largely untroubled between 1999 and 2007; state-based conflict was historically low; much of the ugly and painful work of remaking macroeconomic policy in the poorest parts of the world had already been done. These were favourable circumstances for an ambitious organisation bent on reducing poverty. DFID's objective was to take advantage of this situation and accelerate progress, even though external factors, including aid, are only ever a contributory factor, and, as in most areas of public policy, there is a notable time lag (running into years) between setting the policy, taking the action (including spending money) to achieve it, and then generating the outcomes. The oil tanker analogy is apposite: much of what was put in place by 2003 did not feed through to real-world outcomes until some years later.

That said, DFID plausibly contributed in three ways: through contributions to economic growth and stability (via policy advice, support to the debt relief initiatives, and financial support); through programmes supporting specific MDG goals, especially in health and education; and indirectly through its influence on what other players in the international development system did.

It is clear that the fruits of DFID's engagement across the international development system (which we described in Chapter 3) were substantial. What is striking in retrospect is the scale and breadth of the ambition, and the energy with which it was pursued. In some areas, DFID can reasonably claim to have played the leading role (as in the creation of the MDGs and the Private Infrastructure Development Group). In others it was a loud voice singing alongside a few others to a crowd that was sometimes happy to join the chorus (increasing EU aid levels, and new global institutions for health). And on occasion it was more like a comet, burning brightly but briefly and then fizzling out (untying). Short led from the front. But she was careful to build alliances and seek to collaborate with others on the international scene (sometimes more so than in dealing with her ministerial colleagues at home). That often paid off.

In summary we can confidently say that:

- DFID was clear and consistent in the objectives it was trying to achieve;
- It adopted policies that were, based on international consensus at the time, conducive to those objectives;
- It allocated a growing and by the end of the period significant budget rigorously to seek to maximise its contribution to the development goals, with a strong focus on countries where the needs were greatest and the scope for progress highest;
- It was influential in encouraging other countries, the EU, and multilateral agencies – who collectively were able to make a larger impact – to do the same;
- And the evidence is clear that DFID's projects and programmes were, when you add them all up, largely successful in achieving the individual goals set for them, though the scale of effort was, while bigger than previously, not yet large enough to move the dial as far as would later prove feasible.

It is not possible to quantify in any meaningful way how much of the improvement in life experiences for many people in poor countries from 1997 to 2003 can be attributed to DFID. Our judgement is that, combining its direct and indirect contributions, DFID's role was distinctive and material.

The state of DFID in 2003

The capability, reputation, culture, and effectiveness of the department was, from the valuable but limited embryo of the Overseas

CHAPTER 4

Development Administration, strengthened substantially in these years. What was put in place was reinforced, adapted, and tinkered with over the following 15 years, but it was not fundamentally unpicked. Powerful foundations had been established from which an edifice was built that made a notably bigger impact in the decade that followed.

It is often said that the most important test of leaders is what is retained from what they did years after they have moved on. That question is particularly relevant to DFID after Clare Short, given the role she played from 1997 to 2003 and the potentially destabilising circumstances of her departure.

Some writers have attributed an almost overwhelming weight to her personal role in creating the department. Robert Greenhill, one-time head of the Canadian International Development Agency, who admired DFID, wrote:

> *What drove the difference? In a word, leadership. Short imposed focus and drive on her organization. She believed that DFID should – and could – make a real difference. She recruited the best and brightest from the UK and abroad. She encouraged discussion and debate. She demanded excellence.*[5]

Without diluting Short's contribution, it is clear that things were more complicated than that.

DFID was now regarded as a success story by Labour. Support for international development resonated with the party's values. It was important to be able to demonstrate the effort being spent was achieving results, and that was done successfully.

Even more important than the generality of views across the Labour Party, though, was the attitude of Tony Blair and Gordon Brown, the government's dominant personalities. It is a little paradoxical, given that Short was often publicly and privately critical of Blair, and her relations with Brown also had their ups and downs, that as time passed the interest of both in DFID's work, and their confidence that DFID could deliver, grew.

Brown has written of how, coming into government, he wanted international development to have a higher profile, emphasising his focus on the goal of eradicating poverty and improving development, his admiration of Short's "dynamic leadership", how they worked well together, and the impact of using aid more effectively to reduce poverty.[6] He played a major international role in debt relief, and his interests in development extended and deepened from there. Above all, Brown controlled the money: he exercised an iron grip over the public finances; he took the major decisions in successive spending reviews on how much each department received; and giving such preference to the DFID budget was his personal choice.

Blair formed a positive view of DFID and its senior staff partly as a result of what he saw personally in Kosovo during the 1999 refugee crisis.[7] He made a series of visits to Africa with Short from 1999 onwards; she was sometimes critical of his motives and questioned his understanding, but his interest was genuine and his engagement sustained throughout his tenure and long beyond.[8] At the UN Millennium Summit in September 2000, he made a powerful speech on the need to provide better support for progress in Africa, and he followed through on that.

Labour's manifesto for the 2001 general election accordingly doubled down on its support for development. The coverage was much fuller than in the 1997 manifesto, with a range of commitments and initiatives building on the 2000 White Paper. They embraced new plans to achieve the MDGs, support for economic reform, debt relief, increasing DFID's budget, and a particular focus on Africa.[9] That laid the foundations for a continued priority to development for the remainder of the decade. Short's departure from government in response to Britain's involvement in the Iraq War in 2003 did not derail this, though it was well known that DFID was institutionally sceptical of the wisdom of invading Iraq to depose Saddam Hussein, and the department (like others) was subsequently criticised for inadequate engagement in preparations for the war and its aftermath.

Labour's stance was not at this stage matched by the Conservative opposition. Their 2001 election manifesto[10] offered barely 200 words on aid and development. Many of them were devoted to aid charities (with the remarkable claim that "they are often better placed than governments to relieve suffering"), criticism of the EU, and a plan to appoint an envoy for religious freedom. There was no reference to the MDGs or to reducing poverty or to DFID.

Parliamentary views more broadly were positive. Its development committee (chaired by two successive Conservative MPs) proved an increasingly strong supporter of the department, and a source of valuable policy analysis and proposals. Its 2001/02 report on "Financing for Development" backed increasing the aid budget.[11] In its response to the department's 2003 annual report, it commended DFID's role in directly supporting government budgets.[12] It was also consistent and constructive in identifying areas for improvement, many of which were subsequently taken up.

Clare Short had also pursued initiatives to engage the wider public in discussions on international development. Throughout her period in office, she travelled across the UK, going to schools and universities and meeting other groups. Development was also included in the national curriculum as part of what every child would learn at school.[13] It is not clear what lasting impact such initiatives had. For most of the British population, the government's role in international development was not a significant concern, either positively or negatively. They had other preoccupations. Surveys showed that they wanted their government to play a role in responding to disasters and extreme poverty. But most people acquiesced in, rather than being energised by, the priority Labour increasingly gave to development. Criticism from the right-wing press (which grew subsequently) was in this phase relatively muted.

Our assessment is that the UK system as a whole, including DFID, but also other government departments, Parliament, civil society, and research organisations contributed more than the sum of its parts to global development. That system was significantly enhanced in this period, not least as a result of the role the department played. Britain's influence increased as DFID's reputation grew.

The decision in 1997 to establish DFID had been vindicated. The extent of that vindication became even clearer in the following years.

PART TWO

Delivering on the Job

2003–10

FIVE

The Policy Evolves, the Budget Grows, and DFID's Reputation Blossoms

THIS WAS a phase of consolidation in DFID, and of increased effectiveness and impact. The aid budget grew rapidly. Further increases were locked in; that added to the department's international influence, because others could see that it might be worth strengthening relations with them.

International commitment to the MDGs grew up to 2005, peaking with the Gleneagles G8 summit that year, with its motivating slogan to make poverty history. But from then on, and especially in the wake of the 2008–09 financial crisis, the UK's ambition was ahead of many of its peers.

Tony Blair and – above all – Gordon Brown determined the priority the government gave to development. But the goals they championed had to be turned into reality, and DFID worked hard to do that. It was largely successful; significant progress was made towards the MDGs, especially in countries in which the department made its main effort.

The failures in Iraq after the war which deposed Saddam Hussein, and the revitalisation of the Taliban in Afghanistan, which we will come to in Chapter 6, pointed to the biggest strategic challenge: the countries making least progress were those where governments were not committed to poverty reduction or where conflict derailed development. This was to become a dominant theme for the remainder of DFID's existence.

CHAPTER 5

Still a benign economic context for development

Despite the global financial crisis in 2008, the first decade of the twenty-first century was probably the best period of sustained economic growth and poverty reduction in the developing world in the last hundred years. Helped along, in commodity exporting countries, by steadily rising prices,[1] economic growth in sub-Saharan Africa was high and reasonably stable throughout the decade, generally remaining above 4 per cent per annum, with a brief dip to 3 per cent in the wake of the crisis.[2] Looking at low-income and middle-income countries alone,[3] the performance was even better. Growth was fast enough to outpace the increase in population and support higher living standards.

This strong economic performance was not just manna from heaven. The structural adjustment reforms most countries put in place so they could access financial assistance from the World Bank, IMF, and others, in particular budget support and debt relief, played an important role. Macroeconomic management in this period improved almost everywhere, as inflation was brought under control, and many countries finally enjoyed substantial debt cancellation. All told, there was a truly remarkable turnaround in the economic fortunes of many African countries in this period, and while credit must go to their governments for making the most of good circumstances, the international community helped a lot too.

Even the global financial crisis did not derail this progress: growth dipped, but never turned negative in most developing countries, as it did in Europe and the US. Because this was a banking crisis, its direct impact in countries which were yet to fully integrate into the global financial system was muted, and these countries were also less exposed via trading relationships to the countries worst affected.[4]

Policy evolution

The government published two more White Papers on development, both again under the strap line "eliminating world poverty". Hilary

Benn, secretary of state from mid-2003, had put off the first until after the 2005 election, hoping then to set the agenda for the four or five years of the next Parliament. The White Paper he developed and published in 2006 – with the help of a talented team led by Moazzam Malik (later a director general in DFID and then in the merged Foreign, Commonwealth and Development Office) – presented a sharp analysis and policy proposals framed around making governance work for the poor.[5] The analytical framework, drawing both on recent academic publications and some of the department's most insightful practitioners,[6] focused on how to improve the capability, responsiveness, and accountability of states in poorer countries. It was unapologetic in recognising the central role of the state in every country that had ever developed successfully.

The publication of the 2006 White Paper was also the moment that the penny dropped for many people that the Conservative opposition had changed their tune on development. Andrew Mitchell, recently appointed by the new Conservative leader David Cameron as the shadow secretary of state, took his chance when the White Paper was launched in Parliament on 26 October:

> *We strongly support the Government's goals for international development as set out by the secretary of state today. Support for the British contribution to international development is not a Labour or Conservative policy, but a British commitment, and the secretary of state knows that he can rely on support from across the House. . . . The secretary of state and the minister are, uniquely, doing a good job, and we applaud them for it.*[7]

The department's new tilt towards governance was a forced response to what was increasingly understood as the main threat to the achievement of the MDGs: conflict, fragility, insecurity, and other features of weak and failing states. Often, governments and elites in these places barely even paid lip service to reducing the suffering of their poorest citizens. More ink was spilled on what to do when the government was the problem than on any other challenge.[8]

CHAPTER 5

As Douglas Alexander, secretary of state from 2007, told us:

I felt that as the geography of poverty was changing, we needed to rethink and reset our capability to do development in conflict-affected and fragile states.[9]

Michael Anderson notes another key reason for the paradigm shift:

The Twin Towers [the 9/11 attacks in New York and Washington in 2001] ... shaped the way we thought about things. For the next generation we were all constantly in the shadow of terrorism and how we responded to terrorism.[10]

DFID was on the front foot in its willingness to grapple publicly with the policy dilemmas. (The World Bank had generally been looked to for cutting-edge thinking on development challenges, often in their annual keynote World Development Reports. But the international community had to wait until 2011 for a World Development Report on conflict, security, and development.)[11] The department also worked to build an international consensus on the issues. It contributed prominently to OECD guidance for donors.[12] The DAC reported that the UK was "among the leaders in promoting effective international engagement in fragile states".[13]

The final Labour White Paper,[14] published in 2009, was, at nearly 150 pages, the longest. It had chapters on, among other things, economic recovery, climate change, peace and security, (further) reform of the international system, and ensuring the impact and value for money of aid spending. In truth, though, it broke little new ground in policy terms. Its most important role was in helping lock in the national political consensus on prioritising development even through the UK's economic travails following the global financial crisis.

As Gordon Brown[15] put it in his foreword:

Some argue that in these difficult times the rich world should turn our backs on the Millennium Development Goals and retreat from the promises we have made to the poor. . . . While others might be tempted to shy away from their development responsibilities, the United Kingdom will keep the promises we have made.

Reinforcing his boss, Douglas Alexander made clear in his preface to the White Paper that poverty and the MDGs were still the focus of DFID's efforts.

The fact that the government were doubling down in publishing the 2009 White Paper made it harder for the Conservative opposition to back off. They declined to take the bait. Andrew Mitchell told the House of Commons on 6 July 2009 when the government launched it that:

There is much in the White Paper that we welcome, not least since it adopts a number of themes and specific ideas that the Opposition have been championing now for more than four years. . . . Poverty breeds extremism, incubates disease and drives migration and conflict. Tackling poverty and deprivation is not merely a moral duty that we must discharge with passion and rigour – it is also in our best national interest. It is also a matter of relief to many of our fellow citizens that this is no longer a Labour or Conservative agenda but a British agenda that commands widespread support.[16]

What about other policy issues? Much of the vibrant activity that had, between 1997 and 2003, characterised DFID's engagement in non-aid policies affecting developing countries fizzled out. Multilateral trade talks, in particular, remained bogged down for the rest of the decade. The only real glint of light was in aid for trade. At the World Trade Organization's ministerial meeting in Hong Kong in 2005, an initiative was agreed for more and better coordinated assistance to build the infrastructure, institutions, and skills which underpin international trade.[17] In itself, that opened no new markets, but the projects that followed over the next decade (in which DFID played a notable part) did facilitate a growth of trade among developing countries, especially in Africa.

In his foreword to the 2006 White Paper, Hilary Benn wrote that "climate change is becoming the most serious and urgent problem the world faces". There are more than a hundred references to the climate problem in that White Paper.[18] It assumed even greater importance as time passed. The 2009 White Paper mentions climate change 159 times.[19] In policy and operational terms, the main DFID response was to help developing countries engage in international negotiations, and to adapt their own economies and societies to what was clearly coming.

Corruption also loomed larger as a threat to development. Hilary Benn was appointed as the government's anti-corruption tsar. He regularly convened Whitehall-wide meetings in the Cabinet Office, in an attempt to gee up stronger action from the UK's law and order bodies. DFID funded projects to make anti-corruption agencies in its focus countries more effective. In Sierra Leone that led to the prosecution for corruption of the minister for health. In Nigeria the department helped the economic and financial crimes commission improve national compliance with anti-money-laundering rules. It also funded police units in the UK to investigate allegations of corruption in developing countries involving British citizens or businesses. The DFID annual report for 2009/10 reported that this had led to assets worth £160 million being recovered or seized, as well as the first convictions for foreign bribery.[20]

Under Douglas Alexander, these programmes were reinforced. However, he also saw a risk that the anti-aid lobby would use concern over corruption to undermine public support for development. In fact, aid resources were often less exposed to corruption than countries' own resources, because aid agencies had systems to ensure money got to where it was intended to go. But that was a hard narrative to sell. While there were 78 references to corruption in the 2006 White Paper, the 2009 one contained only 19.[21]

More money

The department's budget continued to grow steadily, as shown in Table 5.1. The poverty focus of resource allocation was further reinforced.[22] It came under pressure in 2003, when the department had to free up resources to spend in Iraq to help with the recovery after the US-led invasion of Iraq. Hilary Benn took a principled decision to stick to the earlier commitment to allocate 90 per cent of regional resources to low-income countries. That meant other budgets had to be reduced to finance activities in Iraq. Senior officials saw this an as opportunity to scale back and close remaining activities in countries which were beyond the MDGs, including in central and south America.[23] Much of the 10 per cent of the budget that was available for countries that were not low-income went to the Middle East – and not just to Iraq. There was a substantial increase in help for Palestinians too, both in the occupied territories and in Jordan and Lebanon.

Some 80 per cent of the increase in bilateral aid between 2001 and 2009 was allocated to fragile states.[24] The share going to the 18 focus countries increased to nearly 70 per cent. In some of them, the increase

Table 5.1. DFID budget and UK ODA 2003/04 and 2009/10

£m (current prices)	2003/04	2009/10
Total DFID	3,528	6,590
Of which regional programmes	1,623	2,666
Of which focus countries	949	1,810
Share	58%	68%
Total UK ODA	4,302	8,452
Of which: bilateral	2,914	5,191
multilateral	1,388	3,261
DFID share of UK ODA	82%	77%

Source: DFID Annual Reports. See notes in Table 2.2.

in DFID funding was dramatic (Table 5.2). Aid to Afghanistan increased 20 fold in real terms in the years 2003 to 2010 compared to the total provided between 1997 and 2003; in the Democratic Republic of Congo there was also a 20 fold increase; in Ethiopia it was 10 fold; the budget for Nigeria (spent mostly in the north of the country, where poverty was severe and endemic) grew by more than five times; in Pakistan it trebled; and in India (still then a low-income country) it grew by two and a half times. There was, in other words, a huge increase in support for big countries where most of the world's extreme poor lived. That was precisely what achieving the MDGs required.

But there were substantial increases elsewhere too: Bangladesh, Ghana, Malawi, Nepal, Rwanda, Tanzania, and others in the 18 all saw their budgets (roughly) doubling in real terms. Increases on this scale were big enough for the UK to make a real contribution on issues like infant mortality and life expectancy, especially because, as we will see in Chapter 7, they came along with sharp increases in DFID funding for multilateral agencies most focused on the MDGs (like the global health funds).

By 2006, the UK's aid as a share of national income reached 0.52 per cent, the highest ever to that point. (It was, however, artificially inflated by debt relief, which reached a peak around then.) In its manifesto for the 2005 election, the Labour Party pledged to reach the UN target of 0.7 per cent by 2013. Given the experience of recent years, the promise was credible. And it was accompanied by a loosening of some of the controls traditionally imposed by HM Treasury. As Nilima Gulrajani notes:

The levels of trust engendered in DFID permitted operational flexibility to "break all the Treasury rules", including the ability to make ten-year budget commitments despite a three-year budget cycle, increased delegated authority to field offices, to embrace risk and innovation as an opportunity for greater returns, and to engage in situations where the obstacles to poverty alleviation are more political than technical.[25]

Table 5.2. Cumulative growth in DFID aid in focus countries

£million	1997–2003	2003–10
Afghanistan	58	1,089
Bangladesh	624	1,185
DRC	36	684
Ethiopia	136	1,143
Ghana	465	814
India	1,166	2,699
Kenya	327	553
Malawi	446	702
Mozambique	274	598
Nepal	188	421
Nigeria	158	832
Pakistan	262	756
Rwanda	204	463
Sierra Leona	240	409
Tanzania	596	1,180
Uganda	589	709
Zambia	271	412
Zimbabwe	148	424
Total 18 countries	6,186	15,072
Total DFID regional programmes	10,105	22,111
Total DFID	25,935	50,332

Source: DFID Annual Reports, adjusted for inflation (2022 prices).

These dispensations were immensely valuable given the concentration of DFID's effort in places where the risk was high and a patient, long-term commitment was essential.

This period also, however, saw an increasing fragmentation of responsibilities for the aid budget across government. In 2006 Gordon

Brown announced the creation of an International Environmental Transformation Fund, with allocations initially amounting to £800 million to the Department for the Environment and the Foreign Office as well as DFID.[26] This expanded a precedent set by the creation of cross-departmental conflict pools in Clare Short's time.

Notwithstanding the substantial growth in the DFID budget, it still accounted for less than 1 per cent of the UK's total public spending by 2010.

The department's political leadership

Earlier studies of DFID have looked at the role of ministers. An ODI report in 2017 commented:

> *Secretaries of State often greatly influence how DFID is managed based on their personal and political party ideology, rather than primarily the complex realities of aid implementation.*

It goes on to observe that politicians should

> *resist the temptation of promising more and better results and value for money, given the implications that this has for target setting in aid management.*[27]

The underlying tone is critical – that politicians somehow are a problem. Our view is different: the job of office-holding politicians is to choose the best technocratic approach to achieving public policy goals which is consistent with what the public will accept (or at least acquiesce in). Politicians can sometimes lead public opinion. Sometimes they have to respond to it. The most successful are those who get the balance right between the two.

Measured by this standard DFID was for most of its life lucky in its political leadership – including between 2003 and 2010. Clare Short had ruffled a few Whitehall feathers in carving out an influential role for the department. Blair now wanted someone more biddable, collaborative, and on-message. Valerie Amos[28] was appointed when Short resigned, but was moved after five months to become the Leader of the House of Lords.

Hilary Benn then took over until 2007; he had come in with Amos as minister of state, having also previously served in DFID as one of Short's parliamentary under-secretaries of state. A poll of those who served on DFID's staff over its lifetime would, we suspect, rank Benn as the most personally popular of all the 11 politicians who served as secretary of state between 1997 and 2020.[29] Some thought he was too nice for his own good. But he was also effective. He worked hard on supporting recovery and reconstruction in Iraq at Blair's behest, and was happy to slide in behind Brown's health and education initiatives. He did his best to make nice with Jack Straw's Foreign Office, but not at the expense of financing foolish ventures or being knocked off the department's core strategy of achieving the MDGs.

Benn also had a steely side. Paul Wolfowitz, one of the architects of the 2003 Iraq War, was in 2005, following a nomination by US President George W. Bush, made president of the World Bank. In April 2007, the *Financial Times* reported that, shortly after being appointed, Wolfowitz had personally directed the bank's human resources chief to give a promotion and large pay rise to a female staff member with whom he was in a relationship.[30] A kerfuffle was thus ignited. Circling the wagons, the US Treasury Secretary and World Bank governor Hank Paulson called Benn (the UK governor) seeking support for Wolfowitz – and expecting it, given the closeness of the Blair–Bush relationship. "I know it does not look pretty" began Paulson. "No", interrupted Benn, "it does not".[31] Wolfowitz's resignation was announced the following month. There were other nails in the coffin, but Benn's was an early and important one.

When Gordon Brown took over as prime minister in 2007, he appointed Douglas Alexander, a long-time close personal aide, as the new secretary of state. Alexander multi-tasked: he also chaired the Cabinet Committee on trade and was in charge of Labour's election planning. Clever, committed to development, and sometimes demanding to work for (as, in fairness, he was entitled to be), Alexander's most seminal contribution was arguably in helping lock in the UK's pledges on development in the wake of the global financial crisis and the run up to the 2010 election. He saw the danger of the Conservative opposition shimmying off its new pro-development stance. As he told us in an interview, "I always regarded the Conservatives' commitment to development as fragile." Labour doubling down, not least in the 2009 White Paper, was no small thing.

Benn and Alexander were supported by junior ministers. Under Benn, the model was as it had been with Clare Short – a single junior minister supporting the secretary of state. Gareth Thomas, another self-declared Blair loyalist,[32] was appointed to that role in 2003. He became DFID's longest-serving minister, staying with the department right up to the 2010 election (for the last two years on promotion to minister of state.) Thomas was unusually (and unnecessarily) self-effacing as a minister, seeing his role as to support Benn, Alexander, and the department's agenda:

By the time I arrived in DFID, the calibre of the staff team was very strong . . . Other countries knew they were talking to very serious people and very capable people . . . [DFID] had a global reputation as a very big player, and . . . serious strategic thinkers in the UK recognised that DFID was crucial to Britain's soft power and influence. . . . The weakness was the department wasn't very political in a British sense. So it didn't always pick up where political debate in the UK was going.[33]

Thomas' point is a good one, though it is also fair to say that senior civil servants looked to their ministers for political direction and a sense of where the wind was blowing.

The DFID ministerial team was more complicated in the Brown premiership from June 2007. Alexander was initially supported by three junior ministers. Shriti Vadera, a "brilliant and fiery City analyst who had been central to Brown's financial and industrial decision-making",[34] was elevated to the Lords and appointed parliamentary under-secretary of state. Shahid Malik, elected as the MP for Dewsbury in 2005, was appointed too, and Gareth Thomas was kept on.

Vadera, who previously had made important contributions to some of the innovative initiatives for financing development Brown had proposed, was moved in January 2008 to help cope with the global financial crisis. She was succeeded by a Commons minister, Gillian Merron, who had served in a range of ministerial posts in other departments, but she, too, was moved on after a few months. Her successor was Ivan Lewis, who also lasted less than a year. When he transferred to the Foreign Office in 2009, the department reverted back from four to three ministers – to the (mostly) unspoken relief of a good number of staff. Malik had been moved in October 2008. His successor Mike Foster lasted until the 2010 election (and after that went to work for a development NGO).

What are the takeaways from this? Douglas Alexander put his finger on the most important point:

Who were the most effective cabinet ministers in the 1997–2001 Parliament? . . . Clare Short, David Blunkett and Gordon Brown. . . . What characteristics did they share? All of them served the full parliament in the same department.[35]

The continuity of political leadership from 2003 to 2010 was valuable for the department. As to junior ministers, Gareth Thomas told us:

how much power the secretary state is really willing to devolve is key to what influence a junior minister can have. . . . If the secretary of state has confidence in the junior minister, and the junior minister is capable, you can significantly improve the capacity of the department. And I like to think that's what happened in particular between 2005 and 2007. Certainly, I knew what I was doing at that stage.[36]

DFID's experience was not much different from that of other departments in the UK system. The right number of ministers (in DFID, that was one junior minister supporting the secretary of state), each genuinely interested in the role, working well together and all staying in post long enough to make a difference was most conducive to making the department effective.

Appointing people to ministerial jobs they are not interested in is not a recipe for success. Ministers serving too short a tenure achieve little that lasts. To quote Douglas Alexander again, "as a broad rule of thumb, too many people move too quickly between jobs". And having more ministers is far from a guarantee of better departmental performance.[37]

So the department's senior political leadership was strong through this era. As Andrew Mitchell, whose job it was to oppose them, has said, the Labour secretaries of state were "dedicated and effective ministers".[38] And, crucially, they enjoyed the backing of the highest level of government.[39]

Structure and operating model

DFID remained a grant maker, a commissioner, and a policy influencer during this period. It did not invest directly for a return (either through loans or by taking equity stakes in enterprises).[40] And it did not hire staff to deliver services directly to people in developing countries.[41] It continued to work in partnerships, above all with the governments of developing countries but also with intermediaries, including multilateral agencies, NGOs, and private contractors.

By 2002, John Vereker, who had been permanent secretary of the Overseas Development Administration and then DFID for eight years, thought it was time to hand over the reins.[42] His successor was Suma Chakrabarti, an economist who had spent several years in the Overseas Development Administration before time in the Treasury and Cabinet Office. He was well known in Number 10; they trusted him, which was important at a time when tensions with Short over Iraq were growing. As a result, Chakrabarti found he was able to protect the department from proposals that would have derailed it from its main mission.[43]

DFID'S REPUTATION BLOSSOMS

Chakrabarti wanted in particular to make management across the department more effective, with the goal of driving even harder on the MDGs. His senior deputies (director generals) had served for many years and were ripe for a move; one of them, Richard Manning, was elected chair of the DAC soon after Chakrabarti's arrival. This was also a moment when governance across Whitehall was evolving, with each department now required to create a management board chaired by the permanent secretary and including external non-executive directors.[44]

Chakrabarti was therefore able to create a new top team. He hired two highfliers, Minouche Shafik from the World Bank and Masood Ahmed from the IMF.[45] Why did high-powered people leave the prestigious international financial institutions to join DFID? For Minouche Shafik:

At that moment in history, DFID was the most exciting, the best bilateral and where a lot of the most creative thinking about development was happening. And so that was a huge attraction.[46]

For Masood Ahmed, it was about where he could make the biggest difference:

I joined DFID for a very simple reason: in 2003 there was no other agency where I felt I could have as much influence on shaping the key issues on the international development agenda.

In another structural change, Chakrabarti created a new Middle East division.[47] That established a much stronger senior-level capacity to work on Iraq and elsewhere in the region, including engaging across Whitehall – which, as some of our interviewees put it, reduced the number of high-level cross-government meetings at which DFID was not represented and was therefore at risk of being bad mouthed.[48] A further example of stronger cooperation between departments saw DFID join the Foreign Office and Ministry of Defence in 2004 to create a post-conflict reconstruction unit. It brought together staff from all three departments to act as a hub for reconstruction operations.[49]

CHAPTER 5

Chakrabarti also oversaw an enhancement of DFID's second headquarters, which had been established in the late 1970s in East Kilbride (near Glasgow) for back-office functions. More policy jobs were moved there, and a principle was established that if a staff member wished to work from East Kilbride rather than London, they should be allowed to unless there were serious operational reasons why that could not happen. That led to a significant shift, which included senior officials. It made the department more attractive to potential staff who did not relish living in London on a civil service salary. The East Kilbride office became – and remained until 2020 – a hub of real policy expertise.

In 2003 Chakrabarti set about what turned into one of the more controversial structural changes in the history of the department, with the creation of a new policy division and changes in the roles of the heads of specialist groups (economists, health advisers, engineers, and others). One account describes what happened thus:

> *Previously, projects had been managed by generalists who could call upon teams of specialists. The latter were grouped into "cadres" . . . The Chief Advisers of these cadres had . . . management responsibility for their advisers. Critics described these as "powerful baronies" and "silos". These structural reforms reduced the power of the Chief Advisers, by taking away their line management responsibilities. It gave members of professional cadres project management roles.*[50]

Some of this was unpopular with many of the specialists.[51] And Chakrabarti's view now is that errors were made in the change process: "We did make some mistakes and I think I was too distant from it."[52]

There was, however, a clear rationale for the changes. The goal was to reinforce the philosophy of getting behind developing country leadership, which was at the heart of what Chakrabarti (like Clare Short) thought made for successful development, by expanding the role of the heads of local DFID offices as the lead interlocutor with local decision makers.[53] Previously, chief advisers had held larger budgets which were sometimes spent with limited engagement from either the DFID local office or their senior counterparts in the partner government. Likewise, having the specialists report through the head of the country office, rather than round their backs direct to their technical chiefs in London, was intended to improve coherence. And giving members of professional cadres responsibility for project management was intended to empower them while also making them accountable for ensuring that their technical advice delivered the desired outcomes in practice. Finally, Chakrabarti thought it essential that senior managers acted as a coherent team, responsible for the department as a whole. He wanted to attack a culture – common elsewhere in Whitehall, and from which DFID was not immune – where senior staff competed with each other as the heads of rival baronies. His successors worked hard to sustain that mindset throughout the department's life.

These changes were reinforced by other bureaucratic initiatives. The department had traditionally had a long rule book setting out the processes for spending money.[54] Like other large public organisations, it tended to accrete processes: more and more were added as time passed to deal with some new requirement or other. A new "Blue Book" of rules and tools was created. The previous huge catalogue of mandatory rules was stripped back to a short volume of minimal "must dos", accompanied by guidance material which could be followed or not according to the professional judgement of the project manager. All staff went on obligatory training courses to absorb the new arrangements. As the DAC put it in their 2006 review of the UK:

> The Blue Book represents a significant rationalisation and streamlining of predecessor manuals and guidelines. In a very compact (100 pages) and user-friendly manner, it explains DFID mandatory requirements while providing useful links and references for the remaining support materials of interest to each area. The Blue

CHAPTER 5

Book has become the one-stop, primary reference document for the effective functioning of DFID's large and highly decentralised operations. It is among the best examples seen in the DAC to date.[55]

Crucially, managers in DFID's country offices were given a lot of authority. As Eamon Cassidy, who headed the DFID offices in Mozambique and Nigeria and later worked for Save the Children, told us:

There was a lot of delegation. In Nigeria, I had delegated authority of £20 million. And that was fantastic. That really distinguished DFID from other donors . . . My opposite numbers in the aid community in Abuja literally couldn't breathe without asking headquarters.[56]

Staffing

The department had doubled in size from 1997 to 2003. Its administration costs in the UK were controlled by the Treasury, but staffing overseas was funded separately, and growth there was unconstrained. In 2003, in the wake of this expansion, the department's top officials decided that more discipline was needed. They introduced a category of total operating costs, and reached an informal agreement with the Treasury to limit them. Cost control across Whitehall then became tighter. And in 2009, in the wake of the financial crisis, tougher steps were taken. As *The Guardian* revealed in early December:

Gordon Brown will announce the biggest shakeup of Whitehall in a generation next week as the government attempts to save billions of pounds by cutting the number of senior civil servants and abolishing a fifth of all quangos.[57]

One consequence was a need to reduce the size of the senior civil service in DFID (the top 100 posts) by 20 per cent.

The upshot of all this was a major challenge. The DAC described it in diplomatic terms:

[DFID] proposes to more than double its current level of aid in the next few years (0.7 per cent target in 2013), to deliver its aid better (aid effectiveness agenda, results monitoring) and to move into countries with more complex and difficult environments for aid delivery (fragile states, conflict). At the same time, it plans do so with fewer staff (10 per cent reduction in DFID staff over the next three years) and expected constraints on its administrative operating funds. It will be a challenge for DFID to undertake all of these tasks while maintaining the quality and innovative character of its aid. DFID recognises this challenge and is approaching it constructively.[58]

Senior officials had cause to rue the decision they had voluntarily taken in 2003 to tighten belts. They were sceptical of the wisdom of the scale of reductions now required. But it did not matter what they thought. They had to play the hand they were dealt. Given the importance and scale of the challenge in fragile states, a decision was taken to increase staffing for those countries. Efficiencies and cuts were made elsewhere. Hundreds of people were (over the passage of several years) seconded to other aid organisations, especially multilateral institutions. That took them off the DFID headcount, but it also brought the department's perspective to other organisations.

There was at the same time (and also as in other parts of Whitehall) a significant effort to increase the professional skills of staff in corporate services – finance, human resources, IT, procurement, communications, and the like. Traditionally, many civil service jobs in these functions, not least at senior levels, had been filled by generalists without training or accreditation in the relevant professional bodies. The change in DFID began as a consequence of a decision across government that public sector bodies should produce accounts based not just on a cash book (recording funds coming in from the Treasury and expenditure going out), but distinguish-

CHAPTER 5

ing between current and capital expenditure and looking at assets and liabilities as well as expenditure. DFID's finance team needed upgrading to handle this.[59] Similarly, a former head of human resources at British Airways was hired to take responsibility for personnel management, and a chief information officer came in from the private sector to oversee IT. As well as new recruits, existing staff across all the corporate services functions studied to earn accreditation to their professional bodies. The benefits were significant. The department was, for example, an early adopter of video conferencing, which transformed communications between headquarters and the country offices. It also began to produce much better management information, so senior staff could see what was going on, spot problems, and amplify successes.[60]

It helped that DFID was fortunate in its most important asset. The department continued to be the top choice among candidates for the civil service graduate recruitment programme, often getting the pick of the best candidates.[61] It also became notably more diverse than it had been 10 years previously. By March 2009, women held a third of the top (senior civil service) jobs, and people from ethnic minorities 12 per cent.[62] As the DAC, again, put it, DFID's "high calibre, highly motivated staff" was "a particular strength".[63] In 2009, as part of a broad programme of civil service reform introduced by Gus O'Donnell, the Cabinet secretary,[64] the government began conducting annual surveys of civil servants to test staff engagement. The idea was that staff motivated by and committed to their jobs would be more productive and effective than those who were not. Hundreds of thousands of civil servants round the country completed the survey. A staff engagement index was produced for each department based on the responses. The median score across departments was 58 per cent.[65] DFID achieved the highest score, at 72 per cent.[66] Gus O'Donnell told the parliamentary Public Accounts Committee that DFID was marked out by the commitment of its staff.[67]

The culture of the department fostered that commitment. As Hilary Benn told us:

In other government departments I was in, you'd have a meeting with officials and the most senior official in the room would lead off. It wasn't like that in DFID. The person who knew the most about the subject led off in front of his or her superiors. That was impressive.[68]

Performance management

The system of Public Service Agreements introduced soon after Gordon Brown became chancellor of the exchequer was sustained. They continued to support DFID's focus on the MDGs. The stability of this framework was a real boon for an organisation whose raison d'être was the achievement of long-term targets focused on 2015.

Suma Chakrabarti highlighted one of the advantages:

I believed in development outcomes. The only way to get people motivated around a PSA is if it describes things they actually care about. If you don't, it doesn't motivate staff. We were fortunate to have such a clear set of outcomes.[69]

With its improving IT systems, the department was able to collect information on more than 34,000 projects and programmes. All projects and programmes over an approved commitment of £1 million were reviewed and scored annually through this system.[70] As previously, the project success rate was high.[71]

There was also innovation. Partly, it was motivated by new legislation requiring the department to publish detailed information every year on progress towards the MDGs.[72] DFID started to estimate the total number of people it was lifting out of income poverty (i.e., above the dollar-a-day line), as well as other outcomes like the number of children it was financing in school and the number of lives saved through its support for immunisation.[73]

This approach later became more pronounced – and attracted a degree of criticism – as we will pick up in Chapter 9. It is worth noting, therefore, that it began in the Labour years. Hilary Benn explained that: "as the aid budget rose, more people asked quite properly what are we getting for it?"[74] The department knew that it could not afford to overstate what it was doing, not least because the data was part of the annual report subject to scrutiny by the NAO. It was never caught out exaggerating. It erred on the side of understatement.

Richard Manning, who worked in the department and its predecessors for nearly 40 years, said in 2017: "when I left DFID [2003] I was relatively satisfied with how we were using the idea of results". Similarly, Adrian Wood, the DFID chief economist from 2000 to 2005, who had previously worked in senior positions at the World Bank, observed in 2016 that:

DFID was constantly engaged in self-appraisal . . . There were a lot of external reviews of DFID's performance, including by the DAC. Every country office had plans and records. People were very definitely held accountable by their superiors.[75]

How effective was DFID by 2010?

We will the assess the contribution DFID made between 2003 and 2010 to the MDGs in Chapter 7. But what, overall, can we say now about its capability as an organisation?

As we have already indicated, there is quite a lot to be positive about. But there were also some additional challenges to the vision many staff held dear of development that would be lasting and sustainable and help make poorer countries self-sufficient. The shift – which began in a relatively gentle way in this era – from focusing on how DFID was contributing alongside others to achieve the MDGs, to giving greater prominence to what the UK could attribute to its own efforts may have been a political necessity. But it did have consequences. In particular it took the edge off the partnership philosophy, the centrality of country leadership, and the commitment to collective donor effort.

As the department's budget grew, so did scrutiny. The old anti-aid lobby looked for weaknesses. DFID's political leaders became more conscious of the risks. One related to corruption and the danger that some of the department's budget might be diverted from the intended uses. As Gareth Thomas said to us:

I started to get concerned about the risk of corruption and aid spending. Hilary and Douglas both got those concerns. We made decisions which were slightly less ambitious than the department wanted, but it meant that there was no substantive attack on development spending, in the time we were there, on corruption and therefore on aid effectiveness because of corruption. I thought one big corruption scandal and we'd be in a lot of trouble.

As Thomas says, there were in fact no major scandals in this period. A more cautious mindset did, however, permeate.

Greater scrutiny also meant that ministers wanted to find ways of communicating and getting credit for what was being achieved. Under the previous government, a favoured tactic was to plaster the Union Jack symbol on aid goods and use photos of them in publicity.[76] Many staff, especially those long in the tooth, were sceptical of such branding. They observed that no one likes being a recipient of charity, and the emotion most commonly expressed by people getting respite from extreme suffering was not gratitude but desperation. They all also had stories of branding backfiring.[77]

But the bigger issue was the one Clare Short and her European allies had identified in the late 1990s. They argued that donor flags undermined the accountability relationship – which they were keen to foster – between developing country governments and their citizens. They wanted people to complain to their local officials and politicians (rather than foreigners) about service failures to put pressure on them to sort things out. Nevertheless, by 2010 branding was starting to come back – and would grow thereafter.

CHAPTER 5

These were, however, straws in the wind of changes that were to become more significant later. They did not at this stage take much edge off DFID's overall effectiveness or reputation. In April 2007, Simon Maxwell, the director of the influential think tank the Overseas Development Institute, observing a brief flurry of media criticism in *The Times* and *The Sun* and on BBC Radio, published a blog asking the question "Is DFID any good or isn't it?"[78] Reviewing the media critiques and observing the limited evidence base underpinning them, he then summarised three more substantive assessments. One reviewed research literature on the country-level impacts of aid. It concluded that recent research "provides overwhelming evidence that aid is effective". A second was the latest DAC peer review of DFID. Maxwell quoted its view of DFID as "one of the bilateral models for today's evolving world of development cooperation".

The third assessment was a capability review commissioned by the Cabinet Office. These reviews, which were another of Gus O'Donnell's initiatives when he became Cabinet secretary, were conducted on all government departments between 2007 and 2010. They were carried out by five senior independent people from other parts of government, civil society, and the private sector. Departments were scored against 10 criteria; in 2007, DFID was scored in the top two categories ("strong" or "well placed") on seven of them. Overall, it had the top scores in Whitehall.[79]

An update to the capability review in March 2009 came to the same conclusion:

DFID is a well-run department. It has impressive leadership that is complemented by high-quality and committed staff. It is admired internationally throughout the donor community and is regarded as a leader.[80]

SIX

Crises and Summits

THERE WAS a notable transition in the exercise of British influence on international development in this era. Between 1997 and 2003, Clare Short, as the secretary of state, had been prominent. Her departure was followed by both Tony Blair and Gordon Brown taking a bigger personal interest. In Blair's case, that was partly an offset to the role he played in the Iraq War – though that is not to say that he was anything but strongly committed to the global poverty agenda. Both as chancellor and then as prime minister, Brown focused much of the time he could carve out for international affairs on development issues, on which he became a leading global voice, enthusiastically supported by the department.

In many Western countries, military interventions overseas, and the reactions they provoked, were high in politicians' minds as they thought about their support for the poorest countries. In some cases that helped motivate and sustain their support for development, which they hoped (and believed) could take the edge off criticism over the deployment of their troops a long way from home. Partly, though, development assistance was seen through the prism of combatting terrorism, extremism, illegal migration, the international narcotics trade (especially heroin from Afghanistan), and organised crime. Defence, interior, and intelligence agencies across Western countries were increasingly interested in the role of aid and development as a buttress against these new threats to their national security.

CHAPTER 6

Iraq and Afghanistan

DFID was inextricably engaged in the UK's major foreign policy preoccupations between 2003 and 2010. The presence of thousands of British troops in Iraq from 2003, and then Afghanistan from 2006, substantially increased public and media attention on what was happening in those places, especially when military lives were lost. In turn, that heightened the focus across Whitehall in how DFID was contributing to the government's overall goals, and on how successful (or, more to the point, unsuccessful) development efforts were in winning hearts and minds among local people. DFID's licence to operate on its global poverty goals could have been undermined had its effort in Iraq and Afghanistan been – or appeared to be – lukewarm.

This was the sharp end of the growing focus on governance and security issues given prominence in the department's policy work, not least in the 2006 and 2009 White Papers. But it proved harder to implement the policy than to proclaim it. In truth aid could make little difference in Iraq.[1] Oil made Iraq rich enough to meet the basic needs of the population, but the fundamental problems – and the vicious civil conflicts at the heart of them – came from internal political divisions which foreign invasion had opened up but could not solve. Domestic politics nevertheless required a visible DFID effort there for several years after 2003. It was wound down in the last years of the Labour government and was minimal by the time British troops, based mostly around Basra in the south, withdrew in 2009.

In Afghanistan, the situation was different. The government's senior figures believed there was no alternative to nation building.[2] It was not so much that they desired to impose Western norms – though there was an element of that – but that no country had ever developed without effective state institutions, and Afghanistan in particular in 2001 had almost none. So there was, through the decade after 2001 and beyond, a major effort to help establish them.

Senior officials recall Douglas Alexander emphasising the importance of DFID's work there in neutralising attacks on the aid programme more widely.[3] The department put its shoulder to the wheel. Progress was significant – school attendance, child survival, and average incomes all shot up. One goal was to support and facilitate NGOs and others in delivering public services. Another was increasing the tax base and seeking to improve the integrity of Afghan tax administration, a zone historically rife with corruption.

There were, however, major failures, above all in politics and the administration of justice, and the consequences became ever clearer as the years passed. The fact that the Afghan government of Hamid Karzai did not build a political system that embraced all sides, and in particular could not ensure that local governance and justice administration operated in a way that carried the confidence of local communities, created space which allowed the Taliban back in. The initial Western response – the large-scale deployment of troops, mostly American but also thousands from the UK – was intended in British minds (which were perhaps too optimistic) to buy time for state building. But it failed to quell the insurgency and provided a target around which many Afghans, especially in rural areas, could coalesce. The Americans were in any case neuralgic about nation building. And the UK, like the rest of the EU, was always a junior partner in this endeavour. The US, which dominated the security response, also threw huge resources at development problems in Afghanistan. The ultimate failure of the whole enterprise was, however, not exposed until 2021, when the Taliban rapidly reassumed control when the last US troops left.

Humanitarian relief

On 15 December 2004, Hilary Benn gave a speech at the Overseas Development Institute in London.[4] The topic was reform of the international humanitarian system. After some typically gracious introductory remarks (referring in particular to "the extraordinary efforts of humanitarian staff" in the Red Cross, UN, and NGOs) he launched into a detailed critique of the inadequacies of global humanitarian response. He was at the time deeply engaged in the Darfur crisis in Sudan, in which millions were killed, displaced, and terrorised. What he saw there led him to believe humanitarian agencies had to do better.[5] His ODI speech set out a six-point agenda for reform, and then moved on to complementary proposals on disaster prevention, the prevention and resolution of conflict, and peacekeeping.

Benn's proposals embraced a stronger coordinating role in emergencies for the UN Office for the Coordination of Humanitarian Affairs, the preparation of common response plans covering all the UN agencies in each disaster, benchmarks and standards for the speed and scale of responses, a new $1 billion humanitarian fund to be managed by the UN's Emergency Relief Coordinator, and a more powerful role for the European Commission Humanitarian Office (ECHO).

This was the most consequential statement on humanitarian relief issues by a DFID minister during the whole of the department's existence. Less than two weeks after Benn's speech, a massive tsunami ripped through the Indian Ocean, killing hundreds of thousands of people in Indonesia, India, Thailand, and Sri Lanka.[6] The speech, the tsunami, and Benn's response to it (he spent much of the remaining three years of his tenure on these issues) elevated the department's humanitarian role to a new plane, and established the UK as among the biggest providers of emergency relief – behind the US, but alongside ECHO. For the rest of the decade, some 10 per cent of the DFID bilateral budget was allocated to humanitarian response, up from around 6–7 per cent (and the total budget was much larger by then, so in volume terms the growth in spending was marked).[7]

The Benn agenda was not fully adopted, but it struck a chord and went with the flow of what some UN leaders thought was needed. Significant improvements were made to the UN's work, including through better leadership and response planning, the creation of the Central Emergency Response Fund (CERF), and the establishment of a suite of country-based humanitarian funds.[8] ECHO was also boosted.

Overall funding for global humanitarian response increased substantially from this point. The US remained much the biggest funder (and they effectively decided who would head some of the most important UN agencies, in particular the World Food Programme and UNICEF). Better quality and more generous humanitarian aid reduced suffering and loss of life in crises (and thereby contributed to the MDGs). DFID carved out an effective complementary role to the US. It became (and remained for a decade) the biggest financial supporter of the CERF and the UN's humanitarian country funds, which were often among the most proactive responders.[9] It also supported coordination and funding for local organisations, and championed the use of cash in emergencies (rather than, as had been typical, simply providing commodities).

Nothing in the department's work caught the public eye more than its responses to major disasters. As Gareth Thomas told us, after the Indian Ocean tsunami:

> *DFID was in the spotlight for two and a half weeks of the Christmas and early new year holidays when there was no other news. The department handled the UK politics adroitly . . . as well as allowing those on the ground to do what needed doing. The perception that DFID did a good job and that it was right to help those who had lost so much underpinned support for development and bought the Treasury political space for the growing DFID budget.*[10]

The 2005 Gleneagles Summit

In 2003 Tony Blair announced that when he chaired the G8 summit at the Scottish golf resort of Gleneagles two years later, his objectives would be increasing aid to Africa and climate change. Civil servants across Whitehall, including in DFID, worried about what could be achieved.[11] The US could in practice veto proposals in the G8. What would they agree to? Not much on climate, it quickly became clear. But partly because President Bush did not want to stick fingers in both eyes of his most important ally on Iraq, and partly because he had his own sympathies with Africa, he was "very pleased" to help there. Blair set up a commission, for which much of the policy work was to be done by the highly regarded economist Nick Stern, recently head of the Government Economic Service. Gordon Brown, who was also pleased with the G8 focus on Africa, joined it, as did Hilary Benn. But most of the members were African leaders. DFID seconded staff to Number 10 and the commission, as well as providing analytical and advocacy support (especially in Africa and with donors). But the main effort was led from Downing Street – as it had to be other if G8 heads of government were to sign their countries up to new pledges. The commission's lengthy report included 90 recommendations. But how many of them would be adopted and acted upon?

The Gleneagles summit agreed $22 billion worth of debt relief to 18 of the poorest countries, 14 of which were in Africa. It also signed up to a $50 billion increase in global aid levels by 2010, with half of it going to Africa. Again, British influence over the US was crucial: on 30 June, a week before the leaders were due to meet, Bush announced that the US would be doubling aid to Africa. American officials were candid in acknowledging that would never have happened without Blair.[12]

Civil society campaigners played a notable role. On 13 July 1985 it was estimated that more than one-fifth of the planet's inhabitants watched the Live Aid concert organised by pop stars horrified by the famine in Ethiopia. It was "the most spectacular charity appeal in history".[13] None of the public events mustered in 2005 by the Make Poverty History campaign got anywhere close to that. The difference was that Live Aid had little political traction with the Thatcher and Reagan governments, whereas in 2005 the campaigners generated it in spades. It was in truth a two-way process, with Brown and Blair's teams egging the campaigners on to ratchet up the pressure. Both sides found themselves having to deny they were in each other's pockets.[14]

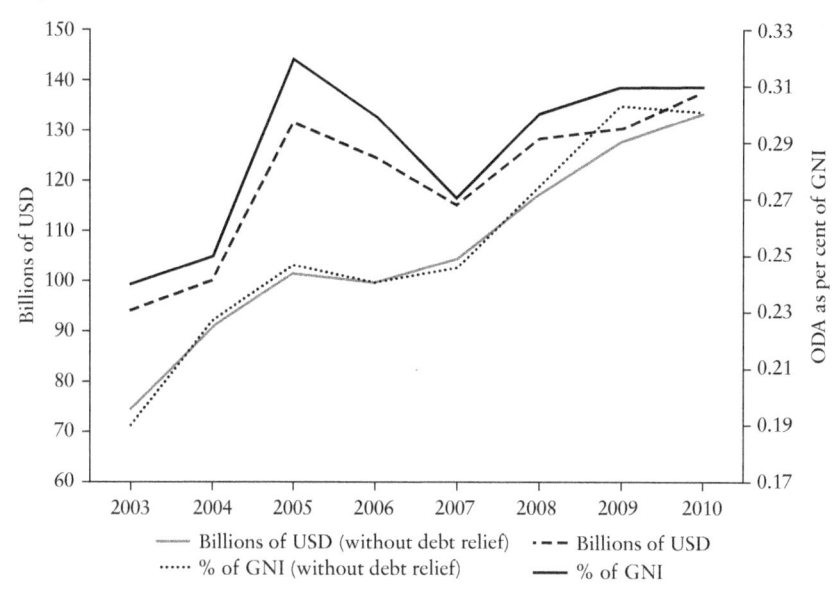

Figure 6.1. Net ODA from DAC countries

Source: OECD Creditor Reporting System (2023) (in billions of USD at constant prices).

There is no question that the commitments on development agreed in Gleneagles from 6–8 July 2005 were substantial.[15] As well as debt relief and aid increases that were not just promised but actually delivered in the years that followed (Figure 6.1), there were other wide-ranging undertakings too, promising to implement 50 of the Africa commission's 90 recommendations. (The pledges on trade, where the commission had asked for an end to agricultural subsidies in rich countries, were notably lukewarm.) DFID wanted to ensure all the promises made were met, and tried to get mechanisms set up to ensure that. But on many of the less high-profile points, the actual track record was mixed. As Andrew Rawnsley put it:

While Britain made good on its pledges, others did not. . . . [Even so] this G8 had much more meaningful product than most summits.[16]

CHAPTER 6

The global financial crisis

In September 2008, UN Secretary-General Ban Ki-moon presided over a summit to mark the halfway point to the 2015 deadline for the achievement of the MDGs. Gordon Brown spent the preceding year working for its success. As John Sawers (then the UK's ambassador to the UN in New York, and later head of the Secret Intelligence Service) put it, "by throwing such energy into development, he forced it back onto the global agenda" – and right at the time all eyes were focused in trepidation on the New York markets as the financial crisis unfolded. Brown's speech at the UN was interrupted several times by spontaneous applause – which is not how the world's diplomats normally react to utterings there.[17]

The global financial crisis in 2008–09 brought growth to a shuddering halt and created enormous financial problems across the planet. The poorer countries were, however, less badly hit than they might have been. As Alan Winters, at that time DFID's chief economist, told us, "this was by far and away the only crisis that developing countries have weathered reasonably well".[18]

Partly that was because earlier debt relief and improved economic policy had made them more resilient. It is true that remittances (the amount of money diaspora populations from developing countries sent home) declined, current account deficits grew (as the value of developing countries' exports fell more than their imports), and inflation increased. This was, though, initially a global banking crisis, and the banking sector in many of these countries was relatively loosely integrated into the global economy and thus insulated from the worst effects.

But the other reason that the poorer countries coped better than in many global downturns was that the international community came to their aid. No one did more to orchestrate that than Gordon Brown. The meeting of the G20 that he hosted in London in early 2009 produced a package not just for the bigger economies but for the poorer ones too.[19] A trillion dollars was added to the firepower of the IMF, including $250 billion in Special Drawing Rights (which effectively made a country's currency reserves more liquid and usable and increased the help they could get from the IMF). A further $100 billion was generated through the multilateral development banks. And there was $250 billion in trade credits. At the end of the meeting, the newly inaugurated President Barack Obama took the floor to pay a gracious and fulsome tribute to Brown. The World Bank's verdict was that the London summit had "broken the fall" of the global economy. Brown's own judgement is right – the event

> *is likely to go down in history as the moment when the international community united to stop a slide into a depression.*[20]

Climate negotiations

In late 2006, following his work on the Africa commission, Nick Stern produced an influential report on climate change. It attracted attention for its implications for developed countries. But it was clear that there were major issues for developing countries too. The Conference of the Parties to the UN convention on climate change met in Copenhagen in December 2009. DFID staff had been intimately engaged in supporting developing countries in their preparations. They were particularly close to the Ethiopian prime minister, Meles Zenawi, who played a leading role as a spokesman for developing countries in the final stages of the negotiations. They helped Meles articulate a proposal for a $100 billion a year climate funding package for low-income and middle-income countries by 2020. Their work and personal, face-to-face discussions between Meles and Obama led to this being agreed in the Copenhagen accords.[21] Implementing it, however, proved harder: it has been a bone of contention ever since.

Aid effectiveness

DFID continued its campaign to improve the effectiveness of the international development system. Agreement at a February 2003 meeting in Rome (between bilateral and multilateral donors and developing countries) on harmonising systems and processes was followed up in Paris in 2005. The agenda included specific targets for aid providers and parallel commitments from recipients. Donors committed to getting behind countries' own poverty reduction strategies, reducing bureaucracy, and providing more of their money through the receiving government's own systems. There was then a third meeting in Accra in Ghana in 2008, at which Douglas Alexander with his US and Dutch counterparts played an important role in securing political agreement to get earlier agreements implemented more fully, to make aid more transparent and predictable and to get a stronger focus on identifying and reporting on what results aid was achieving.

This "aid effectiveness" agenda, for which DFID was one of the main cheerleaders, absorbed a lot of political and bureaucratic energy.[22] Much of the impetus and many of the ideas had their origins in the Utstein collaboration between Clare Short and her Dutch, German, and Norwegian counterparts from 1997 to 2003. Researchers have pored over all the activity trying to work out what difference it made.[23] The key points that emerge are that, first, there were lots of distortions and inefficiencies in the aid system, and transparency about that, as well as trying to address the problems, was desirable. But second, there were declining returns to this effort, especially from 2008, and the long-term benefits have largely evaporated. Up to 2010, the UK (through DFID), and a small number of likeminded northern European countries lived up to the commitments they made. In March 2009, in his foreword to the new development White Paper, Gordon Brown emphasised:

We must ensure that aid flows are predictable and support plans formulated by national governments, not spent on priorities, however well intentioned, imposed by donors from afar.[24]

However, as we noted earlier, a growing tension emerged between, on the one hand, the need to generate information on what aid was achieving and attribute it to particular donors and, on the other hand, the focus on recipient country ownership implied by the aid effectiveness principles.[25] Other donors were more constrained than Britain by domestic political, institutional, and legal factors. By 2008 the air was gradually sapping out of the aid effectiveness balloon.[26]

SEVEN

Lives Getting Better: How DFID Made a Difference

A GROWING budget, clear goals, recognised organisational capability, and a reputation that gave it influence and credibility: these were all powerful assets. But how did the department now use them to improve the life experience of people in the poorest countries? We will look first at how the department's practice followed its philosophy of trying to back poor countries' own poverty reduction strategies. We will also examine DFID's activities on education, health, social protection, private sector development, and scientific and social research. This is far from a comprehensive array of the department's work, but it is illustrative of important features of the approach that was brought to bear and the growing scale of activity.[1] At the end of the chapter we will look at what difference this all made, in aggregate, to progress on the MDGs, and where the department stood as the era of Labour government came to an end.

Backing partner countries

The department under Clare Short had been leading proponents of providing aid as cash injections into the national budgets of countries committed to poverty reduction and the MDGs. This was part of an explicit state-building strategy. The hope was not just that the money would feed through into the delivery of services but also that it would build administrative capability for the long term, strengthen the accountability links between governments and their citizens and buy time to grow the economy and tax base so that recipients could become more self-sufficient.

This was the essence of what the deep development thinkers in DFID believed in. No country, they thought, wants to be dependent on aid. Success was improving people's lives, but also reducing the need for aid in future. It was an optimistic, perhaps idealistic, vision. And it was posited on the proposition that while no country had ever developed successfully without capable state institutions, those institutions also had to be responsive to citizens' concerns.[2]

DFID provided high levels of budget support throughout the 2003–10 period. In the 2009/10 year it gave £426 million in general budget support (i.e., money untied to any particular sector) to 11 countries, and a further £290 million in sector budget support to 10 countries (including six who also received general budget support). That represented in total 27 per cent of the whole bilateral aid programme. The department was transparent in what it was doing, and about the risks of relying on partner countries' systems. The annual report noted that budget support "is spent using the government's own financial management and procurement systems and is accounted for using the government's own accountability systems".[3] In some countries (Nigeria, the Democratic Republic of Congo, and others) the risks were judged too high, and assistance was provided in alternative ways.[4] The biggest judgement was on the underlying commitment of the recipient government to poverty reduction. The department displayed a high willingness to take fiduciary risks where it was satisfied on that.

It also developed subtler tactics for handling problems when they arose. Major concerns (for example over human rights abuses in the wake of Ethiopia's 2005 elections, which were marred by violence) led to publicly announced pauses in support, often as part of a joint approach with other donors. Such difficulties were not infrequent: in 2009/10 the department reported 14 such cases, many of them on budget support and the *casus belli* was often suspected fraud.[5] Pauses were rarely, however, long-lasting: problems were typically addressed quite promptly and funding resumed, so the damage done to the MDGs by the hiatus was limited.

DFID also offered help, typically through technical assistance projects, with strengthening national institutions charged with ensuring accountability and propriety. Audit offices, finance ministries, central banks, anti-corruption bodies, parliaments, and justice departments were all targeted for help. As Minouche Shafik has said:

What really matters in the long run. . . . are strong institutions – the institutions that make sure whatever kind of leadership you have works in the public interest.[6]

It is important to note that creating strong institutions is not primarily a technical challenge. It is fundamentally political. External support can be effective – provided there is a genuine top-level desire to reform.

It is not clear how successfully budget support led to a stronger tax base and greater self-sufficiency in the long run. In some countries receiving significant volumes of budget support (for example Rwanda, Malawi, Mozambique), the proportion of national income collected in tax tended to increase somewhat over time (from low levels). In others, including some receiving very high levels of aid (like Ethiopia), the tax take did not keep up with rapid economic growth.[7] The effect on the political economy is also open to question. In the decade after 2010, too many countries resorted to the international bond markets to finance recurrent expenditure, rather than domestic resources, when aid could not meet their needs.[8]

Overall, however, the evidence points to budget support being a big plus for the MDGs. The department reported the findings of an independent evaluation of general budget support (GBS) in its 2002/03 annual report. The study concluded that budget support could increase state effectiveness, particularly in delivering social services, lead to greater democratic accountability, and reduce transactions costs in the management and delivery of aid. A more analytical paper published in 2010 by Jonathan Beynon and Andra Dusu looked at the impact in more detail. It found that countries receiving high volumes of GBS:

> *have performed better, often significantly so, in all four MDGs assessed (covering primary enrolment, gender parity in education, child mortality, and access to water), as well as in terms of improvements in the Human Development Index, in the period 2002–2007. We also find that even after we control for the quality of the policy environment, income level and aid dependency, high GBS recipients have on average still performed better than other countries. It should be emphasised that this study is an analysis of association, not causality. Nevertheless, the results overall do provide more comprehensive support for the view that countries receiving large amounts of budget support perform better than those receiving little or no budget support.*[9]

A study published by Oxfam in 2008 on the contribution of European budget support to the health and education MDGs in eight African countries reached similar conclusions:

> *The evidence does show that where it [the European Commission] is giving large amounts of budget support, headway is being made in reducing poverty.*[10]

This era saw the peak in the use of budget support by DFID and other donors. Analysis of the sort we have just summarised had addressed all the various concerns (principally fiduciary and political risk). Nevertheless, such problems created headaches. It proved a drawback that the precise effect of budget support on poverty could not be measured when donors increasingly wanted to measure the specific short-term results from their own interventions. And DFID (like other donors) proved not to have the necessary staying power for financial management, procurement and anti-corruption measures alongside budget support so that they could both deal with risks as they emerged and at the same time use their financial heft to strengthen systems and accountability in partner countries.[11] The problem was a change in the political stance in donor countries rather than greater political risk in poorer ones. As Suma Chakrabarti put it, "I think budget support requires great political courage and clarity."[12]

Education

Education was a personal passion for Gordon Brown, both as chancellor and as prime minister (and it is one he has sustained since, including as the UN secretary-general's special envoy for global education, a role he has held since 2012).[13] As he wrote in 2017:

> *I see Britain's commitment to universal education – guaranteeing schooling to the poorest and most vulnerable children in the least promising corners of the world – as the British people demonstrating our internationalism in practice and cajoling other nations to do likewise.*[14]

Brown campaigned on the issue with characteristic energy and determination throughout the 2003–10 period, not least with counterparts in developing countries, urging them to do more to get all their children in school.[15] In 2006, at an event in Mozambique attended by Nelson Mandela, he and Hilary Benn announced that DFID would provide £8.5 billion for education in poorer countries over the following 10 years.[16]

DFID supported education programmes between 2003 and 2010 in all 18 of the focus countries we have looked at particularly closely.[17] (In one, Zambia, its contribution was restricted to indirect funding through its general budget support. Zambia was a prime example of donors agreeing a division of labour across sectors as part of the international effort on aid harmonisation.) The department's education work was everywhere focused on the MDGs: universal access to basic education, and in particular increasing the proportion of girls going to school. DFID sent specialist education advisers to work in these countries, and consistently engaged in policy issues with national and sub-national authorities, as well as on programme funding and implementation.

Education in all the 18 countries received a substantial share of the national government budget, and DFID generally provided the bulk of its aid for education through government systems, either as general or sector budget support. In practice, that meant that most of its resources contributed to paying teacher salaries – which absorb the lion's share of spending on basic education everywhere across the world. But the department also engaged actively on policy issues.

Amassing all the evidence, the department was persuaded that fees were the biggest block to every child going to school.[18] In 2002 DFID had commissioned a six-country study examining how costs deterred poor families from sending their children – especially daughters – to school. Some DFID economists were nervous about the fiscal consequences for governments of addressing this. But, particularly with the backing of Gordon Brown, it increasingly pushed for free basic education. It was able to piggy-back on decisions in a few first-mover countries. From the 1990s, Uganda's President Yoweri Museveni promoted universal primary education. The presidential election in Malawi in 1994 – the first free election after the departure of the long-time dictator Hastings Banda – was won by Bakili Muluzi partly on the back of a promise of free schooling.[19] DFID used its growing budget to underwrite the initial costs of abolishing fees. Crucially, the department could see that once introduced, free services would be well-nigh impossible to roll back.[20]

Progress was impressive: by 2010, there were few countries in which primary fees remained part of government policy (though levies raised, sometimes unofficially, by schools still effectively barred some children). Policy work, often supported by technical assistance projects complementing financial aid, also covered curriculum modernisation, performance management, standards for school buildings, textbooks and other supplies, improving the use of capitation grants provided by government to schools, and stipends for particularly vulnerable groups. As attendance increased, the focus shifted to the even bigger challenge of quality and learning outcomes.

In Bangladesh, by way of illustration, the 2009/10 DFID annual report notes that primary enrolment was on track (at 93 per cent) but that only 55 per cent of children were completing five years of school. Poor-quality schools, materials, curriculum, and teaching were identified as the main problems, with children with disabilities or from ethnic minority groups particularly neglected. The report describes how that year, the DFID Bangladesh programme helped construct thousands of classrooms, train tens of thousands of teachers and distribute tens of millions of books – as well as helping reform teacher training and support national student assessments.

More widely than the 18 focus countries, DFID gave growing priority in its education work to fragile states. They were, after all, the ones in which progress was most needed if the education MDGs were to be achieved. Some 60 per cent of the increase in education spending through the country programmes between 2001 and 2009 went to fragile states.[21]

In addition to its direct contribution through its country programmes, DFID engaged in education in two other important ways (as was also the case in other sectors).[22] First, there were specialist programmes the department ran from London. One, Imfundo, was a public-private partnership involving technology companies, posited on the notion that new information and communications technology might transform education in poorer countries. This was heavily driven by a team appointed by Tony Blair in the Cabinet Office. It was regarded with some scepticism by DFID's education specialists, and by managers in DFID's country offices who thought the main chance was in operating at large scale with governments to expand traditional systems, and who worried about being diverted from that. A second initiative had been promoted by Clare Short from 1999, on skills for development, aiming to address the all too real shortage of managerial, analytic, technical, vocational, and entrepreneurial skills holding back many countries. That floundered for similar reasons to Imfundo. A third venture, launched with backing from Gordon Brown as part of the celebrations for Queen Elizabeth II's jubilee in 2002, was a Commonwealth Education Fund. The concept was strategically insightful and innovative: to create a consortium of leading UK charities (ActionAid, Oxfam, and Save the Children) who would build capacity among local organisations in 16 Commonwealth countries to monitor, scrutinise, and advocate to national governments on progress with the educational MDGs. This had the potential to strengthen national accountability systems, and thereby improve the sustainability and effectiveness of what governments were doing. Unfortunately (as it seems to us) implementation problems emerged, results were expected too quickly, patience was eroded, and the department pulled the plug on future funding in 2008. It might, in retrospect, have been better to have displayed a little more staying power.

The other important way in which DFID engaged in education beyond its country programmes was in seeking to influence what the multilateral agencies were doing. In the health sector, as we will discuss next, this era saw the consolidation and expansion of a series of new multilateral institutions intended to support progress with the MDGs. The experience in education was more chequered. The World Bank played a leading role in creating an "Education for All Fast Track Initiative" (FTI). However, the FTI failed to carve out a niche that was complementary to the core role governments everywhere play on basic education, so the question arose as to why the World Bank did not simply do more on education through its existing vehicles. (The answer, dressed up in different ways, was that the World Bank thought the FTI might enable it to get access to more donor money.) Clare Short had also questioned why the World Bank wanted the FTI to focus on "good performing" countries. She (rightly) thought a higher priority was to do more in the five countries containing most of the children not in school (India, Pakistan, Bangladesh, Nigeria, and the Democratic Republic of Congo). Independent evaluations revealed that the FTI was neither fast (prompting wags to suggest it be renamed the slow track initiative) nor generating significant additional resources. These problems were addressed to some degree in later periods, when there were also important developments in the provision by multilateral agencies of educational support for children forced to flee home for long periods as a result of conflict.

In other sectors, DFID's contribution to the MDGs in this period was matched by at least a small number of other bilateral donors. On education, the scale of the financial resources offered, complemented by top-level political engagement and the contribution both these factors made to the department's ability to persuade partner governments to adopt new policies to get more children into school, meant the UK played a genuinely leading role. And the impact was enhanced because the approach was sustained (and in some ways extended) in the years after 2010, as we will see in Part III.

Health

The health-related MDGs – covering infant mortality, maternal mortality, HIV/AIDS, malaria, and other major diseases – were through this period DFID's largest area of activity. There were, as with education, large-scale programmes in the 18 focus countries. But in addition there was substantial financing through multilateral channels, especially the new global funds. There was also some striking innovation in international health financing. And there were notable investments, often in partnership with the Bill and Melinda Gates Foundation, in developing new health products and other technologies.

The department provided direct support to strengthen government health systems in all 18 of our selected focus countries.[23] There were well qualified DFID health teams in all these countries (and in other places too). The focus of their work varied according to local needs and what other donors were covering. But in many places the department made particular contributions on obstetric and ante-natal care, enhancing the size and quality of the health workforce (especially female health workers), financing issues (including support for phasing out user fees and improving social insurance schemes), and nutrition programmes.

In the large majority of the focus countries, immunisation programmes were supported (and they were quite diverse, depending on the particular disease burden in each country and often also on the gaps left by other donors and national programmes). Contraceptives, and insecticide-treated bed nets to prevent malaria, as well as malaria treatments, were provided in most countries too. Where HIV/AIDS was a significant problem (which was most countries other than Rwanda and some of the South Asian focus countries), the department frequently supported public health campaigns and sometimes provided antiretroviral drugs directly. Generally, however, it preferred to rely on others to take the lead in supplying antiretrovirals, particularly the US and the Global Fund to Fight AIDS, Tuberculosis and Malaria, both of whom were by this time financing huge HIV/AIDS programmes.

DFID was also an important financier of some of the more sensitive health services which other donors wished (or were forced by domestic regulations) to avoid, including safe abortion services and programmes to combat sexual violence. Such programmes were reported in the 2009/10 annual report in the Democratic Republic of Congo, Ethiopia, and Malawi, but they were more widespread than that. In some cases partner governments wanted help but did not want it to be widely advertised; in others implementing agencies preferred to avoid the problems that might have arisen with greater publicity. The department was adept at navigating these waters.

Achieving the health-related MDGs also benefitted from rapidly expanding and highly effective multilateral initiatives. The Global Fund to Fight AIDS, Tuberculosis and Malaria was the largest and had the highest profile. No development challenge received more public or political attention than the fight against HIV/AIDS. That was partly because it attracted the most creative, ingenious, and effective public lobbyists, with media celebrities consistently in pole position. But it also reflected the gravity of the issue and that it was now possible, as antiretrovirals became cheaper, to prevent HIV/AIDS being a death sentence. The US was by a country mile the largest financier, but the UK through DFID was consistently in second place. That owed much to the priority given to it by both Hilary Benn and Gareth Thomas.

Hilary Benn told us how his concern arose:

The department's position was that it's no good talking about antiretrovirals, because if you haven't got a strong health system, it's pointless ... The first country I went to was Malawi and I met Justin Malawezi, the vice president ... [he asked] how could we bring antiretrovirals to people. And I was profoundly affected by this because I thought we are behind where the country that is in the midst of this crisis is.[24]

DFID's contribution on HIV/AIDS was material, but on immunisation it played a bigger, leading role. The department had long understood the cost effectiveness of immunisation, constantly explaining to questioners that for a cheap, one-off intervention, children could be given a life-long protection against a range of killer diseases. Nothing else provided the same bang for buck in reducing infant mortality (and hence increasing life expectancy). And yet immunisation coverage was far from universal, above all in the poorest countries. The core problem was a shortage of funds. Working closely with Bill Gates, Gordon Brown successfully championed a novel solution: a buy now, pay later scheme called the International Finance Facility for Immunisation (IFFIm). An entity was created to borrow $4 billion over 5–7 years through bonds sold on the capital markets. A consortium of donors (with DFID as the largest) undertook to pay the interest and principal back over 20 years. An accounting ruling from the EU statistical agency meant that the donor financing was registered as public spending only when the debt was serviced, not when the money was borrowed.[25] The financial aspects were managed by the World Bank, and the funds raised from issuing the bonds were channelled through Gavi, the vaccine alliance. IFFIm facilitated a dramatic expansion of Gavi's operations.

An independent evaluation in 2011 calculated that since 2006, IFFIm had financed hundreds of millions of vaccinations and so far saved more than 2 million lives, with a projection that another 2.5–3.5 million lives would be saved in future years.[26] Nearly two-thirds of Gavi's spend had been financed by the IFFIm. By 2009/10, DFID was spending more than £300 million a year in servicing IFFIm debt, twice its contribution to the Global Fund.

One of the underlying insights behind the IFFIm was that the poorest countries had a huge requirement for medical interventions barely needed in richer countries, but because they lacked purchasing power there was little incentive for pharmaceutical companies to develop the necessary products. In a further collaboration with the Bill and Melinda Gates Foundation, DFID started investing in a series of product development partnerships, trying to create new technologies to tackle tropical diseases. One of them, the Vector Control Consortium based in Liverpool, developed a new kind of mosquito bed net that had two insecticides rather than one. It took nearly 10 years, but the new nets proved 40 per cent more effective for reducing malaria than the previous ones. Another of the product development partnerships generated the pentavalent vaccine for developing countries. It provides immunisation against five diseases, including diphtheria, whooping cough, and tetanus, in a single shot, dramatically reducing the cost and difficulty of protecting infants against killer diseases.[27]

The most significant innovation was on advanced market commitments, through which donors sign a forward-looking binding contract guaranteeing a viable market for target vaccines. The concept gained wider attention as a result of a paper published by the Center for Global Development in 2005.[28] In 2009, after years of negotiation and analytical work, a group of donors led by the UK and the Gates Foundation signed an agreement to accelerate the development of pneumococcal vaccines that met the particular needs of developing countries. The pilot aimed to prevent 7 million childhood deaths by 2030.[29] The innovation in advanced market commitments spread. Leading pharmaceutical companies, including GSK, Pfizer, and, more recently, the Serum Institute of India, all developed qualifying vaccines. By 2020, more than 150 million children had been immunised, saving an estimated 700,000 lives.[30]

This range of initiatives established a long-lasting collaboration between DFID and the Gates Foundation that led Bill Gates in later years to describe DFID as the foundation's "best partner". DFID was blessed with a unique combination of attributes for its global health work – sustained high-level political backing, a voracious focus on its poverty goals, a large and growing budget, and a culture that combined technical expertise at headquarters with professional capability in the poorest countries and an appetite for financial and scientific innovation.

Social protection[31]

The department had historically been suspicious of welfarism. In the prevailing mindset, development was about promoting self-reliance, principally through economic growth, and the general view was that the poorest countries needed to get richer before they could afford social safety nets. But in this period, inspired in particular by observation of government provision of conditional cash transfers to poorer families in Brazil and Mexico, that began to change. DFID's top mandarins were particularly impressed by the work of Armando Barrientos, an academic at the University of Manchester sometimes described as *the* world expert on cash transfers and social protection.[32] They were struck by the obvious point: if our goal is to make sure everyone has an income of a dollar a day, why not just give a dollar a day to more of those who currently don't?

The idea of cash transfers in low-income countries was hitherto viewed with scepticism not just for affordability reasons, but also for fear of the right-wing critique that recipients would fritter away the money on alcohol or other "wasteful" expenditure. So when DFID gradually developed what by 2010 had become a diverse portfolio of pilot projects for social protection across about 10 countries in Africa and South Asia, there was alongside them the largest programme of evaluations and analytical studies the department had ever embarked on. Many of these studies drew on the techniques of randomised controlled trials commonly used in the development of medical technology.[33]

Two other factors made DFID a willing pioneer on social protection. First, while wherever possible the department wanted recipient government backing (not least so that over time they would take on the financial burden), these schemes could be run by independent groups even in the absence of government involvement. That was particularly attractive in those countries where the authorities were in practice not seriously bought into poverty reduction or the MDGs – countries which were a growing concern. Second, as we will come on to, DFID played a crucial role in this era in the development of mobile money (cash payments through mobile phones). That was an ideal platform for social protection programmes. The synergies were exploited with alacrity, initially in Kenya and before long in countries across Africa and South Asia.

Over the years a growing body of international evidence has confirmed that social protection schemes are effective and that recipients typically spend the money on food, education for their children, and some form of enterprise to generate a higher family income. (One consequence was that what were originally *conditional* cash transfers increasingly became unconditional, as it was shown that the conditions added little value and were expensive to administer.) DFID was between 2003 and 2010 a first mover in this area, and others, in particular the World Bank, later followed with larger programmes. In the wake of the global financial crisis, the World Bank marketed a Rapid Social Response Programme at the G20 summit in London in early 2009. DFID promptly provided £200 million.[34] The fact that the majority of poorer countries now have social protection schemes of

Private sector

In many developing countries in the 2000s – especially the poorer ones – the private sector largely comprised small and informal enterprises that were held back by weak infrastructure, red tape, corruption, insecurity, police and courts that did not work for them, banks that would not lend to them, political volatility, and the poor health and education of many of their workers.[35] Outside oil, gas, mining, and plantations there was little inward investment. Most multinational corporations and international investors were deterred by small market size and exchange rate uncertainty as well as the risks faced by local firms.

The private sector in this state was not generating enough income, jobs, innovation, growth, or taxes to reduce poverty. DFID set out a new approach in a 2005 publication *Working with the Private Sector to Eliminate Poverty*.[36] The melange of inter-connected difficulties facing private enterprise called for reforms to improve the business environment, coordinated with pioneering investment to demonstrate that good business could be done.

The enthusiasm of DFID's private sector specialists for backing enterprise development was moderated by concerns – voiced not least by the powerful cadre of economists – about market distortion and about unfairness (in giving grants to some firms but not others). The department tried to address these concerns by using new approaches to allocate funding. It launched a series of competitive challenge funds, covering financial deepening, business linkages, tourism, the food retail industry, and the garment sector. These funds aimed to catalyse private sector innovation that would benefit the poor – breathing life into ideas that businesses had in mind but were loath to fund by themselves. DFID would invite applications, select the best proposals, and then share the cost of trials.

The funds stimulated a wealth of innovation. In 2003, a grant of £300,000 from the financial deepening fund was given to the UK mobile phone company Vodafone, and its Kenyan affiliate Safaricom, to pilot the use of text messages from mobile phones to transfer money and make payments. Alongside that, and arguably even more important, DFID provided technical advice to the central bank of Kenya on changes to regulations to make money transfer by text message lawful. In 2007, Safaricom launched its M-Pesa product. Kenya became the first country anywhere in the world to introduce mobile money. (It took several more years before it took off in the UK and other richer countries.) M-Pesa now provides more than 50 million customers in seven Africa countries with a range of financial services including transferring money, and paying bills and salaries.[37] And, of course, similar products are now used by billions of people across the world.

In total, DFID spent about £1 million in supporting the creation of M-Pesa. It is probably, in terms of the development benefits generated, the best single investment the department ever made. It happened because of DFID's unusual combination of attributes: the relentless focus on what would improve the lives of the poor; a belief in hiring professional staff with distinctive skills, including in negotiating with local decision makers; a delegated system for deciding what to spend money on (no one in London had to be consulted on M-Pesa: the decisions were taken in the DFID office in Nairobi); and a culture which valued innovation and risk taking.

DFID also used its position as shareholder and a growing funder of multilateral institutions to promote policies and programmes to help the poorer developing countries become better places in which to invest and do business. It funded a good deal of the research for the World Bank 2005 World Development Report "A Better Business Climate for Everyone", which the *Financial Times* described as "among the most important the World Bank has ever produced".[38]

A stream of global, regional, and country initiatives followed. In 2008, DFID played a key role in establishing the Africa Investment Climate Facility, the International Growth Centre (led from Oxford

CHAPTER 7

University and the London School of Economics) and the International Commission on Growth and Development. They all made material contributions to policy and research promoting growth from which the poor could benefit.

The department also took forward the reform started but not completed under Clare Short of CDC, its investment business. It needed to resolve how Actis, the new fund management company, would take over the management of CDC's capital, and how staff should be remunerated. Remuneration needed to be generous enough to attract private equity professionals and incentivise them to produce good returns – but not so high as to attract criticism, given that CDC was a public entity whose purpose was poverty reduction. Actis adopted the standard private equity model of reward comprising a percentage of profit (or "carry") realised above a base rate of return ("hurdle"). It was agreed that whilst Actis management would receive the then standard 20 per cent carry over an 8 per cent hurdle on new funds, they would accept a lower share of profits on CDC's existing investments (5 per cent for power investments, 10 per cent for the rest). The CDC Board, consulting with the department, decided on a remuneration structure for CDC senior managers heavily dependent on their performance. Incentive plans would reward CDC staff to the extent that CDC generated good financial returns, sold previous investments for good prices, mobilised third party capital, and met its investment policy targets.

Actis got off to a flying start. It sold several of its stakes in businesses for a lot more than had been expected and won a competitive tender to manage a new $150 million Canadian Fund for Africa – to which CDC committed another $200 million. At the time of the 2004 demerger, Actis managed $900 million for just one investor – CDC. By 2010, Actis managed $4.8 billion for over 100 investors. More than 50 per cent of its investments were in Africa – and 25 per cent in South Asia.[39]

CDC, too, returned strong results. Its net assets grew from just over £1 billion in 2004 to £2.8 billion by 2010. Its financial performance exceeded private sector benchmarks in the places it worked.[40] In a 2012 paper commissioned by CDC, Harvard Business School researchers concluded that CDC "has had a transformative effort on its markets of interest".[41]

Yet the apparent successes were overshadowed by growing criticism and censure. DFID was slated for selling the fund management business to Actis management too cheaply. CDC was condemned for making investments (such as in shopping malls) that critics believed did not contribute to poverty reduction, and for channelling its investments through subsidiaries in tax havens. Executive pay also came under the spotlight. Under the CDC board's application of the new performance-related remuneration policy, in 2007 it paid the chief executive £745,000 in bonuses, on top of his £220,000 salary – a total of nearly £1 million. The NAO criticised

lapses in oversight and governance of executive remuneration since 2004, with significant departures from the agreed framework, which also contained ambiguities.[42]

In late 2008 the parliamentary Public Accounts Committee conducted a televised grilling of DFID senior officials and the CDC chair and chief executive. They then published a scathing report. Media criticism, not least in *Private Eye*, added salt to the wounds.

Research

It is in this period that DFID became a true powerhouse in the global research ecosystem for international development (and indeed, international issues more broadly). Over the next 15 or so years, until its merger with the FCO, DFID consistently punched above its weight in financing high-quality and influential research, published in the best journals and with substantial policy impact. The quality of DFID's research work was commented on positively in the DAC's 2010 review of the UK, which particularly noted the closer links being established between the research the department funded and its own policy and programming choices.

CHAPTER 7

Alan Winters is well placed to judge DFID's contribution on research for development. He was director of research at the World Bank before becoming DFID's chief economist, and was later, returning to academic life, a recipient of research grants from the department. He told us:

> *[DFID] was immensely influential on research. And the model of creating research centres, giving them space, holding them accountable, focusing ... not on just "is it coming out in the top journals", but is it actually useful ... can you point to someone who's living better as a result of what you've been doing? ... By a long way DFID was the best of the organisations ... [funding research] We did very much like dealing with DFID.*

Three aspects of DFID's approach to research are worth drawing out here. The first is institutional. DFID brought its research and policy functions together with its international work under one director general during this period; this built a bridge between the learning that DFID was funding and the policies it pursued. Similarly, the department hired a number of research fellows – academics of good standing who worked part-time in DFID and aimed to keep their colleagues apprised of the latest information from the research world. It also hired a chief scientist to work alongside the chief economist. In 2009, Chris Whitty was appointed to that role. A practising NHS consultant and professor of public and international health at the London School of Hygiene and Tropical Medicine, Whitty proved adept as a civil servant. He engaged broadly in the department,[43] quickly becoming influential.

The second aspect of the department's research role deserving comment is to do with resources. In 2008, DFID committed to spending £1 billion over the next five years, an outlay that would make it one of the most important funders of global development research in the world. DFID made research markets, and its high and predictable funding made possible ambitious work, spanning many years. On example was the Young Lives project at the University of Oxford which followed 12,000 children from three countries over 20 years.[44]

The third important point relates to the department's approach to funding research – in other words, how it went about it. Rather than directly hiring a large corpus of academics who would then conduct research, as the World Bank does, DFID hired highly competent sector specialists who would design calls for research but would never carry it out themselves. This approach helped leverage the expertise of academics much more established than those the department could hire full-time as civil servants, while still (through the influence of the research fellows, chief economist, and chief scientist) holding them to the highest standards. By setting research questions relevant to policy, led by civil servants with practical subject-matter expertise, DFID ensured that research effort went on questions of policy importance that would support poverty reduction and the improvement of human welfare. Notably, the department increasingly funded research organisations in developing countries.

Multilateral agencies and NGOs

DFID's funding of the oldest multilateral aid agencies (notably the World Bank and UN agencies) changed in a strategically important way as a result of the new pressures it faced by 2010. The staff cuts we explained in Chapter 5 reduced the department's capacity to manage government-to-government projects. Growing risk aversion made it convenient to have intermediaries – who could be blamed if things went wrong – between DFID as the funder and partner governments. The upshot was a big increase in the amount of money the department's country offices channelled through multilateral agencies. In the 2009/10 year, nearly £800 million of the £1.4 billion DFID gave in total to the World Bank (i.e., more than half) went through this unattractively named "multi-bi" channel. For UN agencies it was more than three-quarters of the £800 million contribution.[45]

This was not the best approach, or even second best. It undermined the department's direct dialogue with partner countries. It added cost. (Multilateral agencies are often effective but rarely efficient.) And there were important differences in approach between DFID and the multilaterals. The World Bank, for example, was slower, more centralised, and had fewer decision makers based in partner countries. It struggled to embrace the realities of working in conflict-affected states. UN agencies tended to compete against each other and to want to profile and publicise themselves. They were replete with their own branding and logos and managed a lot of detailed implementation in-house rather than through government bodies. That was inimical to the prize of building state capacity and the accountability relationship between citizens and those who governed them.

The DAC was gently critical. It suggested DFID develop a better strategic vision for funding multilateral organisations, in cooperation with other bilaterals. However, it was not clear that the options actually available were better. The department's decision makers thought putting more money into the core budgets of the multilateral agencies – for the most effective of which DFID was already contributing more than its fair share – might simply have invested further into their weaknesses. In retrospect, the department should have tried harder to build stronger strategic alliances in each country with other bilaterals and partner governments, in order to pursue reforms in how the multilaterals operated. As it was, the underlying problems persisted into the following decade. (Separately, the department did try to improve multilateral performance by engaging with their HQs, but that did not often filter down effectively to the country level.)

Clare Short had not been in love with the development NGOs. She disagreed with some of their policy positions (for example on debt relief and hostility to the private sector) and was sceptical that the kind of small-scale initiatives they carried out could transform countries. She certainly believed NGOs had a valuable role to play, but she was not ready to pander to them. Gordon Brown and Hilary Benn, by contrast, placed more value on the NGOs' campaigning work and their role in sustaining public support for development. Relations were accordingly warmer from 2003 to 2010. And the department's funding for NGOs expanded too. As the DAC noted, the UK had:

> [a] strong network of civil society organisations . . . the annual total spending of the 300 UK based voluntary organisations working in international development and development education amounted to £1.37 billion in 2005.[46]

Total DFID expenditure through UK NGOs amounted to £114 million in 2000/01. By 2008/09 it had nearly tripled to £317 million. There was a modest allocation to match the funding smaller NGOs raised themselves for their projects. A bigger deal was long-term strategic funding for the larger NGOs through partnership programme agreements. NGOs were also particularly important in humanitarian response, both because much public funding arose through disaster appeals, and because they built effective capacity to provide high-quality help promptly.

Shrewder DFID officials started to worry at this time about the risk that NGOs might become over reliant on government money. Most British NGOs ran mainly on private donations – VSO (Voluntary Service Overseas) being an exception, receiving 75 per cent of its funding from a partnership agreement with DFID. The DAC reported that most NGOs they talked to said they would not want more DFID money "if it implies compromising their independence". For too many, however, the trap proved hard to avoid, and that had unfortunate consequences in the decade after 2010.

The scorecard at the end of the Labour years

Life for many millions of people in the poorest countries improved materially between 2003 and 2010. Globally, extreme poverty fell from around one-quarter of the world's population to less than one-fifth between 2000 and 2010;[47] the decline covered most countries

CHAPTER 7

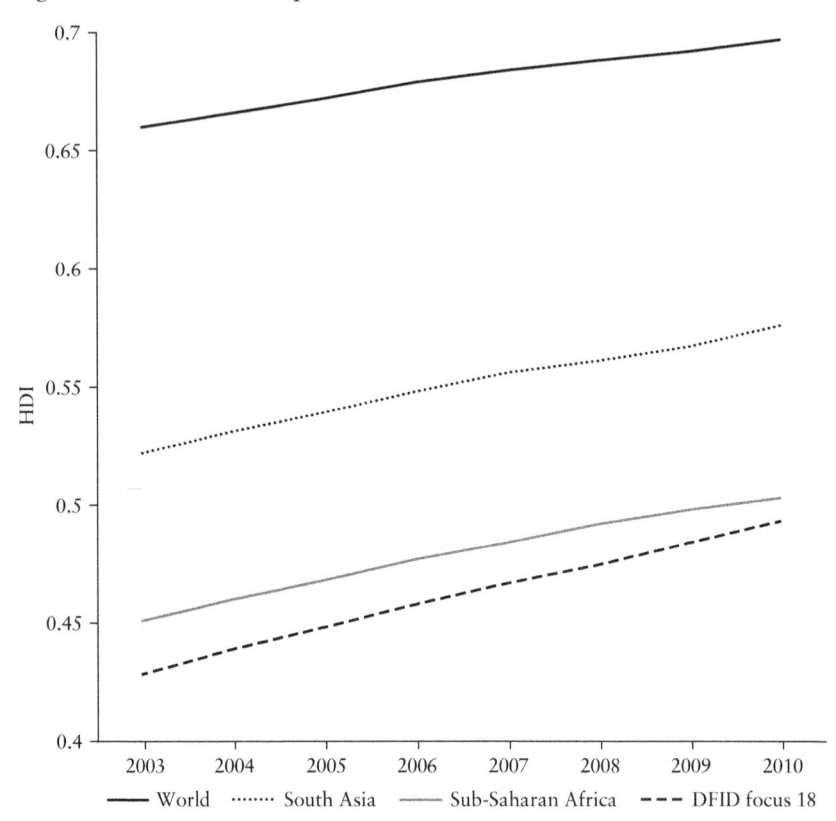

Figure 7.1. Human Development Index 2003–2010

—— World ········ South Asia ——— Sub-Saharan Africa --- DFID focus 18

Source: World Bank World Development Indicators, accessed through the R Package "WDI".

and regions of the world. Similar progress was observed on many other dimensions of social progress. Life expectancy increased, more children went to and stayed in school, fewer died while young, and more of their mothers survived and emerged healthy from pregnancy. That is all reflected in the data. Figure 7.1 shows how the Human Development Index improved across the globe in these years. It also shows that the rate of improvement was faster in many of the poorest countries than in richer ones. That was particularly the case in the 18 DFID focus countries. As is evident in the figures in Appendix B, life expectancy, child survival, and average incomes were all higher in

2010 in each and every one of the DFID focus countries than they had been in 2003. In some cases, the improvements were quite dramatic.

So progress was being made on the objectives DFID was created to pursue. The MDGs were advancing. It is not possible to attribute with any degree of precision how much of the progress made in these countries arose from what the department itself was doing.[48] Changes in average incomes in particular are the outcome of a huge number of factors both internal and external to a country over a protracted period. It would be outlandish to argue that DFID did not contribute to growing incomes in countries like Ethiopia and Rwanda in this period, given how much they increased and the volume and nature of the department's support. But the scale of that contribution cannot be meaningfully quantified.

It is possible, though, to go a little further on the health and education MDGs. Progress on both was impressive across the 18 countries. There was a huge increase in the volume of DFID assistance to them in the 2003–10 period compared to 1997–2003.[49] Much of that extra money went into well-evidenced and well-run programmes for the health and education MDGs. Aid from all sources, especially that going into government budgets to finance services to achieve the health and education goals, was more important in these countries from 2003–10 than previously. And DFID was a big player. By 2010 it was the largest or second-largest donor in all bar four of the 18 focus countries.[50] It therefore had a prominent and influential role in the local donor community. And it had a real voice with the national authorities. It is reasonable to conclude that the DFID contribution to overall progress in health and education was substantial, and certainly markedly greater than in the 1997–2003 phase. If the first years of the department's life under Clare Short were about setting the compass for eliminating world poverty, this era was about delivering on the job.

We should be clear-eyed, not least given what happened in the following decade, that improving the average life experience of vulnerable people in very poor countries, while intrinsically desirable and beneficial, is not the same as setting their nation as a whole on a

CHAPTER 7

path of self-sustaining long-term development. As we have said, the Achilles heel of the whole endeavour was that in fragile and conflict-affected countries, or places where the authorities were not really committed to the MDGs, improvement could turn out to be limited – and in a few of the worst cases, might not be permanent. The department was well aware of that. It had been too optimistic on the prospects for quickly building effective states which would grow the economy and raise and manage public finance well. It was, though, seized of the problem and trying to develop better levers.

What DFID contributed to the achievement of the MDGs up to 2010 is one thing. It also needed to sustain enough support at home to keep going into the future. It worked hard at that. Relationships across government generally improved. Ministers led the way.[51] But officials followed. Minouche Shafik, who took over as permanent secretary from Suma Chakrabarti in 2008, got on well with her counterparts at the Foreign Office and Ministry of Defence.[52] Especially as a result of their shared experiences in Iraq and Afghanistan, the UK's national security institutions increasingly saw that DFID understood the environments they were all working in, and had something useful to offer in achieving the collective objectives. More Foreign Office officials, especially at senior levels, appreciated the soft power that flowed from the UK's global reputation on development.

Domestically, despite the best efforts of the NGO Make Poverty History campaign, public support for the priority the government accorded to development reached a peak not long after the 2005 Gleneagles summit. DFID's own annual report for the 2008/09 year mentions public opinion surveys showing popular support for aid spend decreasing, even if only slightly. Critical stories in right-wing newspapers became a growth industry – though they never uncovered scandals on the scale of some that had occurred between the 1970s and 1997. In July 2009, the government introduced a new UK aid logo for use in the UK and overseas in the hope that it would show their constituents the good that aid was doing. For similar reasons, it created a new scrutiny body, the Independent Advisory Committee for Development Impact.[53] More and more effort was put into communicating to the British public the results that were being achieved. This was all indicative of growing political nervousness. In fact, some of these measures misdiagnosed the issue. It was not so much that people in the UK doubted the effectiveness of foreign aid. It was simply that, especially in the wake of the financial crisis and belt tightening at home, more of them feared it may be getting too much priority over domestic problems.

We should not overstate all this angst. There were indeed a few fraying edges. But the opposition Conservative Party underwent something of a transition in its approach to development in this period. A quiet beginning was made from 2004, when Alan Duncan (later a DFID minister) became the shadow secretary of state. The 2005 manifesto was an advance, albeit a modest one, on the 2001 version, making clear that "fighting world poverty" would be "a key element" of the foreign policy of a Conservative government.[54]

There were more dramatic changes once David Cameron became the party leader after the 2005 election. With his backing, Andrew Mitchell adopted many of the government's development policies. Why? Well, three successive electoral defeats concentrated the mind. Cameron thought things had to change if he was to win power. Shedding the Conservatives' reputation as the nasty party was one of them. He also thought, having observed the Blair and Brown governments, that support for development burnished the UK's soft power, and that helping poorer countries was necessary to help stave off global threats like extremism. There was, too, a recognition that DFID spent the money competently. The biggest factor, though, was more personal and high-minded. Cameron – and Mitchell – were of the Live Aid generation. They had seen enough of the world to understand the misery of extreme poverty. They genuinely wanted, in office, to do something about it.[55]

The fact that the Conservatives were now emulating their approach was one of Labour's most important successes. Making development a matter of cross-party consensus was significant. It meant there were nearly 10 more years after 2010 for a capable, well-resourced, and influential department to continue to bash away at making poverty history.

Minouche Shafik, interviewed in 2023, captured the mood at the end of the Labour years:

> *We were incredibly proud at that time because DFID was providing not just huge resources to development – with a strong focus on the poorest in the world. It was also providing leadership to the whole international system and mobilising resources from other countries and international institutions.*[56]

People then working for the department were highly energised by the opportunity they had to make a difference, and still optimistic about future prospects. They were sometimes rose-tinted, and on occasion unrealistic about what aid and external support for development could achieve.[57] But their enthusiasm was infectious, and they were productive. Douglas Alexander told us that:

> *the intellectual horsepower, the personal commitment, the energy and engagement that officials brought in DFID was as good as anything I saw anywhere else in Whitehall.*[58]

But everything in the garden is never rosy. In its normal diplomatic way, the DAC alluded to that in its 2008 review:

> *DFID is well-placed to respond to the new challenges ahead both in terms of the increased scrutiny attached to a rising budget and in providing global leadership at a time of economic crises and weakening international consensus on poverty reduction.*[59]

A generous compliment but also a clear – and prescient – warning of choppier waters ahead.

PART THREE

Headwinds Slow Progress
2010-16

EIGHT

The Problem Gets Harder

BETWEEN THE mid-1990s and 2010, sub-Saharan Africa and South Asia, home to most of the world's extreme poor, outperformed the rich world in terms of GDP growth, as well as in increases in GDP per capita. The poor were, by and large, catching up after a long period of falling further behind. This was the case both in countries where experts believed policies and governance were conducive to reducing poverty, and in those where they thought policies and governance were worse. This "unconditional convergence", however, started to unravel in the period we move on to now.[1]

Through the 2010s, South Asia continued to grow faster than the rich world: its catch-up continued, and in some cases accelerated (Afghanistan being the major exception). But in sub-Saharan Africa (excluding high-income countries) the growth in per capita incomes did not keep pace with that in the rich world. That was also true, for different reasons, in some of the most populous countries in the Middle East. Overall, reducing poverty was getting harder. That was partly because the easier fruit had by now been picked, but also because existing challenges were biting deeper and new ones emerging.

This was still a period of economic growth. Living standards continued to rise year on year in most developing countries, though more slowly.[2] And in those countries which were peaceful and politically stable, there remained potential for the kind of social spending and productive investment that can support growth and higher living standards into the future. Long-term interest rates were declining steadily throughout this period. Easy credit was available on good terms. African countries in particular borrowed widely: from the multilateral development banks, from China, and by selling their own bonds to private investors.[3] The rise of "non-traditional" donors led by China gave developing countries a wider range of partners to engage with. This was good for countries with credible development plans, giving them options and allowing competition between donors to support their plans. But for countries where there was no clear development plan, it made it more difficult for outsiders to influence their priorities in a more developmental direction.

Some countries took the opportunity of cheap and easy money to finance productive investments likely to generate returns which could be used to service growing levels of debt. Others, particularly if they were borrowing largely to finance recurrent expenditure, were sowing the seeds of future problems. The risk of debt distress was not prominent in discussions in international economic fora in 2010, but it became so before the end of the decade. There were no full-blown debt crises in the first half of the decade, but there was gathering unease, especially as China increased its lending to developing countries on less transparent terms than the Western donors had been typically using.[4]

The bigger problem, however, was that the so-called "long peace", the era between the end of the cold war and the end of the first decade of the new century, was not sustained. Globally, the numbers of conflicts, the deaths of soldiers on the battlefield and total casualties had fallen for nearly 20 years after the early 1990s. Data collected by Uppsala University in Sweden shows a 40 per cent reduction in armed conflicts from 1993 to 2005, and a fall of nearly 80 per cent between 1998 and 2008 in high-intensity civil wars (those with more than a thousand battle deaths a year).[5] The geopolitical environment between 1990 and 2010, with a dominant US and its Western allies often able to deter would-be insurgents or troublemakers, was conducive to these trends in most places, notwithstanding the traumas of Afghanistan and Iraq.

THE PROBLEM GETS HARDER

But in the 2010s, conflict, war, and instability knocked many countries back and prevented others from building on recent progress. The advent of the so-called Arab Spring from 2011 accelerated and complicated these changes. Emerging as a series of mostly peaceful mass protests fuelled by economic and political grievances in Tunisia, Egypt, Syria, and elsewhere, which some commentators initially thought might be harnessed to force democratic and market-friendly reforms, the Arab Spring soon took a darker turn. Some governments were toppled, others sought to survive by instigating their own violent crackdown on their civilian populations. The result was a series of civil wars: in Syria, Yemen, Iraq, and Libya. Many millions of people were displaced, and there was a huge spike in the numbers of people fleeing across borders as refugees in neighbouring countries. Instability spread further afield, notably to many countries across the Sahelian belt, from Mali in the west to Somalia bordering the Red Sea. All this posed a severe threat to rapid progress in reducing global poverty. It also sent the demand for humanitarian assistance sky-rocketing.

It was by now also clearer how big a threat climate change and other environmental problems posed to global development and better lives for the poorest populations. The global warming deniers were losing the argument. It was increasingly accepted both that more action was needed to slow down the increase in temperatures, and that developing countries were being harmed by, and needed help to adapt to, changes already baked in.

The development problem was getting more complicated in another, more surprising, way, too. Since the late 1990s, as we described in detail in Parts I and II, there had been a broad global consensus that the most important goal of international development efforts should be the reduction in extreme poverty. That was encapsulated in the agreement and then energetic pursuit of the MDGs. But the end date for the MDGs had been set as 2015. That raised the question, which was live from the beginning of the new British government's tenure from May 2010, of what should follow the MDGs.

The MDGs had always had their critics. The agenda was quite narrow. The eight goals were underpinned by 18 indicators, of which 14 were quantifiable. Some complained that it was not obvious that the indicators chosen were always the right ones, and many good things were not included, and were thus invisible to the large machinery monitoring MDG progress. Others argued that the MDGs "defined development down" and undermined the bigger picture of what international development should be.[6] But for all their flaws, the MDGs focused effort and mobilised international support. The counterfactual was neither a broader, wider, but equally impactful set of targets, nor a more expansive, profound understanding of international development and how to achieve it, but most likely a continuation of what development aid looked like before the mid-1990s: less effective, less focused on poverty or the poorest places, and less accountable and closely scrutinised.

It was obvious by 2010 that progress against the goals was mixed, ranging from extraordinary success to rank failure.[7] A superficial view suggests that the MDGs were a failure: of the 14 quantifiable indicators, nine were found in analysis after 2015 to have been missed. But that does the progress actually achieved a huge disservice. Their proponents had seen the targets as aspirational, and even where they were missed, the progress induced by them was sometimes remarkable, and often far beyond what most felt possible when the goals were set. The headline goal was the halving of global extreme poverty; this was overshot significantly, as the baseline figure of 47 per cent was reduced all the way down to 14 per cent by 2015, well below the 23.5 per cent target. Gender disparities in educational enrolment were eradicated; the increases in the incidence and new cases of malaria and tuberculosis were both arrested and went into reverse; and the proportion of the global population without access to safe drinking water was more than halved. Progress on the goals that were missed has a flavour of success too: the incidence of hunger did not halve as required by the target, but it came very close to halving; child mortality declined from 90 per 1,000 births to 43, some way short of the target of 30, but nevertheless impressive progress. As Hannah Ritchie and Max Roser wrote: "Often the story is that the world has achieved progress, but not as fast as needed to reach the MDGs."[8]

Because in the early 2010s there was a widespread international view that it had been a good idea to have adopted the MDGs, and because their end date was now looming, there was huge interest in whether a global agreement could be reached on what should replace them – and in who would make the running in answering that question.

Preparing for change

The 2010 general election was the first since 1992 to deliver an outcome that could not be predicted several months in advance. Opinion polls in the six months from the late autumn of 2009 pointed in different directions. The uncertainty was unsettling for many in DFID. As Minouche Shafik, permanent secretary at the time,[9] commented to us, DFID was one of two departments that were seen as Labour's creations.[10] Most staff had never worked under any other political party.[11] There were two undercurrents of concern. The first was over how a change in government would affect civil servants as they went about their day-to-day jobs, and how they should prepare; the second was about what a change in government might mean for how the UK approached development altogether.

Shafik tasked one of her director generals, Martin Dinham, who had started his career in the 1970s and was among the department's longest serving officials (as well as one of the most trusted), with speaking to staff who had no experience of a change of government, and explaining their duties as civil servants. He reminded them that

> . . . in the years since 1997 our agenda has of course grown and developed and become more complicated . . . and the ability to work with, across and through the rest of Whitehall has become essential to our task . . .

CHAPTER 8

We've had 13 years of a Labour government, which means particular policies, a particular use of language, particular behaviour . . . If there is a change of Government party . . . things will be quite a lot different.[12]

Dinham went on to stress that DFID had no policies independent of what the ministers of the day decided; the role of civil servants was to provide ministers with evidence and analysis, and then implement whatever decisions they made. And, he intimated, though they had committed to an independent department and to increase aid spending, a Conservative government would likely make many changes.

As it happened, the election on 6 May 2010 resulted in a hung Parliament. No single party had an overall majority. The Conservatives had the most seats, with 306, but this fell just short of the 311 needed for an outright majority. The Liberal Democrats, with 57 MPs, were the kingmakers: whichever party, between Labour and the Conservatives, they decided to support could form a government. Within a week, it was clear that would be the Conservatives under David Cameron.

The coalition negotiations revolved around two main points: policy and ministerial appointments. Though on domestic policy, there was clear daylight between the Liberal Democrats and Conservatives, and thus much to negotiate over, their manifesto pledges on international development were similar. Both said they would retain an independent development department; both promised not only to increase the aid budget to 0.7 per cent of GNI by 2013 but also to enshrine this commitment in law; and both committed to achieving the MDGs.

On appointments, the issue was how many Cabinet and other ministerial posts would go to Liberal Democrats, and which ones. For international development, the Conservative candidate was clear: Andrew Mitchell had been the spokesman covering DFID since 2005.

As the son of an MP with a public school, military, and City of London background, Mitchell was on the face of it an unlikely champion of international development. But he (like Cameron) was firmly in the "one nation" Conservative tradition, which thought the role of the state was to give people enough room and freedom to make the most of themselves; it was not a stretch to see conditions of extreme material deprivation as a severe constraint on the achievement of individual potential.

Mitchell had spoken to previous Conservative ministers for development, including Lynda Chalker and Chris Patten, who told him "that even on a bad day, to be DfID Secretary was a very good job indeed, and on a good day . . . it might be the best job in the world".[13] He had launched himself into the brief with great vigour. He made good use of his years in opposition, travelling and reading widely. He created and ran a development project in Rwanda – Project Umubano – to bring Conservative politicians and party activists to a developing country to do some form of useful work (teaching, or building basic infrastructure), in part to socialise his party to the value and importance of development work.[14] He took a particular liking to Paul Collier's book *The Bottom Billion* about the world's most disadvantaged people (Collier would be a regular visitor to DFID's offices in time).[15] Together with Cameron, he developed and articulated what he described as a Conservative agenda for international development, "One World Conservativism", launched in 2009 at the Save the Children offices in London.[16] He bought into a great deal of what the Labour government had done. As he says in his autobiography:

> *Once I had assembled my team, I used to tell them we would find it very hard to score any political runs against Hilary [Benn], but we would learn a great deal from him. It is an uncontroversial point to make that the Labour Secretaries of State for International Development, Clare Short, Valerie Amos, Hilary Benn and Douglas Alexander, and particularly Clare, were dedicated and effective ministers.*[17]

CHAPTER 8

And:

> *I realised it was going to be a waste of time attacking Labour, who had made a huge contribution to the fight against international poverty and were respected around the world for it.*[18]

Mitchell was looking forward with great anticipation to leading the department. Observing from the sidelines the horse trading after 6 May between the Conservative and Liberal Democrat leadership teams on potential ministerial appointments, he had a nerve-racking few days, fearing that "his" post might be sacrificed.[19] In the end, partly because William Hague, who was to be foreign secretary, wanted an all-Conservative external affairs team, the Liberal Democrats settled for other roles and Mitchell was appointed on 12 May. He was given two junior ministers. Alan Duncan, who had a strong background in the subject matter as well as experience spanning many decades in the Middle East, was appointed as a minister of state. Stephen O'Brien, who knew Africa well, became a parliamentary under-secretary. They worked together for two years, before Mitchell and O'Brien moved out of DFID in late 2012. Those two years set a direction for DFID that was largely sustained for much of the rest of the decade.

Mitchell's successor was Justine Greening. She had little background in international policy and, according to newspaper reports, was not happy at being given the DFID job rather than a Cabinet position on domestic policy.[20] But in time she was won over and became a staunch champion of Britain's development efforts.[21] An accountant who had studied economics and gone to business school, Greening held the role up to 2016 and largely doubled down on the new focus on value for money that, as we will come to shortly, Mitchell initiated. There was more turnover among the junior ministers in the department, including with the appointment of two Liberal Democrats, Lynne Featherstone from 2012 to 2014 and Lindsay Northover from 2014 to 2015.

The Cameron factor

David Cameron was a champion of international development throughout his tenure. That set the tone for the government as a whole. According to Seldon and Snowdon's account of his premiership, questioning of the aid budget and the 0.7 target was one of the few issues over which Cameron would lose his temper. His commitment did not waver during years of fiscal austerity, when others including the Liberal Democrat leader and Deputy Prime Minister Nick Clegg suggested delaying beyond 2013 the date for getting to 0.7.[22] Cameron's closest ally and chancellor of the exchequer, George Osborne, went along with his boss; but he was less interested. He never played (or seemed to aspire to) the role on the international stage, especially in the IMF, which Gordon Brown had played for 10 years before becoming prime minister. One effect of that, which we will pick up later, was that the previous sympathy among senior Treasury officials for development waned.

Cameron beefed up the UK's central coordination and policymaking machinery on external affairs, establishing a National Security Council which included most of the government's big hitters and met weekly under his chairmanship. He made Mitchell a member, ensuring that the development perspective was brought in to the key cross-government international affairs structure. The new National Security Adviser, Peter Ricketts (previously permanent secretary of the Foreign Office), was impressed. These arrangements gave Mitchell a platform to show how DFID's work contributed to UK national interests, and the ways in which intelligent development work could complement the work of diplomats, the Ministry of Defence, and others with national security responsibilities.

By instinct a liberal interventionist much in the mould of Tony Blair, Cameron developed his own views on development. He was taken with Daron Acemoglu and James Robinson's best-selling book *Why Nations Fail*.[23] He believed that there was a "golden thread" at the heart of successful development, running through "stable government, lack of corruption, human rights, the rule of law, and transparent information".[24] Cameron's vision was an idealist's view of how development happens, and left open the question DFID ministers officials were constantly grappling with over whether and how best to support countries that may in practice be committed to few of those ideals.

Cameron's values were strongly reflected in Britain's response to the Arab Spring, which became a dominant foreign policy concern through his tenure. His desire to support change in Libya (girded by a visceral dislike of its long-standing dictator Muammar Gaddafi) underpinned a limited military intervention in 2011; he felt equally strongly about Syria, though was unable to secure parliamentary agreement to a military involvement there in 2013.[25] Just as had been the case with Afghanistan and Iraq in the previous decade, the Arab Spring and the spread of conflict and instability in more countries created a new agenda for DFID. The department had to respond to the political imperative from the top of the new government to play a constructive role. It needed to build up its knowledge and capacity to operate in the Middle East, where its experience was, despite the engagement in Iraq, still limited. And as time passed, and the humanitarian consequences of increasing numbers of long-lasting conflicts mushroomed, it had to pour vast resources into mitigating them.

The new focus in the Middle East reinforced what was by now a widespread understanding within the department that the scope for continuing rapid progress in reducing poverty was tied up inextricably with trends in conflict and governance.[26] The department's thinking was influenced by Stefan Dercon, its chief economist from 2011 to 2017. In a paper and series of presentations he argued that the department faced an "Anna Karenina problem".[27] While all stable countries were making progress against the MDGs in roughly similar fashion (and thus similar kinds of programmes and policies could bear fruit across them), the fragile countries in which DFID worked were all fragile in different ways. There were no one-size-fits-all programmes that could either resolve fragility or work around it. The work of diagnosing the problems and determining the response would need to be carried out for each place individually. There were no shortcuts, and very often, no obvious answers either.

As time went on, the department developed new tools for diagnosing the problems and developing solutions. A number of analytical exercises were undertaken: country poverty reduction diagnostics, aiming to understand what the constraints to poverty eradication were in each country and how DFID's resources could be arrayed to solve them; and later growth diagnostics doing the same work for inclusive economic growth.[28] These processes produced good analysis (and did so much faster than, for example the World Bank's more detailed growth diagnostics), but often failed to fundamentally shift DFID's programming focus. Project renewal cycles were not aligned to the analytical processes. But the bigger issue was that solutions to intrinsically wicked challenges which were both likely to work and carried the support of all key interest groups were hard to craft. Reconciling what elites dominating decision making were ready to accept and promulgate with what would serve the interests of the broader population in order to create some sort of "development bargain" (as Dercon described it) was easier said than done. This was the defining challenge DFID faced in the second half of its existence – and it remains a defining challenge of the fight against poverty today.[29] No development agency has come up with a fully convincing approach to solving these problems, largely because they are beyond the power of outside actors to fully control.

It was in against this more difficult, more complex context that the new government sought to put its stamp on the department.

NINE

Old Wine, New Bottles

ANDREW MITCHELL wanted to achieve the same objectives as his Labour predecessors. But he believed it was possible to do things better than they had. And he was from the outset conscious that, notwithstanding the strength of Cameron's commitment, there was a growing chorus of dissenting voices who had to be kept at bay. Mitchell thought that if he could show that DFID was achieving results on issues people cared about in a way that was demonstrably good value for money, then public doubts and criticism from the press and the right wing of the Conservative Party about the priority the government was giving to aid could be assuaged.

In this chapter we cover the internal reforms arising from that starting point which he and then Justine Greening pursued. We move on to discuss the way the government handled the increase in the development budget so that, from 2013, the UK finally met the longstanding 0.7 per cent target. The next chapter will then explain how the department spent its share of that growing budget, and how that supported further progress in reducing poverty.

The organisational structure of the department remained as it had been under Labour. The efforts made over the previous decade to improve organisational effectiveness were sustained.[1] And one major constraint was eased. In the years from 2010, staffing numbers were allowed to increase again, rising from 2,383 in 2010 (the lowest level since 2001) to 2,970 in 2015; notwithstanding a blip in 2016, staffing continued to increase for the rest of the decade.[2] There was a significant new influx of mid-career technical staff (health advisers, economists, etc.) including many non-UK nationals. A new graduate entry programme was established too, which was highly competitive and initially brought in up to 50 able and enthusiastic university leavers a year. Staff engagement and morale remained high through this period, as reflected in the department's continuing position at the top of Whitehall surveys. All this helped maintain DFID's effectiveness and reputation, and provided the additional capacity needed for the Mitchell agenda.

Results

One of the key changes that Mitchell implemented as he took over was to switch the talk from spending money to achieving outcomes. As he put it in a 2016 interview, "the worst sentence in the development lexicon is 'we are going to spend a million pounds on x'".[3] The so-called "results agenda" was an approach to justifying development spending by focusing attention (and effort) on what specific things were done with the aid provided by the UK. In private discussions with top officials before the election, Mitchell had agreed that the department would instigate three major reviews as soon as he arrived. One covered bilateral aid and was conducted largely internally; one dealt with funding through multilateral agencies, which was supported by a steering group of leading academics; and the third covered emergency response and was led by the former Liberal Democrat leader Paddy Ashdown, who had in recent years worked for the UN on conflict in the Balkans. Each review looked at DFID's work and partnerships, and all were published. The idea behind them was that a careful, public examination of DFID's work would improve the quality of its portfolio; and as an added bonus would give cover from accusations of waste, and reassurance to those who might make them.

The bilateral aid review was the main vehicle through which the results agenda was promulgated across DFID. A range of spending targets adopted by the previous government (like the commitment to

CHAPTER 9

spend £8.5 billion over 10 years on basic education which Gordon Brown and Hilary Benn had announced) were dropped. They were replaced by commitments to achieve results, which were generated through a bidding process across the department. DFID's country teams all set out what outcomes they could achieve in the following years to reduce the poverty headcount, get more children into school, reduce child mortality, and on other (mostly MDG-related) goals. A price tag was then attached. The results were analysed so that ministers could choose which bids to fund.

For the multilateral aid review, the department developed a methodology which looked first at how well the objectives of each agency were aligned with the MDGs, and second at how well each agency managed its affairs to maximise their contribution to them. The published report was widely circulated and discussed internationally. The approach was repeated at regular intervals, and similar exercises were conducted by a number of other donor countries. Recent analysis has shown a strong correlation between the level of funding allocated to different multilateral organisations and their effectiveness as assessed in the reviews.[4] Some multilateral organisations saw big increases in their funding from the UK; others lost out. This was not always popular with the agencies, but it did more than many previous initiatives to incentivise improved performance. It gained traction because the exercise was conducted professionally, with a credible methodology; because DFID was widely respected across the donor community; and because the agencies could see that money from a well-heeled funder was at stake.

Mitchell made results the central plank of his approach to development. As he explained in his foreword to the 2010/11 DFID Annual Report:

> *We will never forget that the money we spend is taxpayers' money. That's why I instituted an immediate root and branch review of our bilateral and multilateral aid so that we could be certain we were focusing our efforts in those areas where we*

could achieve most. We emerged from those reviews with a clear plan of action for the next four years and a clear understanding of the results that we will work to achieve. We will, for example:

- *educate 11 million children – more than we educate in the UK – but at 2.5% of the cost;*
- *save the lives of 50,000 women in pregnancy and childbirth; and*
- *support freer and fairer elections in 13 countries with more than 300 million voters.*[5]

The same tone ran through the whole report. The "we wills" describing the results that would be achieved were ubiquitous: the phrase is used 40 times in the first 31 pages. The results focus also suited Justine Greening. She liked to be able to see where the money was going and what it bought. She wanted to incentivise an approach that matched her idea of what a more efficient department should look like. In the everyday life of the department, discussions about policy priorities and resource decisions were shaped by promises on results. The upshot was that DFID's activities were increasingly driven by what could be counted and attributed. The 2012/13 DFID annual report, the first to be signed off by Greening, is thick with statistics; virtually every paragraph about DFID activities includes the number of things that were built or people that were reached or items that were bought.[6]

The results agenda gave DFID concrete lines in defence of accusations of waste at a time when it was one of the few government departments with a protected budget. Mitchell, and Greening after him, could point to specific things that would be lost by cutting aid, and quantify what could be gained with the additional resources promised. The department was alert to the drawbacks of this approach. Not everything that mattered was susceptible to such quantification. In some sense, it was a Faustian bargain. By focusing on what aid "bought", it turned the department towards short-term achievements, potentially at the expense of other investments with a long-term payoff that would make more lasting improvements to lives. It incentivised direct delivery of programmes to get children into school rather than investments in a schooling system that works without outside help. This accelerated a change that had already started under Douglas Alexander. Clare Short had of course been focused on results. That was what the DAC goals and MDGs were all about. But her original vision was of an international contribution to developing countries' own strategies for long-term development driven by economic growth and the creation of locally managed systems, paid for by domestic taxation, that delivered basic social services and necessities to the population. The focus now was not on the contribution the UK made alongside others but on what could narrowly be attributed to the UK's particular efforts. Clearly, this change owed more to the political imperatives of the donors than to what many developing countries wanted or needed.

These trends were reinforced by a marked change in the way in which DFID channelled its resources. As we saw earlier, in the first half of its life, DFID tried hard wherever possible to work through the budgets, systems, and institutions of the developing countries it was supporting. The willingness to tolerate risks associated with that diminished – as in 2011 when Andrew Mitchell closed down budget support in Malawi after financial management problems there were exposed. (Clare Short had typically been ready to offer help fixing the problems, with the carrot of then resuming financing.) The proportion of country programme budgets which DFID disbursed to state institutions in partner countries fell markedly between 2010 and 2020.[7] Part of the previous approach was abandoned completely: in 2015, Justine Greening announced that the department would no longer provide general budget support anywhere.[8] (Years later Labour politicians covering the development brief heard a lot from developing country leaders about the need to restore a partnership approach: often, what they meant was they wanted support directly from the UK, in the form of financial aid – whether through project or budget support - not via a host of intermediaries.)

The bulk of resources spent through the country programmes now went as grants through intermediaries – multilateral agencies, NGOs, private contractors, and occasionally other UK public bodies. Those intermediaries then often passed resources on to state institutions in developing countries. And the department still engaged in dialogue with governments in the countries it supported. But its programmes now frequently operated at one step removed from them. The philosophy of partnerships behind countries' own leadership of their development was corroded.[9]

Moreover, the switch to operating through intermediaries swapped one set of difficulties (trying to get governments to spend aid money on the MDGs) for another (trying to manage and scrutinise the activities of the intermediaries, and ensure that the overhead costs they charged were not excessive). It also compounded the centralising effect that much of the value for money agenda produced, which we will say more about in a moment. DFID was previously a very decentralised organisation, which allowed for good decisions to be taken in complex situations – because they were taken by officials based in each country, who were closest to the situation, and had the best knowledge of the particular political, economic, and delivery constraints to be navigated. Some of that was now lost.[10]

Scrutiny and transparency

In his first major speech after taking office, Mitchell announced the creation of the Independent Commission on Aid Impact (ICAI). The goal was to get external validation of the value for money of aid spending. Mitchell called it a sign that "the UK Government is dispensing with the power to sweep things under the carpet". The first commissioners were not development experts – they included a chartered accountant, a lawyer, and a management consultant.

ICAI replaced the independent advisory committee on development impact which Hilary Benn had established.[11] It conducted published studies of its own choosing on programmes the department was financing, and it reported to the parliamentary development committee, buttressing its independence. It adopted a traffic light methodology

CHAPTER 9

to judge programmes, providing a media-friendly kite mark of a red or green rating. The department in its turn published formal responses to ICAI's recommendations and answered questions in parliamentary hearings.

One of ICAI's early reports, in 2013, was on Trade Mark Southern Africa (TMSA), a programme seeking to promote greater trade across the countries of the region.[12] The report was critical, giving the programme a red rating, and describing "serious deficiencies in governance; financial management; procurement; value for money; transparency of spending; delivery and impact". Notably, ICAI found no corruption or theft or misappropriation. The department commissioned its own internal auditors to take a look. They found a payment had been made to the government of Zimbabwe, in contravention of DFID policy. The saga generated criticism from the parliamentary development committee and negative media stories. The programme was closed.

TMSA had a number of deficiencies, and it was clearly managed poorly. Yet reading back over the ICAI report, it is striking how little is said about the actual final impact TMSA would have on its development objectives. Much of ICAI's early work was in this vein. The approach was akin to that of an auditor: were required processes being followed and was the money spent on the things agreed? That is different to saying whether some defined aspect of life would improve sufficiently to justify the expenditure – that is, whether the benefits exceeded the costs – which was ultimately the more important question.

That failing was addressed in later years, with the appointment of commissioners with more experience of development and greater expertise in impact evaluation. ICAI has been an important net positive for the UK's development policy. Its scrutiny, applied to DFID and other government departments has shone a light on the relative quality of different activities. It has generally been positive in its assessments of DFID's programmes.[13]

A complementary reform was the institution of much greater transparency on what the department was doing. From the early

2010s, DFID started publishing detailed information on its portfolio: not just the amounts spent at aggregate level, but transaction-level data, organised by project, and accompanied by virtually all, largely unredacted, project documents. That opened DFID up to scrutiny not just from formal bodies like ICAI but much more widely, and it brought not just criticism but also helpful external advice and insights. The International Aid Transparency Initiative, together with Publish What You Fund, ranks donors by the transparency of their funding and the ease with which information can be accessed. The UK's 2010 ranking was third, after the World Bank and the Netherlands.[14] By 2012, UK institutions were being disaggregated because of how far DFID was moving ahead of the others, and DFID was ranked first.[15] This commitment to transparency continued until the department was absorbed into the much less open Foreign Office.

Centralising controls

More important than external scrutiny and transparency were changes to the department's internal systems. This was a principal focus of Justine Greening's tenure as secretary of state. As she said in 2015, "When I arrived in DFID three years ago, I came armed with my accountant's eye."[16] Greening centralised decision making, reducing the level above which ministerial sign off was needed for spending from £40 million to £5 million. Reducing the threshold increased the *number of projects* that went to ministers for final approval but did not substantially increase the *share of the budget* they signed off, because the proportion of overall spending that went on activities in the £5–40 million range was quite small. (The bulk of the budget was spent on larger programmes, which were already going to ministers.) Senior officials were sceptical that the reduction in delegated authority would improve quality, and unsurprised to observe that it was followed by a large increase in the number of projects approved by mid-level officials with budgets just below the new cut-off point.

CHAPTER 9

A more effective innovation was the establishment of a quality assurance unit supervised by the chief economist, which carried out an independent technical scrutiny of every spending proposal above £40 million. They assessed whether the proposal was in line with academic and research evidence of what was likely to work, made suggestions for improvement, and wrote a short report which went to ministers along with the project approval documentation. This was a return to the approach that had prevailed in the 1980s and 1990s, when a senior multi-disciplinary projects committee chaired by a director general signed off proposals. Ministers consistently accepted the advice of the quality assurance unit, and it reinforced the department's reputation for using evidence and analysis effectively.[17]

Ensuring that spending proposals looked good at the outset was one thing. Whether they were then delivered successfully was quite another, particularly when the timescales for many DFID programmes ran to five years or more, during which period much could change. Senior officials spent much of their time in these years strengthening the supervision of activities under implementation. All significant programmes – a number running into the thousands – were subject to an annual review which was supposed to involve people independent of those with day-to-day responsibility for implementation. The purpose was to establish whether programmes were achieving the goals envisaged when they were approved. They were rated on a scoring system designed to expose problems, and the results were aggregated and reviewed every three months by a board chaired by the permanent secretary. Underperforming activities were listed individually in the reports sent to the board; if the problems were not fixed, the pressure to redesign or close them grew. An overall portfolio quality index was created and became an important performance measure published in the department's annual reports and discussed between DFID and the Treasury. This work was not very glamorous and attracted little ministerial attention but was of fundamental importance in ensuring a growing portfolio was managed effectively. While a small minority of projects failed, most delivered the intended results and a good number went beyond what had been expected. The portfolio quality index rose as time passed.

These reforms were buttressed by other changes too. The department's internal audit function was beefed up, enabling them to carry out comprehensive reviews every two years to assess whether each country office was complying with key controls. A category of senior responsible owners was introduced, attaching accountability to a named individual for every project. The contracting function for those activities which were carried out by private companies (which remained a minority, but grew over these years) was professionalised, with more staff specifically trained as procurement experts. In a speech in 2015, Justine Greening explained how in the Democratic Republic of Congo, there was a programme

> *reaching 2 million people at a cost of $13 per person. We re-tendered it and put in place a results-based contract, and we were able to reach 7.5 million people, but at a cost of $7.40.*[18]

Such calculations were part of attempts to stimulate competition among providers, in theory leading to better value and more effective programmes. Many of these changes were formalised and extended with the development of Smart Rules in 2013, which were a further iteration of the requirements that had been set out in the Blue Book 10 years previously.

Trade-offs

Part of the motivation for the reforms we have just described was to head off the allegation (often surfacing in the right-wing press) that a lot of aid money would be lost to fraud and corruption. It was obvious corruption was a major problem in many of the countries where DFID worked. It did not follow that the department was bound to lose a lot of money: that depended on how well the risks were managed. The NAO published a report on that in 2017. It noted that, as a result of DFID's work to increase fraud awareness and reporting requirements, more allegations were reported – 475 of them in the nine months to 31 December 2016. But confirmed losses were small – 0.03 per cent of DFID's budget in 2015–16, according to the NAO. And they noted that since 2003, the department had recovered around two-thirds (by value) of reported fraud loss.[19] The fact that DFID took a very hard line on recovering losses, even where implementing agencies were not obviously grossly negligent, did however have consequences: a number of valuable programmes (including one on malaria in Tanzania and another on education in Pakistan) were closed, to the detriment of the beneficiaries as well as the department's wider reputation as a reliable partner.

There was a recognition in the department that the results and value for money agenda, together with the move away from programmes implemented through developing countries' own systems to ones that operated through intermediaries, was double edged.[20] On the one hand, many of the measures taken undoubtedly improved the quality of programmes, and as scrutiny grew, DFID had to make sure that its growing budget was being spent well and achieving valuable real-world reductions in poverty. On the other hand, sharper accountability and creation of the senior responsible officer role disincentivised risk taking, especially when projects needed to contribute reliably to the results being counted for public consumption. There was also a concern that some of the changes made the department slower and less responsive. Richard Manning, among the most respected and knowledgeable former Overseas Development Administration and DFID officials, held a number of external roles in these years which gave him a good perspective on the department. He told us that:

> *there was a point when I became concerned that DFID was becoming increasingly hard to deal with, as it became perhaps overfocussed on measuring detailed outputs (often by rapidly-changing staff) and as it outsourced in the end too much of its "intelligent customer" capacity.*[21]

Bill Gates captured the point well when he observed (in an exchange with Lowcock during a meeting in 2023) that adding costs of perhaps 5 per cent to deal with a problem that might be affecting 2 per cent of the department's effort looked questionable.

At the end of the day, however, Mitchell and Greening thought that a much stronger story on value for money, and extinguishing the political risk of writing cheques directly to developing countries' own institutions – which by definition were weaker and riskier than those in richer countries – was essential if a substantial increase in DFID's budget was to be tolerated. That was a judgement they were entitled to make. That said, the huge effort made on value for money failed to head off right-wing critics. They were technical and evidentiary responses to what was ultimately a political problem.

0.7, finally

George Osborne confirmed in his first spending review as chancellor of the exchequer shortly after the 2010 election that the aid budget would in 2013 reach 0.7 per cent. The increase in the DFID budget was heavily back loaded to the 2013/14 year, but it was then substantial.

It is important to remember the context for such a substantial increase in the development budget. Overall public expenditure was severely constrained in the 2010–16 period, barely growing in real terms (in marked contrast to the years of the previous Labour government). As a share of total public spending the DFID budget was always small, rarely more than 1 per cent, and even at its 2013/14 peak less than 1.4 per cent. But DFID was unusual among government departments in seeing its budget grow substantially – by more than 25 per cent in cash terms (Table 9.1). It was this contrast between the treatment of DFID and other departments that attracted increasing attention, rather than the absolute amounts of money at stake. Many departments faced real-terms cuts.

The most senior Treasury officials disliked the priority being given to aid. But it was a political choice and there was nothing they could

Table 9.1. DFID budget and UK ODA 2010/11–2015/16

£ million (current prices)	2010/11	2013/14	2015/16
Total DFID	7,552	9,921	9,479
Of which regional programmes	3,178	4,511	4,009
Of which focus countries	2,172	2,752	2,387
Share	68%	61%	60%
Total UK ODA	8,629	11,701	13,377
DFID share of UK ODA	88%	85%	71%

Source: DFID Annual Reports. See notes in Table 2.2.

do about it. What they could do, however, was to ensure that everything possible was scored as ODA, to minimise the financial cost of the 0.7 pledge. One gap they identified was expenditure in supporting refugees arriving in the UK in the first year after their arrival. The DAC had for many years allowed such spending to count as ODA, but the UK had not previously made use of the dispensation. That practice now changed (ultimately at huge cost to the rest of the aid programme, as we will come on to in Part IV).

In a similar vein, the Treasury also encouraged other departments to look at their spending and see what parts of it might be repackaged to enable it to be scored against the 0.7 target (using the ODA rules), or what new ideas they could come up with in their areas of responsibility. Several departments were able to take advantage of that and mitigate the overall spending cuts they were facing. They notably included the Foreign Office and the business department (which now had responsibility for some international climate spending, as well as the UK's research councils, which often funded work on international issues). The result was that, as Table 9.1 shows, even as the total UK ODA budget grew after 2013/14 in line with growth in the economy, the DFID budget fell, both in cash terms but especially as a share of total ODA.

It is clear that other departments were less likely than DFID to use their ODA budgets in a way that prioritised the reduction of poverty.

They operated not under the terms of the 2002 International Development Act, which required a specific focus on poverty, but under whatever legislation governed their general activities. They did of course have to use the money in a way that met the DAC definition of ODA, but that was weaker than the 2002 Act, requiring only that spending "promotes and specifically targets the economic development and welfare of developing countries".

The Independent Commission on Aid Impact has conducted a number of reviews covering ODA spending by departments other than DFID. Ian Mitchell and Sam Hughes at the Center for Global Development looked at nearly 80 reviews ICAI published between 2011 and 2020. Most covered DFID expenditure, and ICAI scored more than 70 per cent of its graded reviews on DFID as green or amber-green (its highest ratings). For the Foreign Office, by contrast, only 20 per cent received positive scores; 80 per cent were given one of the lowest two ratings, red or amber-red. The results on other government departments were similar.[22] One of the programmes ICAI looked at was the £1.3 billion Prosperity Fund set up by the Foreign Office, aimed at economic development in places where the UK might build future commercial or economic interests.[23] Such a programme could be valuable: there is no reason good development work should have no positive effects on the UK economy. But it was, in the end, conceived and implemented poorly. The Foreign Office lacked the expertise and systems to design and run a large set of economic development programmes well, and failed to meet high standards of transparency. None of the projects the Prosperity Fund backed ever truly took off. This is not to criticise the Foreign Office, merely to observe that managing aid money well requires capabilities that are for good reasons not prioritised in diplomacy.

The Treasury also introduced another innovation to reduce the cost of achieving the 0.7 target. It created a new category of capital spending, beyond the traditional system of capital grants, which it christened non-fiscal capital. This was money that was to be used for the purchase of financial assets (which could in principle later be sold). The money still had to be raised, so it scored against the government's borrowing targets and the deficit. But non-fiscal capital was treated as not adding to the national debt (the value of the asset bought was netted off), so if it could be used to help pay for the 0.7 commitment, that was attractive. The Treasury initially flirted with the idea that the UK's contributions to the World Bank, which had always counted as ODA, could be scored as non-fiscal, on the grounds that were the World Bank ever to be wound up, contributions might be returned to shareholders. That was far-fetched, and the idea was dropped. Treasury officials then decided to include a sizeable allocation of non-fiscal capital in the DFID budget and let the department work out how to use it. The department's most senior officials were sceptical that it had the capabilities necessary to invest successfully for a return in developing countries. The only sensible large-scale use for such money they could see was to capitalise CDC, the government owned, independently managed private sector arm for which DFID was the shareholder.[24] As we will explain in coming chapters, several billion pounds were pumped into CDC in the years from 2015.

All we have just described exposes the fact that the emphasis on the 0.7 per cent target as a goal in itself had real drawbacks, especially under the acute pressures of austerity in the UK's public finances from 2010. It is not that these various wheezes were a complete waste of money: some good things were achieved. But it is clear that this approach was not calculated to maximise the UK's contribution to ending world poverty.

A toothless law

The 0.7 target became an even bigger bone of contention when Parliament passed legislation making it the law of the land. Months before the 2010 election Andrew Mitchell had questioned the wisdom of promising to legislate: in his retelling, he advised Cameron and Osborne to fudge but was overruled.[25]

Both the target, and the idea to write it into UK law, were controversial. Based on a calculation more than 40 years previously, the reasoning behind 0.7 as a magic number was out of date; the idea of defining the adequacy of the aid target by what donors give rather than what recipients need was flawed; and it perpetuated the idea that development was something that could be simply bought, and was primarily about the amount of money made available.[26] Against this, it was an effective lobbying tool. Very few people seriously thought that the existing levels of aid provided in the 2010s were sufficient to meet the needs of developing countries: any mechanism to mobilise additional resources tended to be popular among development activists. DFID spent most of the 2000s and early 2010s steadily increasing its capacity to spend its budget effectively. The target may have been arbitrary and poorly formulated, but, in the UK at least, movement towards it generally meant a greater contribution to ending poverty.

The decision to legislate, however, arguably did more harm than good. It drew more attention to the controversy. The Treasury, for good reason, hated such declaratory legislation: a functioning government could set the aid budget at whatever level it wanted and did not need a standalone law to tell it what to do. (That view attracted a good deal of sympathy from officials at the top of DFID.) In office, the government proved, in practice, lukewarm to actually implementing the manifesto pledge to legislate. Despite a substantial campaign from NGOs, mobilising vast numbers of letters to the department asking when the target would be made law, the official line was the legislation would be introduced when parliamentary time allowed.[27] The government had other legislative priorities and was quite happy for the 0.7 bill to be kept on the backburner.

But not all parliamentary time is given to the government of the day: there are a small number of opportunities for MPs not in the government to table so-called Private Members' Bills. Twice, bills legislating the target into law were introduced. Both times, the government gave them its support. The first attempt laid bare the divisions within the

Conservative Party over aid: Peter Bone, a well-known right-wing aid sceptic, "talked the bill out" – filibustering until the time allotted for discussing it ran out.[28] His was not an isolated voice: one research paper estimated that of the 308 Tory MPs sitting in Commons at the time, 94 were sceptical of the target (and aid more generally) and a further 24 were outright opposed.[29]

However, Michael Moore, a Liberal Democrat who previously served as secretary of state for Scotland, secured a new slot to reintroduce the bill. This time it survived the opposition and passed into law in March 2015.

In fact, as events were to show, the law was toothless. All it required was that the government tell Parliament in advance in any year when it expected aid spending not to reach 0.7. At the time it was passed, the Act merely formalised what had already been achieved. In 2020, when the government no longer wanted to spend 0.7, it complied with the law simply by telling Parliament it was cutting the budget.

TEN

Better Lives

Reprise

THE DEPARTMENT had a lot more money at its disposal from 2010 to 2016 than earlier in its life (Table 10.1). What did it do with it? The short answer is more of the same, at a larger scale and with refinements around the edges.

We will illustrate that now, looking as we did for earlier periods at DFID's long-standing priorities of health, education, humanitarian action, and support for economic growth through private sector initiatives. We will also look at three additional themes that were prominent under Mitchell and Greening: support for women and girls, governance, and responding to climate change.[1] Before we get to that, there are a number of preliminary points to be made.

First, most of the money the department spent in the first three years of the Cameron-led government arose from decisions taken, or work started, under Labour. Unlike Clare Short in 1997, Mitchell did not want to change DFID's priorities: he, too, wanted to deliver the MDGs. There was therefore a high degree of continuity in what DFID actually did, even while the narrative around it and some of the processes and aid channels changed.

Second, as Table 10.1 also shows, there was still a strong concentration on the original 18 focus countries. None of them were dropped.[2] The bilateral aid review did lead to some rationalisation, but that was mostly by phasing down smaller country programmes, for example in East Asia (including Vietnam and Cambodia), which

Table 10.1. How DFID's spending power increased between 1997–2002 and 2010–16

£ million	1997–2002	2003–09	2010–16
Total DFID	25,935	50,330	77,735
Total 18 Countries	6,184	15,069	21,344

Source: DFID annual reports. Figures are adjusted for inflation, based on 2022 prices. The 1997–2002 figures are for the financial years 1997/98–2002/03, and likewise for the subsequent periods.

had by now largely eradicated extreme poverty. There was also a new emphasis on supporting the UK's overseas territories, notably Montserrat and St Helena, but the scale of resources they absorbed was, in the big picture, small.[3]

Third, while the increase (in real terms) of nearly 40 per cent in contributions to the core budgets of multilateral agencies was not as large as for the rest of the DFID programme, it was heavily concentrated on those agencies with the potential to make the largest contribution to the MDGs – in particular the World Bank's fund for poorer countries (IDA), the Gavi vaccine programme and the Global Fund to Fight AIDS, Tuberculosis and Malaria.

The consequence was that the department remained focused, both culturally and operationally, on supporting the poorest countries and the poorest people – to a much higher degree than most other donor countries.[4]

Doubling down on health...

The department's health portfolio remained its largest. In June 2011 the government hosted a major international fund-raising conference on immunisation, the headline goal being to reach 250 million children by 2015. David Cameron pledged that DFID would vaccinate 80 million under-fives (at a cost of some £600 million, which was de-emphasised in the publicity around the event, consistent with

Mitchell's desire to focus on results, not money). This perpetuated the UK's position, established under Labour, as the leading international financier of immunisation in developing countries. As well as other governments and foundations, businesses were encouraged to contribute, and incentivised by an offer that DFID would (up to a limit) match what they provided with additional resources. It was estimated that 4 million lives would be saved.

This approach was replicated in 2012. A summit on family planning produced what a government press release called:

a historic global breakthrough giving access to family planning for 120 million women. The milestone will help stop 200,000 women and girls from dying in pregnancy and save the lives of 3 million babies across the world's poorest countries.[5]

In the margins of the London Olympics later that summer, a similar event was convened, together with Brazil (as the next Olympics host), on nutrition. It generated a major European Union commitment to take responsibility for reducing the number of stunted children in the world by 7 million by 2025. DFID was successful in using such events to make pledges which locked in the department's own future activity. In 2020 ICAI reported that DFID had reached 50 million people with nutrition services since 2015, making "significant contributions to reducing malnutrition".[6]

Also in 2012, the department announced a five-fold expansion of work on neglected tropical diseases, aiming to protect 140 million people in particular from lymphatic filariasis (elephantiasis), onchocerciasis (river blindness), schistosomiasis (bilharzia), and dracunculiasis (Guinea Worm).[7] Those diseases were estimated to affect more than a billion people and to kill half a million a year. That work, too, was sustained and reinforced for the rest of the decade. In February 2016 former US President Jimmy Carter (then in his nineties) visited London. The Carter Center had begun leading the international campaign to eradicate Guinea Worm disease in 1986, when there were

CHAPTER 10

an estimated 3.5 million cases annually in Africa and Asia. By 2015 progress was such that only 22 people worldwide had contracted the disease that year. Carter met staff in the department and took delivery of a further DFID pledge to help complete the eradication of the worm. He acknowledged the UK as one of the world's largest supporters of the campaign.[8]

There was a similar story on polio. In 2011, David Cameron announced funding to fully vaccinate an additional 45 million children.[9] In 2017 the then secretary of state Priti Patel extended the commitment further, to immunise 45 million children against the disease each year until 2020. As the press release her team issued put it, as a result of UK (and other) support since 1988

more than 16 million people are walking today who would have otherwise been paralysed, and the number of people contracting the disease has been reduced by 99.9%.[10]

These initiatives were all part of what was by now a deep partnership between DFID and the Bill and Melinda Gates Foundation, which had first taken off in the Labour years and expanded over time both in scale and breadth. And alongside them, the department was scaling up all its other activity on malaria, HIV/AIDS, health systems strengthening, safe motherhood, and research into health problems and solutions for them. Among other donors, only the US matched the scale of DFID support to improve health in low-income countries. And there was a direct link between what the department was doing and visible year-on-year reductions in infant mortality, maternal mortality, and loss of life through HIV/AIDS, tuberculosis, and malaria, and increases in life expectancy, both in the department's 18 focus countries and globally (see Appendix B). In no other area did the department in these years (as previously) draw as successfully on its carefully curated combination of assets: top-level political engagement, technical expertise and in-country presence, partnerships, long-term funding, and convening power.

. . . And education

The department's spending on education doubled to more than £1 billion a year between 2010 and 2016 and was sustained near that level until 2020. The impact was not as transformational as in the first years of the department's existence: most children in the countries where DFID focused were by 2010 enrolled in school, which many had previously not been. If anything, the department became less influential on policy issues as it focused more on the results it could attribute directly to its own activity, rather than the broader contribution it could make by helping improve education systems. Nevertheless, DFID support helped sustain enrolment, and it focused increasingly on the quality of learning. The evidence is now clear that the introduction of free primary education across many countries led to a rapid increase in literacy rates – though they remained shockingly low in too many countries.[11]

The department extended its work into new areas, too, especially trying to get (and keep) more girls in classrooms. It also engaged in the controversial issue of low-cost private schools, which were championed by right-wing think tanks and loathed by some NGOs and teacher unions. The department's approach was pragmatic, taking as the starting point the observable fact that millions of parents, especially in rapidly growing mega-cities like Nairobi and Lagos, were choosing to pay a few dollars a month to send their children to such schools (which were mostly run by former teachers). That was either because there were no places at publicly funded schools, or because they thought the education was better. DFID looked at the regulatory environment for these schools with the goal of improving standards. In the wake of the protracted Syria war and other long-lasting crises, it also played a leading role in supporting educational provision as part of humanitarian responses.

Among the most important initiatives (which, unusually in this period, addressed the education system as a whole, not the narrower

CHAPTER 10

question of what the UK was specifically buying) was in Pakistan, where Michael Barber, who had run Tony Blair's Delivery Unit, acted for several years from 2009 as DFID's (unpaid) special representative on education. He struck up a strong relationship with Shehbaz Sharif, who between 1997 and 2018 served several stints as chief minister of Punjab (Pakistan's most populous province, with more than 120 million people). Barber introduced to the Punjab education sector the approach he had brought to the Blair government. It combined the setting of ambitious goals with rigorous, intensive, and persistent monitoring of implementation by the chief minister and his top team, all using continuously updated data on student attendance, teacher presence, the quality of facilities, and inspection visits to drive up performance.[12] Barber summarised some of the results:

As of January 2014, on a conservative estimate, there are over one and a half million extra children enrolled in school since 2011. Student attendance daily is now over 90 per cent. Over 110,000 new teachers have been hired on merit. More than 35,000 extra teachers are present at school every day. Over 90 per cent of schools have basic facilities compared to less than 70 per cent when we began.[13]

ICAI published a complimentary assessment in late 2012 which came to similar conclusions.[14]

In 2022 ICAI published a broader and, again, notably positive review of the impact of DFID support for education globally. Much of what they looked at had started (or had its origins) before 2016. They corroborated DFID's own assessment of the scale of its impact: they said the government's claim that it supported 15.6 million children in education programmes was "reasonable".[15] They concluded the UK was a global leader in addressing inequalities in education, with 80 per cent of projects costing over £1 million having targeted activities for girls; that it had a strong influencing role which helped strengthen multilateral education programming, not least the Education Cannot Wait fund, which had supported 4.6 million children in conflict zones to access education since 2016; and that it had (at least on occasion) helped strengthen national education systems. All that said, it is notable that no serious effort was made in this period to extend the department's education work beyond primary to the secondary, tertiary, or vocational levels.

A shift towards emergency response

Humanitarian crises were more numerous, larger, and longer lasting in these years than in the previous 15 years. Nothing attracted more public attention to the department's work; and nothing except a massive corruption scandal (of which there were none) had the same potential to undermine its reputation, both with the public at large and with decision makers and opinion formers around the Westminster village. The fact that DFID throughout this period was universally recognised as performing well in this area was therefore important.[16] Its record was not unblemished. Like everyone else, it was too slow to spot and respond to the famine that took 250,000 lives in Somalia in 2011 – the only large-scale famine seen in the world over the 23 years of DFID's life.

In mid-2014 an Ebola outbreak emerged in West Africa, concentrated in Guinea, Liberia, and Sierra Leone. Ebola is an unusually nasty disease, transmitted through contact with the bodily fluids of an infected person. It is less infectious than, say, COVID-19, but many who contracted it died. (There are now effective vaccines.) When a handful of cases started appearing in the US and Europe in the early autumn, it became an international crisis, closing borders and flustering stock markets. At its peak in November 2014, Sierra Leone was reporting more than 500 new cases a week, and the fear was that the numbers could rise exponentially.

DFID was at the head of a government-wide effort to help Sierra Leone, which included sending more than a thousand uniformed public servants, mostly soldiers, to the country. The department threw more than £400 million into ending the outbreak. Justine Greening's summary, in the department's 2014/15 annual report, is fair:

Britain has led the international response to the Ebola outbreak in Sierra Leone. Our investment built emergency treatment centres, supported more than half of all treatment and isolation beds for Ebola patients, funded burial teams, trained healthcare workers, and provided testing laboratories to rapidly diagnose Ebola and minimise spread.[17]

The crisis was also a major moment of international cooperation: the US, UK, and France worked together to provide the support to contain the crisis, each focusing on one of the three most affected countries.[18] As had been the case with the 2004 Indian Ocean tsunami, the department was perceived in Whitehall to have performed well, and Cameron enjoyed the plaudits of his counterparts (notably President Obama and Chancellor Angela Merkel). The outbreak was the kind of complex challenge DFID was designed to address. There were logistical difficulties in getting people and supplies to the right areas; equipment and new buildings that were required to house the sick; and cultural barriers (in particular, practices around death and funeral arrangements) that needed to be both understood and sensitively handled to contain the spread of the disease. The outbreak was brought under control by early 2015, but Sierra Leone was not finally declared Ebola free until March 2016; 11,000 people had died there and in neighbouring Liberia and Guinea, after around 30,000 cases.[19]

The humanitarian crisis spawned by the civil war in Syria from 2012 was of a different order of magnitude.[20] Both for altruistic reasons (the scale, brutality, and duration of the horror kept it at or near the top of the news cycle for several years, with the public in many countries wanting their governments to intervene to ease the suffering) and for more self-interested ones (concerns over security, a terror threat, and mass migration) it became a dominating foreign policy preoccupation. Aid was poured in to help Syrians inside the country as well as those who had fled to Turkey, Jordan, Lebanon, and elsewhere. In 2015 nearly a million people caught up in crises – most of them Syrians – walked to Europe. It was immediately clear that was politically unsustainable. As part of the response, David Cameron hosted a UN conference in London in February 2016 aiming to raise enough money to persuade Syria's neighbours and the refugees that they were better looked after closer to home. It proved the most successful event of its kind ever, with pledges on the day amounting to $12 billion for 2016 and subsequent years. Britain announced £2.3 billion, a doubling of the previous DFID commitment.[21]

As the number, complexity, and duration of crises grew as the decade progressed, so did the proportion of the department's budget allocated to humanitarian response, reaching 15 per cent of total UK ODA in 2016. (One consequence was, inevitably, that the share available for longer-term work on reducing poverty fell.) The US, as it had always been, remained by far the larger financier of humanitarian agencies. But the department was at the forefront of efforts to make humanitarian aid more effective. It pushed the agencies to provide more help in the form of cash to beneficiaries rather than simply giving them commodities; to do better in meeting the particular needs of women and girls; to provide more comprehensive help going beyond the traditional focus on food, water, and shelter (for example in education for displaced children, as we noted earlier); and to act earlier when it was clear that a new crisis was about to erupt (for example as a result of drought). Making the humanitarian response system work better could not prevent or end crises, but it undoubtedly mitigated their impact and saved many lives.

Promoting private sector growth

Early in his tenure Andrew Mitchell announced an intention "to put the private sector center-stage".[22] The department established a new private sector department, hired additional specialist staff, and published a new policy paper.[23] In each of its partner countries it examined what held back economic growth, and in particular the kind of growth that would most benefit the poor, and then examined how closely each country office's portfolio mapped to the issues identified. It refreshed its approach to jobs, shifting from a supply-side approach (focusing on, for example, training) to a demand-side approach (with greater emphasis on growing businesses which needed to hire workers).

These changes gave DFID a more sophisticated understanding of economic growth in its partner countries. But they were also partly borne of necessity, reflecting a larger change in how DFID worked. Clare Short had emphasised that economic growth was critical for development, but much of the activity that followed in DFID's earlier years focused on macroeconomic policy in relation to budget support (through, for example, insistence on adherence to IMF programmes). As the role of budget support atrophied, there was a shift from macro-influencing to a more microeconomic approach. That led to work to improve the business climate and develop markets that worked better to create jobs for poor people. By 2014, DFID was backing programmes in 24 countries to reduce the costs and time to register a business, secure title to land, clear goods across borders, and enforce contracts in local courts. (In one example that became well known, the department supported the establishment of Africa's first one-stop-border post between Zambia and Zimbabwe, which cut customs clearance and waiting times by 66 per cent.) This approach sometimes worked well, but mistakes were also made. DFID had been an early champion of microfinance but was slow to divest from it even as the evidence mounted that most microfinance programmes had little or no effect on income generation and productivity.[24]

Changes in the government's approach to its private sector arm, CDC, were more consequential. In mid-2011, following a period when CDC hit the headlines for the wrong reasons,[25] Andrew Mitchell announced three key reforms to its mode of operation.[26] First, it would now invest only in Africa and South Asia, and only in the poorer parts of the richer countries there.[27] Second, it would increasingly make its own investments and not simply operate through private equity funds managed by others, a move that would both increase the risks it faced but also give it more control over the impact of its portfolio. And third, its success and performance would be measured by its development impact, not just its financial returns.

The government also decided that, for the first time in decades, it would now put new money into CDC.[28] In 2015, following lobbying by the department and others, the DAC changed its rules so that an ODA credit could be registered when the government gave CDC new capital – the corollary being that negative ODA would be incurred if the government ever took a dividend or sold shares in the institution. (The previous system had looked through into CDC and scored positive ODA in years where its new investments exceeded realisations, and negative ODA when the opposite occurred.) The government immediately announced it was going to give CDC £735 million.

This did not inoculate CDC from controversy. The NAO, which looked repeatedly at CDC, published a report in 2016, saying it should do a better job in working out what impact its investments had on development. Their conclusion was striking: despite improvements in looking ex ante at potential impact, it

> *remains a significant challenge for CDC to demonstrate its ultimate objective of creating jobs and making a lasting difference to people's lives in some of the world's poorest places. Given the Department's plans to invest further in CDC, a clearer picture of actual development impact would help to demonstrate the value for money of the Department's investment.*[29]

ICAI came to similar conclusions in 2019, issuing a critical report saying that many investments failed to achieve the development impact that had been expected when they were approved.[30]

CDC did things that DFID was not equipped to do. It tackled different constraints to growth and development. The organisation was now being better managed than previously. But the story of this period is of an increase in ambition and investment that was not proven to be more effective in contributing to the MDGs than alternative ways of using the scarce ODA money used to capitalise it.

Near the end of her tenure, Justine Greening defended the department's approach:

The last 15 years have shown us that investing in economic development and jobs is the only way we can defeat poverty for good. The World Bank predicts 600 million new jobs are needed over the next decade to keep up with young people entering the job market. That is why I have doubled the UK's investment in jobs and growth to £1.8 billion in 2015/16. We are helping to create jobs and livelihoods, particularly for young people, in Africa, the Middle East and Asia, to tackle the root causes of poverty and migration, as well as building future markets for UK trade.[31]

DFID's portfolio promoting economic development performed well enough, in the sense that its activities typically met their objectives. But the line of sight between that and improved incomes and reduced poverty is harder to see. That is partly because the linkages between the inputs and outcomes are particularly complex in this area (unlike, say, in immunisation, which leads directly and inevitably to lower child deaths). But it is also questionable whether the department operated at a big enough scale in economic development to materially move the dial (unlike, say, the World Bank or private investors), or whether it was as influential here as it was in some other domains. It was not a major investor in, for example, infrastructure (like roads and water systems) or agriculture, which were more clearly linked to faster growth, and the efforts it made in analysing what was holding growth back rarely led to transformational change.

Women and girls

Gender became a much stronger focus of DFID's work. For many years the department's strong cohort of social anthropologists had drawn attention to the way discrimination and restrictions over the rights of women and girls held development back. The analysis was often presented in terms of gender politics and power relations, in ways that – however unintentionally – made it harder for others across the department (who were for the most part sympathetic) to answer the "so what shall we do?" question. The result was that programmatic activity was limited.

On the centenary of International Women's Day in March 2011, the department published a new strategic vision for girls and women, committing to new large-scale initiatives in four areas: giving women more control over economic assets; getting more girls through secondary school; delaying first pregnancy and supporting safer motherhood; and tackling violence against women and girls. This initiated a step change in DFID's level of effort, with greater transparency and regular reporting on progress.[32]

The new approach had initially been driven largely by senior officials, with Joy Hutcheon, one of the director generals, playing a prominent role. But from 2012 Justine Greening, who had a personal passion for the topic, picked it up. Lynne Featherstone was also energetically engaged, especially in campaigns on violence against women and girls. And shortly before she became prime minister, Theresa May spent a Saturday attending a conference in the department on empowering girls and women.

In 2014, the commitment to do a better job in this area was translated into law by the International Development (Gender Equality) Act, which amended the 2002 International Development Act. It required that development assistance must now, as well as reducing poverty, be "likely to contribute to reducing inequality between persons of different gender". Humanitarian assistance had to be provided

in a way that takes account of any gender-related differences in the needs of those affected by the disaster or emergency.

The law also instructed the department to report on its actions to support gender equality.

CHAPTER 10

These were important changes. Inequality needed to be tackled not only through specific programmes focusing on gender, but through the design of other activities that may previously have had no explicit gender focus in their conception. Earlier ways of doing things could unwittingly entrench existing gender disparities or disadvantage girls and women. The Act, given effect through procedural changes to the business case process by which all aid spending was agreed, forced all programmes to consider whether this was the case. It also forced consideration of whether the design of the support needed to be tweaked so that it actively furthered gender equality. In this respect, DFID was ahead of the curve: Canada adopted its feminist international assistance policy in 2021.

ICAI reviewed DFID's work on eliminating violence against women and girls in 2016, looking at 23 programmes with a budget of £184 million.[33] In one of its most positive reports, it applauded the department's "high quality and innovative" programming, and said it had

> *demonstrated strong global policy leadership, through initiatives such as the 2014 Girl Summit, and has made a significant contribution to knowledge and evidence on preventing abuse, including on global challenges such as child marriage and FGM [female genital mutilation].*

It was not just the legislation and programming that changed. Under Justine Greening girls and women became an increasingly visible part of the UK's development policy and identity, quite literally in some ways: following the Girl Summit in 2014, a large sculpture spelling out "GIRL" was moved into the foyer of DFID's London headquarters building in Whitehall. It was one of the first things staff and visitors saw.[34] Greening encouraged staff to listen to girls and invited classes from girls' schools across the UK to visit the building. Gender was now a stronger part of DFID's identity than it ever had been before, and remained so until the end of the department's life.

Governance

Improving standards of public administration and tackling corruption were, in principle, a significant focus before 2010. The department reported that around 17 per cent of the bilateral portfolio between 2004 and 2009 supported governance objectives. In some countries (including Tanzania, Afghanistan, and Bangladesh), it was more than 25 per cent. These figures, however, mask the fact that much of what was scored took credit for the fact that a governance dialogue was included in budget support arrangements. There had also been targeted projects trying to strengthen institutions responsible for public administration, financial management, and promoting accountability. They tended to have most traction when technical assistance was combined with finance into the budget to improve how well it was managed.[35] However, as we have said, budget support was substantially scaled back after 2010 – so some of the department's ability in practice to engage in governance issues was lost.

Nevertheless, with the arrival of David Cameron, DFID's work on governance became more visible. There was a renewed focus on corruption, looking at both developing countries and the role of the developed world (the UK not least). Cameron called corruption "the cancer at the heart of so many of the world's problems";[36] in 2012 Stephen O'Brien gave a speech at a roundtable on transparency, accountability, and good governance in which he declared:

> *Corruption is bad for development, bad for poor people and bad for business. It causes huge damage to developing countries and wastes precious resources. We know, too, that poor people feel the effects more harshly than those who are better off. The uncertainties of bribery stifle business development and inward investment. And more widely, corruption corrodes the fabric of society and public institutions and is often at the root of conflict and instability.*

CHAPTER 10

At the heart of DFID's work to tackle corruption is the recognition that in the modern world the problem of dealing with corruption cannot be confined within a country's own borders.[37]

Strong words. But this was a tough nut to crack. In developing countries, dealing with it meant uncovering corrupt practices (itself difficult), stopping them, and then helping to recover the money. Clearly, those profiting were actively obstructive. Nevertheless, there were some successes. The team leading DFID's work set itself a target of freezing £96 million and recovering £50 million of corruptly acquired funds from developing countries by 2014.[38] It overshot the first mark, reaching £120 million, and substantially undershot the latter, achieving £13.75 million.

ICAI published a review that was critical of the department's approach in part because it was insufficiently focused on the poor.[39] That was a harsh assessment: to focus more directly on the poor would have meant prioritising petty corruption rather than grand corruption, though the consensus was that the latter likely did more damage.

Cameron held a flagship anti-corruption summit at Lancaster House in 2016. It was co-hosted by Muhammadu Buhari and Ashraf Ghani, heads of state in Nigeria and Afghanistan. On the eve of the conference Cameron was caught on camera telling the queen that both countries were "fantastically corrupt", an assessment to which Buhari took no exception.[40] The summit was a qualified success. Much of the action focused on the ways in which developed countries facilitated grand corruption. Britain created a public register of the ultimate "beneficial owner" of property purchased by UK companies, making it harder to stash ill-gotten funds in expensive UK properties; and pledged to automatically share its register of the beneficial ownership of UK companies with a number of other countries. It also promised to make open contracting the norm in public procurement. These were useful improvements. But the pledges were undermined because a number of the UK's Overseas Territories dodged participation. Given the importance of places like the British Virgin Islands and the Cayman Islands as tax havens, shrouded in the secrecy necessary to hide corruptly obtained funds, that was a blow. In September, a few months after the Lancaster House summit, another ICAI review was critical of the effectiveness of UK aid in tackling tax avoidance and evasion.

The department also tried to work in a more "politically smart" and "politically informed" fashion. There was a view that political constraints were commonly a prime barrier to growth. Loosening or working around these constraints required nimbleness and a willingness to engage with local politics that was missing in the large multilateral organisations. An internal review of DFID's performance found many examples of good practice and programmes that successfully followed this approach, but no systematic adoption of it.[41]

The department funded a growing programme of research on governance topics, yielding 130 peer reviewed articles and 19 books by 2011 – and more thereafter.[42] They often confirmed the fundamental truth that improving governance was hard unless it was a genuine priority of local political leaders.

Climate

It was in this period that DFID's spending on climate change-related activities really began to ramp up. By 2010/11, climate change was universally understood as a threat to development. A cross-departmental international climate fund, building on the model Gordon Brown had initiated, was set up with a commitment to spend £2.9 billion.[43] By 2015/16, it had doubled in size to £5.8 billion.

Climate aid could be spent in one of two ways: on adaptation (essentially, diversifying economic activity and building resilience to climate shocks) or on mitigation (reducing carbon emissions and thus slowing the pace of climate change). A great deal was spent on the latter, particularly by departments other than DFID. Within the department, climate change was addressed in part through dedicated

CHAPTER 10

projects and in part by "mainstreaming" climate considerations across activities; much of the effort eventually focused on promoting "climate-compatible development". There were some successes: the Productive Safety Nets Programme in Ethiopia, already a lifesaving social protection programme, was redesigned to increase the focus on resilience and food security.[44] There were also substantial contributions through multilateral organisations, notably £720 million to the Green Climate Fund set up in 2010 under the UN climate change convention.[45]

Yet, overall, the sum seemed rather less than its parts. ICAI was broadly positive about the international climate fund in a 2014 report, but their review was notable for how little it said about the actual development impact of what was being done.[46] The parliamentary development committee, reviewing years of work in 2019, was less complimentary. They found it "highly disconcerting that there does not appear to be an active strategy underpinning the Government's International Climate Finance spending".[47] They were particularly concerned that ministers could give few examples of climate funding focused on poor people in poor countries; much of the action was in middle-income countries, and there was little monitoring of the poverty impact of spending. The results described in the government's own reports include quantified metrics on mitigation, but nothing on poverty or incomes of the poor.[48] If adaptation meant trying to ensure the poor had the means to cope despite climatic changes, it was not being systematically measured. DFID's role on climate had to be coordinated with other departments, including the Foreign Office and the departments dealing with energy and the environment, all of which at various times held ODA budgets for very similar purposes. It felt to top officials like more effort was spent in cross-government dialogue on the next international negotiation than in ensuring that the money already available was spent to maximum effect.

There were areas where a more strategic approach might have yielded significant results, notably in agriculture, where investments were necessary to help farmers stay ahead of changing weather pat-

204

terns. But DFID's portfolio was not focused sufficiently on that problem. Indeed, the parliamentary report noted that climate change was not a central concern of DFID's agriculture work. Given the increasing volumes of funding dedicated to climate change, there is a strong sense of a missed opportunity.

After the MDGs, and a new narrative

In the summer of 2011, Andrew Mitchell invited his political advisers and DFID's top officials to his Nottinghamshire home for a day's brainstorming on the forward agenda. Much of the discussion was about how the UK could influence what would follow the MDGs when they expired in 2015. The mandarins said that if the prime minister were willing to put personal time into the endeavour, the UK may be able to carve out a leading role, reflecting the kudos its commitment to global development had generated over the last 15 years. Otherwise, Britain would end up just another voice in the cacophony. Mitchell sounded out Cameron, who was interested. One idea was for him to set up an international commission, along the lines of Blair's Africa commission in 2005. But it became clear through informal soundings that the UN secretary-general, the former Korean diplomat Ban Ki-moon, wanted the UN to be in pole position.

In the summer of 2012, Ban announced the establishment of a high-level panel to make recommendations to him. It was to be co-chaired by Cameron and the presidents of Indonesia and Liberia. One of DFID's director generals, Michael Anderson, was seconded to Number 10 to run the team supporting Cameron. The challenge was clear from the outset: because the MDGs were viewed as having made a difference, the champions of every issue relating in some way to global development wanted the next framework to include their pet project. Cameron and Anderson well understood that if everything was a priority, then nothing was a priority. They wanted a simple and clear agenda, with focused and quantified goals covering the 15 years up to 2030. But it was difficult to contain the mission

CHAPTER 10

creep, particularly with a groundswell of global opinion determined to ensure that environmental issues, of which there were many, got more prominence this time.[49]

Cameron was conscientious in devoting significant time to the endeavour and a skilful facilitator, but he ultimately had to accommodate many competing views. At the end of May 2013, the panel issued a report setting out an illustrative list of 12 goals and more than 50 measurable targets to replace the eight MDGs and their 14 quantified indicators.[50] That was bad enough. But by the time the sustainable development goals, as the new framework was called, was adopted in 2015, machinations among diplomats from all the UN's member states in New York had increased the package to 17 goals and 169 targets. The poverty-focused goals were still there, but the Christmas tree now contained every other bauble too. The MDGs may have been imperfect, but the fate facing the sustainable development goals was worse: irrelevance.[51] As Costas Michalopoulos has put it, the new goals "do not address the problem of how to strengthen developed country commitment to help address global issues", noting that, other than on climate change, that commitment is weaker now than at the beginning of the century.[52]

In their manifesto for the May 2015 general election, the Conservatives adopted the same stance on development that they had in 2010. They recommitted to DFID, 0.7, and untied aid. Undertakings on eradicating extreme poverty, promoting human development (including by reducing child and maternal death), and gender equality, as well as good governance, were all still prominent.

In November 2015, however, the government published a new aid strategy, largely developed in the Treasury to accompany the announcement of the spending review setting departmental budgets for the years ahead. It was presented to Parliament jointly by George Osborne and Justine Greening (though neither she nor DFID officials had much input into it). The branding was quite different to the focus on ending extreme poverty which had been the hallmark of Britain's development effort since 1997. The title was "UK Aid:

Tackling Global Challenges in the National Interest".[53] The introduction explained that the government knew its commitment to aid was controversial, so it was going to take:

> *a new approach... that we believe will command public confidence... Our aid budget will be restructured to ensure that it is spent on tackling the great global challenges – from the root causes of mass migration and disease, to the threat of terrorism and global climate change – all of which also directly threaten British interests. We want to meet our promises to the world's poor and also put international development at the heart of our national security and foreign policy.*

The content was different too. There were now four "strategic objectives": strengthening global peace and security; strengthening resilience (e.g., to health threats) and crisis response; promoting global prosperity; and – last – tackling extreme poverty.

What accounts for this change of tack? Politics is the main answer. Since 2010, Cameron had resisted Conservative aid sceptics partly by hiding behind the Liberal Democrats, pointing out that delivering on the development agenda was not just a Conservative manifesto commitment from 2010 but an element of the coalition deal with them too. How true that really was is not the point: it was useful cover. When, against the expectations of many pundits, the Conservatives won a clear majority in the 2015 election, that prop was lost. The government now decided to rely more heavily on the argument that the aid programme served the UK's narrow national interest. The re-branding reflected that.

It did not work. The aid sceptics were unpersuaded. According to polling, the wider public had their doubts too: backing for 0.7 was not strong, but the support base it did have arose from a view that reducing extreme suffering overseas was a moral imperative, not something to be justified by self-interest. The champions of development were running out of road.

CHAPTER 10

The bottom line

What can we say about overall development progress in this period in the 18 countries where DFID was still making its main effort? The aggregate Human Development Index for them continued to improve. Life expectancy and incomes were increasing year on year in most of the countries, and under-five mortality was still falling everywhere (see Appendix B). The rate of progress in reducing the global poverty headcount, though, started to slow down, reflecting both a more difficult economic climate and the fact that many of the easier things in countries committed to reducing poverty had now been done, so what was left was tougher challenges in less conducive environments.

More broadly, the fates of the 18 were bifurcating, becoming a microcosm of the broader environment that UK development policy needed to navigate. Some of them, such as India, Ghana, and Bangladesh, were – despite setbacks and various real and persistent problems – broadly stable, growing, and on a more-or-less defined development path.[54] These countries kept improving, and, as they got richer, they became less dependent on aid, and less susceptible to outside influence over their development path. That was all to the good: no country wants to be reliant on outsiders.

In other countries (particularly those characterised by conflict and fragility) the development path was determined by the internal politics which set limits on economic progress, on how resources were distributed, on how effective the state was and what it was seeking to achieve. In these countries outsiders could still do good: they could fund vaccinations, health clinics, and so on, and deliver results in other areas too. But everything was harder and slower.

In terms of DFID's contribution to ongoing progress, all the caveats we explained earlier still applied: aid was just one of the factors that contributed to improvements, and DFID just one donor.[55] Earlier in its life, DFID had been influential on policy issues – like the adoption of the MDGs, the deal on debt relief for reform, encouraging governments to make basic education free for all, and the introduction of social protection systems. Now, partly by choice (giving up budget support, its best tool for supporting policy dialogue, and the way it handled the focus on results and value for money), and partly because of the way the development context evolved, with fewer countries as dependent on aid as they had previously been, the department's policy influence was weaker. The direct impact DFID had in improving the lives of the world's poorest may, because it now had a lot more money, have peaked between 2010 and 2016. But something precious was also fading. The department had resumed a little of the defensive crouch that had characterised the Overseas Development Administration in the 1990s. It was still quite widely admired, but it became more focused on protecting itself at home, less outwardly engaged, and, it seemed to some, less confident, agile, and responsive. Then things got worse.

PART FOUR

Fall

2016–20 and Beyond

ELEVEN

The Last Gasp

THE GOVERNANCE of the UK in the years after the Brexit referendum was characterised by chaos. The shenanigans over the negotiation of the deal under which Britain would leave the EU, which stymied Parliament for four years from 2016, absorbed all the country's political bandwidth – and much of the capacity of its governing institutions. Foreign observers watched with a mixture of amazement, amusement, and increasing concern as the UK demolished the reputation it had built over many decades as a stable and predictable country and a consistent champion of international agreements, the rule of law, and Western liberal values.

When Theresa May won the Conservative Party leadership election and became prime minister in 2017, there were rumours that she would drop the UK's commitment to 0.7, and perhaps not retain DFID as a separate department. Neither proved true. She did however appoint a well-known aid sceptic, Priti Patel, as the department's new secretary of state. The years from 2016 onwards were ones in which party management played an even bigger role than is normally the case in determining the composition of the Cabinet and other ministerial appointments. Patel was selected not because she was interested in – or equipped to lead – DFID. She got the job because May thought that, as a leading Brexiteer, she had to be brought into the Cabinet, and with Justine Greening moving to cover education, that was the available vacancy.

CHAPTER 11

Political turmoil, policy confusion

DFID was affected as badly as other departments after 2016 by the game of musical chairs which saw Conservative politicians move from one post to another – and in and out of government – at an ever more dizzying rate. Between mid-2016 and 2020, there were six different secretaries of state for international development.[1] Patel had taken over from Justine Greening in July 2016. She was fired in November 2017, having lied about an unauthorised visit to Israel earlier that year.[2] Penny Mordaunt assumed the role. She brought a degree of stability and common sense, but only lasted until May 2019 and was then replaced by Rory Stewart. The best qualified of the sextet, by interest and experience, Stewart also enjoyed the shortest tenure. He departed when Boris Johnson became prime minister in July 2019. Alok Sharma took over up to February 2020, when he was reshuffled to the business department and replaced by Anne-Marie Trevelyan. This is what the writer and former politician Chris Mullin, who had previously been a DFID minister, had to say about that:

> *By far the worst appointment made by Boris Johnson in his cabinet reshuffle last month was that of Anne-Marie Trevelyan as secretary of state for international development. An ardent Brexiteer, Trevelyan has no known interest in international development; just about her only previous public utterance on the subject was an observation that "charity begins at home".*[3]

There was just as much churn at the junior ministerial level. A total of 15 Conservative politicians (11 MPs and four members of the House of Lords) held junior ministerial positions in DFID from 2016 to 2020. Several simultaneously held office in other departments too, reducing the time they had for development work. None lasted longer than two years, many much less. Some – like Rory Stewart, Alistair Burt, and Liz Sugg – were knowledgeable, principled, and serious, and applied themselves in a dedicated way to their responsibilities.[4] Others were merely ships passing in the night.

Within this period, 2019/20 was a bumper year: a total of 14 ministers are listed in the department's annual report for that year, including four different secretaries of state. One, Lord Goldsmith, was described as having three different DFID ministerial portfolios in the same year.[5]

If there was no continuity in its political leadership, did the department at least have a clear and stable policy agenda to work to? The manifesto Theresa May published for the 2017 election provides some pointers:

British aid helps millions and is a powerful statement of Global Britain's place in the world. It protects our interests: by building a safer, healthier, more prosperous world, we can protect our own people from disease, conflict and instability. This is the right ambition for a country with a global outlook, so we will maintain the commitment to spend 0.7 per cent of our gross national income on assistance to developing nations and international emergencies.[6]

There are references to the sustainable development goals, ending extreme poverty, saving children's lives, support for women and girls, and harnessing British research capacity to address global health threats. There is a commitment to "combat the brutal slave trade", on which Theresa May had a long-standing personal track record.

There is also a bizarre proposition that the government will only subscribe to the DAC rules for ODA if it likes them, and the statement that if ODA rule changes it wants cannot be agreed with others, the government will

change the law to allow us to use a better definition of development spending, while continuing to meet our 0.7 per cent target.

This was an oxymoron: if the government wanted to create a new category of spending for its aid, fine; but the ODA definition is

CHAPTER 11

determined not nationally but by agreement in the DAC, and they would credit the UK in international statistics only with aid as they defined it. This was just one example of the government building a track record of announcing an intent to flout international agreements it had often played a major part in creating. The madcap scheme on the ODA rules never went anywhere.

One of the other places to look, if we want to try to understand what the government thought it was trying to do in its development policy from 2016 to 2020, is the forewords written by secretaries of state for each year's annual report to Parliament. We earlier noted that in the Clare Short era and the years that followed, these statements were characterised by a consistent (indeed, mind-numbingly repetitive) focus on ending extreme global poverty. No one, at that time, could be in any doubt about what DFID was trying to do.

Priti Patel in July 2017 put an emphasis on the national interest, British leadership on the world stage, economic growth, trade, investment, managing migration, the reform of multilateral institutions, and "the moral responsibility" to maximise cost-effectiveness. She made only one reference to poverty, saying "if we stand back . . . we are allowing other countries' problems to come closer to our shores".[7] Patel also while in office mooted the possibility of tying development spending to pursuing free trade deals, but her ideas did not become government policy.[8] She was highly attuned to the wishes of the right-wing press. She closed a major programme supporting adolescent girls in Africa when they attacked it as a frivolous waste of money, despite the fact that Justine Greening, her predecessor, had been a particular champion of it.[9]

In 2018, Penny Mordaunt emphasised the importance of responding to humanitarian crises, tackling climate change, and gender issues. There was one brief mention of "the great opportunity we have to end extreme poverty", and a statement that we "remain committed to leave No-one Behind". She drew strong links between UK interests and the threats that global problems pose to the UK. "Britain's leadership as a great global nation is needed more than ever", she wrote.[10]

She emphasised more help for people with disabilities, on which she worked hard during her tenure. And, in the wake of a scandal in Oxfam, she stressed the importance of safeguarding people caught up in humanitarian crises from sexual abuse and exploitation.[11]

In the 2019 annual report there was a stronger statement of strategic intent. The first sentence of Rory Stewart's foreword was about eradicating poverty, and he reinforced the point in its last paragraph. In an echo of the posture struck in the first half of DFID's life, he also emphasised international collaboration and the need for collective global action (not least on climate change), marking a difference with the "British leadership" narrative more common in these years.[12]

Boris Johnson called a general election in December 2019. His manifesto did not say as much on development as some earlier Conservative ones had done, but nor was there any hint of a change in direction:

> *[We will] proudly maintain our commitment to spend 0.7 per cent of GNI on development . . . We are proud of . . . our record in helping reduce global poverty . . . We will stand up for the right of every girl in the world to have 12 years of quality education . . . We will end the preventable deaths of mothers, newborn babies and children by 2030 . . . We will lead the global fight against climate change.*[13]

And finally we have Anne-Marie Trevelyan's statement in the annual report published in the summer of 2020. This was the high point globally of the COVID-19 pandemic. She described the humanitarian and economic ramifications for poorer countries, before claiming that "British innovation, technology and expertise is at the forefront of the global response". She made a brief reference to the "global goals" (the SDGs). "The UK's prominence and global leadership in development" was exemplified, she said, by the presentation of the UK's first voluntary national review (of its contribution to the SDGs) at a UN high-level political forum in July 2019 and by hosting the

UK-Africa investment summit in January 2020. (This was a business event.) She also repeated the government's commitment to 0.7 (though as we will see below, she must have known it was not to last much longer).[14]

Reading more deeply into this, the last of the DFID annual reports, we find a longer description of the current policy goals, which built further on those in the 2015 aid strategy produced by the Treasury. DFID now had six "strategic objectives". One of them (it was the fourth one, which tells its own story) was "tackling extreme poverty". That came after "peace", "planet", and "global prosperity". Fifth was "partnership – a strong and resilient international system" and lastly "quality" – improving value for money and transparency.[15] The annual report still included lists of activities and results. But there was very little aggregation and almost no material on levels or trends in poverty or other development goals, either globally or in countries where the department was still focusing its effort. In other words, the nearly 300 pages of detailed text, mostly on financial and governance issues, say very little to build a picture of what the department was actually spending its money on, or how the countries it was supporting were faring, or about the policy challenges DFID was grappling with. Equally, there was very little on the international development system or collaboration with others on shared goals. This is all in glaring contrast with the approach between 1997 and 2015.

There remained a strong parliamentary constituency for development, which was supportive of the department. The development committee continued to produce a good number of thoughtful and well-evidenced reports. In 2017, for example, it issued a useful critique of DFID's work on education, recognising that historically the department had played an important role, but urging that it now needed to go further to support girls and children with disabilities, and focus more on learning outcomes.[16]

And in one of its more prescient and pointed contributions, and a rebuke to the authors of the 2017 Conservative manifesto, the committee in 2018 produced a report on the definition and administration of ODA. They warned that:

> *unilateral action by the UK to develop and use its own oda definition would be an own goal . . . [that threatened the UK's] reputation as a leading development actor . . . DFID is an experienced administrator of oda and should play the leading role in equipping other government departments with the skills required to ensure consistently excellent levels of oda administration, from transparency in reporting to poverty reduction driven programming . . . Moving increasing amounts of oda outside of DFID also creates inherent risk in three areas; coherence, transparency and focus upon poverty reduction. . . . The secretary of state for international development should have ultimate responsibility for oversight of UK oda.*[17]

And they made their own proposal on what the strategic goal of the UK's development effort ought to be:

> *Poverty reduction should underpin all the UK's oda, helping the poorest and more vulnerable and ensuring that no-one is left behind.*[18]

What can we take away from all this? First, the general chaos and tumult in the national political environment from 2016 to 2020 was unsurprisingly reflected in the political leadership of DFID. Second, to the extent that they had any policy agenda at all on development, the government's narrative focused in an increasingly transactional way on a few issues – especially health, education, humanitarian response, and help for women and girls. Too often, when these topics are mentioned in policy statements, they come across as box ticking rather than overarching policy goals and intent. Third, there was a deluded desire to pretend that Britain mattered more, and had greater influence on the world stage, than it did. That was reflected in the ever more hubristic claims to global leadership on development. (The parliamentary development committee, no doubt in an effort to shore up support for DFID, unfortunately contributed to that. Others did too, including by repeating the claim that the UK was "an aid superpower", a boast of dubious merit which irritated others internationally.) Consequently, there was, fourth, little interest in collaboration with other richer countries on development, or acceptance that there were real limits to what Britain unilaterally could achieve. There was no appetite for the truth that collective action, including through multilateral fora and institutions, was still essential if global problems were to be tackled well – or any recognition that in the wake of the Brexit fandango other donors had increasingly shut their ears to what British ministers were saying.

The final takeaway, however, is the fact that international development issues barely broke the surface in the political maelstrom that was Theresa May's three-year premiership. Anthony Seldon and Raymond Newell reviewed her tenure in a book running to nearly 700 pages, which was published a few months after she stood down. In contrast to Seldon's books on the premierships of Blair, Brown, and Cameron, international development simply does not figure. There are no references to DFID, aid, or international development in the index. The closest they get is two paragraphs on Priti Patel's departure in 2017. Brexit drowned out everything else.[19]

The machine trogs along

One of the most powerful forces in public policy is hysteresis: activity that persists into the future even after its original cause has been removed or is permanently changed. The political leadership and drive for the department to reduce poverty had largely disappeared. Senior officials spent a lot of their time on the thankless task of managing political dysfunction. There were changes in their ranks too. (Lowcock left in 2017, after more than six years as permanent secretary.[20] Matthew Rycroft, recently the UK's ambassador to the UN in New

Table 11.1. DFID budget and UK ODA 2016–20

£m (current prices)	2016/17	2019/20
Total DFID	10,012	10,661
Of which regional programmes	4,457	4,134
Of which focus countries	2,621	2,258
Share	58%	68%
Total UK ODA	14,059	14,470
Of which: bilateral	8,803	9,533
multilateral	5,256	4,945
DFID share of UK ODA	82%	77%

Source: DFID Annual Reports. See notes in Table 2.2.

York, was appointed.) But most of the senior management remained in place, and they were also able to ensure that in the engine room the changed political context made little difference to the everyday work of many staff. And so, until the middle of 2020, quite a lot continued much as previously.

In particular, the DFID budget remained substantial, and its share of total UK ODA stabilised after the significant reductions since 2014 (Tables 9.1 and 11.1). The focus on the 18 poor countries in which the department had concentrated much of its anti-poverty work since 1997 was also sustained, at least to a degree. By the 2019/20 year (i.e., before the budget cuts later in 2020) total spending in those countries was 20 per cent lower in real terms than in 2016/17 but remained at a level allowing a genuine impact to be made.

The department also now for the first time made use of the power provided under the 2002 International Development Act to issue guarantees allowing some countries to borrow more from the World Bank than would otherwise have been possible. Egypt and Iraq were early cases considered for that. This was later done on a larger scale for Ukraine following Putin's invasion.

CHAPTER 11

The government also doubled down on CDC. Under the 1999 CDC Act, a ceiling of £1.5 billion had been set on the capital that DFID was allowed to provide. The announcement of new capital in July 2015 had taken the total to the limit. But the Treasury were keen to keep pumping in new money, since this was a cheap way of meeting the ODA target. So in 2017 the government had Parliament pass legislation increasing the financial limit to £12 billion. CDC remained for the moment focused on the poorer countries in Africa and Asia, and on the whole performed creditably. In the five years from 2016, it invested an average of £900 million a year, which was financed largely by the billions of new money provided from DFID. In 2020 it held investments in more than a thousand companies, employing nearly a million people. These companies paid more than $2.2 billion in tax in developing countries in 2020. CDC made losses in some years, but on average from 2010 to 2020 returns amounted to more than 6 per cent a year.[21]

DFID's long-established systems to ensure value for money and successful programme implementation continued to function effectively. The department's own tools for assessing that, in particular the portfolio quality index which senior managers reviewed for the whole department every three months, showed that on average projects and programmes achieved more than had been intended at the time they had been approved. The index remained above 100 (the baseline level, at which projects were in aggregate achieving their objectives) every year from 2016 to 2020.[22]

The NAO in 2019, however, questioned whether other government departments which had been tasked with managing larger volumes of ODA since 2014 were doing so effectively and criticised their continuing lack of transparency:

Widening ODA expenditure to other departments has increased risks to effectiveness and it is not clear whether the intended benefits of drawing in wider skills have been realised. Government's desire to demonstrate the value secured from ODA spending is fur-

ther undermined by its lack of progress improving transparency, a key objective of its own aid strategy.[23]

Devanny and Berry have reinforced the latter point:

No department could reportedly match DFID's transparency in ODA spending. The 2020 Aid Transparency Index also reported a significant disparity between DFID and FCO (the next-largest ODA spender) in ODA expenditure transparency, with DFID ranked second [in the world] and the FCO 21st.[24]

As noted earlier in the chapter, the department's final annual report, published in July 2020, contains examples of its continuing impact. There was a focus on the people who were receiving help through DFID responses to humanitarian crises, including in a persistent new Ebola outbreak in the Democratic Republic of Congo and ongoing conflicts in Syria, Yemen, and elsewhere. There was also, inevitably, emphasis on helping developing countries cope with COVID-19, in good part by redirecting existing programmes. The department was sustaining assistance for basic health and education, especially for women and girls. Programmes tackling climate change and supporting economic growth were continuing.

DFID still making a difference

What about the real-world impact of all this on the lives of poor people in the countries where DFID was making its main effort between 2016 and 2020? As previously, we have looked at the infant mortality rate, life expectancy, income levels, and the Human Development Index in the 18 countries.

The infant and child mortality rate continued to fall in all of them, though in many it did so at a slightly slower rate than in the recent past. Life expectancy continued to grow in many countries up to 2019, albeit more slowly. But in most, the impact of COVID-19 (comprising both the direct health impact of the virus, and the pandemic's effects on the economy and on other health services) was to reduce life expectancy in 2020. Average incomes were more volatile in several countries in this period. They fell in Afghanistan, Nigeria, Sierra Leone, Zambia, and Zimbabwe. In the majority of the 18 countries, however, they continued to grow, in some cases quite briskly. Overall, the Human Development Index for the 18 countries was higher in 2020 than in 2016, even taking account of the COVID-19 dip in the last year. And the gap with the rest of the world continued to narrow too, if only slightly.

It's also worth saying that DFID's growing humanitarian response expenditure, reflecting the progressive growth in global humanitarian need especially from 2012 onwards, undoubtedly made a notable difference in saving and improving lives for people beyond our 18 focus countries, especially in Somalia, South Sudan, Sudan, Syria, and Yemen. These were all countries in which the department had huge and long-lasting humanitarian programmes – reflecting their dire straits.[25] In the 2019/20 year, DFID spent more than £1.1 billion – more than 10 per cent of its total budget – on humanitarian response in those five countries.[26] It is impossible to calculate the numbers of lives saved, but the benefits included better health and nutrition and lower mortality for tens of millions of people. The UK in this period remained among the top three providers of humanitarian assistance globally, as well as an influential contributor to policy innovation.

All that said, the rate of global progress in reducing poverty was slowing. Between 2003 and 2013, the proportion of the global population in extreme poverty fell by 14 percentage points. From 2013 to 2023, it is estimated to have fallen by only 3 percentage points.[27] This partly reflects the simple fact that getting to and supporting the very poorest is harder than helping those nearer the poverty line to leapfrog it. It was also a reflection of the lack of elite interest in some poor countries in helping the most vulnerable. The easier pickings had been harvested, leaving more difficult work to do. But what Britain was about to do was hardly going to help.

TWELVE

"The Writing Is on the Wall"

A SURPRISING number of people, not least among the technocratic commentariat in the aid sector, took at face value the claim made by ministers at the time of the abolition of DFID and the merger of its functions with the Foreign Office that the new arrangements were intended to increase the developmental effectiveness of British aid by improving cross-government coordination. They were duped. That was not remotely the intent of the merger.

The aid sceptics put the knife in

Over the decade running up to 2020, right-of-centre aid sceptics became ever-sharper in their attacks. They could smell blood and were amply and continuously reinforced across all their favourite media outlets, whether it was tabloids like the *Daily Express*, *Daily Mail*, and *The Sun*, or the broadsheet *Daily Telegraph* and its stable mate, the more cerebral weekly magazine *The Spectator*.

The arguments they made were not new – indeed they came straight from the 1980s. Aid was misused or wasted through corruption; the UK should be prioritising domestic over foreign issues; Britain should practise "trade not aid"; aid should not be used to reduce poverty for moral or altruistic reasons but instead should promote British national interests, including by helping businesses win contracts overseas.[1] Some went even further. Esther McVey, who had been the secretary of state responsible for Britain's welfare system

CHAPTER 12

during most of 2018, wrote in the *Daily Telegraph* that aid "fostered a culture of welfare dependency on a grand scale, something Conservatives should know does nothing to eradicate poverty" – which is not something she would have dared say so bluntly about the UK's own welfare system, either when she was responsible for that system, or afterwards.[2] The attack addressed both the level of aid spending and the existence of DFID.

Serving ministers were held back from joining this chorus by both David Cameron and Theresa May. But out of office they let loose. In January 2019, not long after resigning as Theresa May's foreign secretary, Boris Johnson used an interview with the *Financial Times* to propose that DFID be closed.[3]

Months later, a backbench conservative MP, Bob Seely, published a report, *Global Britain: A Twenty-First Century Vision*, advocating merging DFID and the Department for International Trade into the Foreign Office. Boris Johnson provided a foreword praising Seely's proposals to ensure aid does "more to serve the political and commercial interests of the country".[4]

Johnson was prime minister by July 2019. He called an election on 12 December, winning a large majority. His manifesto said nothing about DFID: as noted in the last chapter, it contained no hint of a significant change in direction on aid and development. But within days the plan was out. *The Guardian* reported on 19 December that sources inside DFID said they expected the department to be merged with the FCO once the UK had finally left the EU.[5] Johnson initially appointed multiple junior ministers covering both the FCO and DFID, but retained separate secretaries of state. Then on 14 February 2020 the BBC ran a news story, clearly well sourced, which mooted the merger.[6]

By now everyone could see what was happening. In the 19 March edition of the *London Review of Books* Chris Mullin published a careful, analytical essay summarising what DFID had achieved over the years, describing the history of the Conservative Party's internal arguments over development, and noting that under Johnson the sceptics were dominant. He quoted some of Johnson's anti-aid statements since 2017. His final sentence said it all: "The writing is on the wall."[7]

The following day, shrewd observers picked up another hint. Matthew Rycroft, who had been the permanent secretary at DFID since early 2018, was moved to the Home Office. No competition was launched for his successor, as would normally have happened. Instead, it was announced that Nick Dyer, one of the DFID director generals, was being appointed to the role on a temporary basis.

On 9 June, the parliamentary development committee published a new report.[8] The committee was now chaired by Sarah Champion, Labour MP for Rotherham. But a majority of its members were, following the 2019 election, Conservative: there were seven of them, as well as four Labour and one SNP. They did their best:

> *The Committee is aware of the excellent reputation of UK aid across the world . . . UK aid has made major contributions to global development goals. DFID has a high international standing, built up over many years, for its excellence in managing and delivering development assistance, and its transparency and effectiveness. . . . This Committee advocates strongly for the retention of the current standalone Ministry of State model for international development.*

The report also recommended retaining ICAI and that the committee's own role be broadened to cover all ODA spend, not just what was managed by DFID.

Then on 16 June Johnson finally told Parliament of the decision to close DFID and create the Foreign, Commonwealth and Development Office (FCDO). He said in his statement that aid spending had "been treated as some giant cashpoint in the sky that arrives without any reference to UK interests". He argued that:

> *it is no use a British diplomat going in one day to see the leader of a country and urging him not to cut the head off his opponent*

and to do something for democracy in his country, if the next day another emanation of the British government is going to arrive with a cheque for £250 million.

That is, of course, something that never happened – the choice of words was characteristic of the misleading and mendacious communication style that was Johnson's stock in trade. The real reason came in his next sentence: "We have to speak with one voice: we must project the UK overseas in a consistent and powerful way."[9] The aid programme, in other words, was merely a tool in support of wider foreign policy objectives, British influence, and the national interest.

The merger announcement was accompanied by some classic double speak from people close to Johnson on the intention on aid resources. As Devanny and Berry note,

Writing on the day of Johnson's announcement, James Forsyth, the Spectator's political editor, claimed that "bringing DFID into the Foreign Office will make the 0.7% aid target more politically sustainable. It'll now have the protection of one of the great offices of state".[10]

The truth, however, was that DFID was already under instruction from the Treasury to plan for substantial in-year budget cuts. One result of the COVID-19 pandemic was a projected reduction in UK gross national income in 2020. Since the aid budget was set as a proportion of national income, that implied a cut in aid. The Treasury told the department to plan for an immediate cut of 30 per cent (far higher than the slight reduction that transpired in national income). The merger took effect from the beginning of September. Two months later, the chancellor of the exchequer, Rishi Sunak, announced the aid budget would be cut by 40 per cent, from 0.7 per cent of GNI to 0.5 per cent, with immediate effect. The saving – from what was the largest in-year cut in a significant departmental budget in modern times – was estimated at £4 billion. It was a knock-out blow for the aid programme, but the saving was trivial in relation to the UK's overall public spending in 2020.

Blowback

How were these announcements received? There was limited public reaction (perhaps unsurprisingly given the universal focus on the ongoing COVID-19 pandemic) but predictable criticism in Parliament from the opposition benches, as well as from the NGO sector. The critique focused on the weakness of the intellectual rationale for what was being done, as well as on the costs and the likely deleterious impact on the ability of both departments to function effectively.[11]

Nick Westcott, a senior British diplomat of long standing who had also served in a top job in the EU's External Action Service and was now head of the Royal Africa Society, exposed the flaws in the government's strategic logic by debunking the notion that the merger would boost British influence overseas:

the full absorption of DFID into the FCO is a loud statement to the world at large that the UK will be pursuing a "Britain First" foreign policy from now on.

Far from enhancing the UK's influence, he argued, that would undermine it. He also dismissed the argument that the move was justified to improve coordination. In his experience (including as a British ambassador in Africa):

there was little difficulty in coordinating between the diplomatic and aid side of our missions on the spot: all it needed was openness, mutual trust and shared objectives.[12]

Most telling, though, was the reaction from some of the government's own supporters. All three living former Conservative

CHAPTER 12

prime ministers (Major, Cameron, and May) criticised the severe cuts to the aid budget in the middle of the pandemic, as did the Brexiteer and former Cabinet minister David Davis. Cameron and May also spoke out against the merger, Cameron tweeting that:

> *More could and should be done to coordinate aid and foreign policy, including through the National Security Council [which, under Cameron and May had met most weeks, but largely fell into abeyance under Johnson], but the end of @DFID_UK will mean less expertise, less voice for development at the top table and ultimately less respect for the UK overseas.*[13]

Conservative-dominated parliamentary committees chipped in too. The influential foreign affairs committee, chaired by the up-and-coming MP Tom Tugendhat, concluded that the merger risked:

> *weakening the cultures of each Department and raises the possibility of the loss of highly-skilled staff who have helped build the UK's reputation as a leading provider of aid.*[14]

And the development committee, just a month after its report advising against the merger, returned to the charge:

> *We have significant concerns that the merger may jeopardise the ongoing effectiveness of future UK aid spending. . . . The loss of an independent DFID, with poverty reduction at its heart and years of specialist development expertise, risks damaging the quality of UK aid and undoing hard won development gains.*[15]

No one was more coruscating than Andrew Mitchell. He found it

> *astonishing that a British Prime Minister would deliberately dismantle UK leadership in this area. . . . The decision to abolish the Department for International Development, taken secretly*

and with no consultation, is in my view a quite extraordinary mistake which has been greeted by our friends all round the world with dismay and incomprehension. . . . DFID [is being] destroyed (let no-one think that adding a silent "D" to the FCDO changes anything) . . . It is hard to think of any coherent reason to justify such an act of vandalism.

He piled in on the aid cuts too:

a political and not an economic decision, designed to please those in the so-called Red Wall seats [parliamentary constituencies the Conservatives won from Labour in 2019]. . . . most of these cuts fall on British humanitarian support and so we have seen the unconscionable decision of British ministers announcing cuts of more than 50 per cent in our humanitarian aid to Yemen . . . in the certain knowledge that this will lead to children dying of starvation and in agony as a result.[16]

Why did they do it?

It is important to be clear about why DFID was abolished. There has been a good degree of finger pointing towards senior diplomats. Certainly, the Foreign Office for years worried about its declining role and became increasingly desperate over the parlous state of its finances. Getting more of its functions paid for through the ODA budget was therefore attractive. A lot was done on that from 2010 onwards, and it did not require the merger. In a panel discussion convened at the Institute for Government to rake over the coals, Alan Duncan, who had been a minister at both DFID and the Foreign Office, accused his fellow panellist Simon Macdonald, who had been permanent secretary at the FCO until Boris Johnson removed him in September 2020, of being behind the merger. But civil servants follow rather than lead political decision makers. They picked up the politicians' explicit public signalling, reinforced by private hints and conversations, saw the direction of travel and then followed in the slipstream, wanting to make sure, as they always do, that they were perceived as getting with the programme. That was especially important in the Johnson government, given its tendency to get rid of permanent secretaries when they didn't like them, or simply when a fall guy was needed for some departmental or ministerial cock-up.

Labour figures we asked said there was no need to seek a complicated explanation for the merger. As Douglas Alexander put it:

We've watched the Conservative party move into a reactionary populist conception of Britain's national interests and they've all been on that train. And if you have a sustained period of Conservative government, you end up with no development ministry. So to those people who say it's not really about party politics: it's all about party politics.[17]

Hilary Benn said the same: "Hey, that's what Tory governments always do."[18]

It is, however, a little more complicated than that. As we noted earlier, there were divisions within the Conservative Party. And some were willing to resist their government. Immediately after the merger announcement, Dominic Raab wrote to Sarah Champion asking her to wrap up the parliamentary development committee. That's not up to you, she replied. Parliament will decide for itself. She told us how the committee was then subject to "very aggressive back channels trying to shut us down. . . . It got very bloody, very quickly."

The committee survived, Champion says, because the "one nation" wing of the parliamentary Conservative Party "all rode in behind me".[19]

The government may not have obtained parliamentary approval for the merger, but they did not need it. On that the development sceptics could have their way, because their faction was now dominant in the administration.

As Devanny and Berry have concluded, the merger was:

a fundamentally <u>political</u> decision . . . to satisfy a core constituency of grassroots conservative supporters and a particular cohort within the parliamentary Conservative Party. . . . Arguments that the merger was motivated by a desire to improve efficiency are unpersuasive and unsupported by evidence . . . Instead Johnson intended to subordinate development (and particularly the objective of global poverty reduction) to an ill-defined conception of the British national interest. . . . Moreover, the merger is highly likely to lead to reduced effectiveness in development policy and diminished influence for development perspectives in inter-departmental policy discussions.[20]

That, of course, was the point: the goal was to relegate developmental considerations. The detailed design of the merger was determined by that goal.

A committee of officials was set up by Number 10 under the chairmanship of the then Cabinet secretary, Mark Sedwill.[21] The process was tightly controlled, with the most knowledgeable DFID staff, who could have advised on the pros and cons of different approaches, kept out. As it happened, they had done some contingency planning ahead of the 2019 election on merger options, concluding the best approach would be simply to recreate the arrangements that prevailed between 1979 and 1997 when the Overseas Development Administration reported to the Foreign Office. That option was now discounted. Instead, a "full integration" model was chosen, in which all the functions of DFID were dismantled and parcelled out across various different parts of the Foreign Office. The result was, as intended, a comprehensive destruction of the structure, skills, accountability system, and processes which had been fundamental to DFID's ability to spend a large budget well to achieve the development outcomes ministers had decided to prioritise.

CHAPTER 12

Hence there was no junior minister for development in the new FCDO structure, as there had been under the Thatcher-Major governments. Likewise, no senior official below the permanent secretary – who was responsible for the whole FCO-led merged department – now had responsibility for development work. Some senior FCO officials worried about that, suggesting that a dedicated permanent secretary role be retained to ensure adequate supervision of development work in the new department. (They had clearly not understood what the real purpose of the merger was.) Reporting lines for previous DFID staff in the UK and overseas made them subordinate and accountable to diplomats charged with pursuing the UK's political and commercial objectives overseas.

The intent was to allow decisions on aid spending to be driven by considerations beyond whether they represented value for money in achieving development goals. In fact, of course, the main decisions to be taken for the next two years were not about new projects to fund. The issue was what to close down and abandon in order to stick within the newly reduced budget.

THIRTEEN

Aftermath

FOR MORE than two years from the second half of 2020, the government implemented a rolling series of increasingly severe cuts to the UK's aid budget. Ministers presided over the destruction of much of DFID's capability to manage development policy and programming, and a tarnishing of the UK's international reputation.

What budget cuts meant

Some people believed when the government decided to reduce the aid budget from 0.7 to 0.5 per cent of national income that this would establish a budget that was, if lower, at least stable and predictable in the medium term. In May 2021 ICAI published a report on how the aid cuts were managed. The government's mantra was "cut once, cut deep", which, ICAI said "meant that cuts to bilateral aid were ultimately more drastic than they needed to be".[1] Little did they know that more cuts were then in the offing.

In 2021 and 2022 a big new pressure emerged: the need to pay for the costs of hosting new influxes of refugees and asylum seekers reaching the UK as a result of the Taliban coming back to power in Afghanistan and Putin's invasion of Ukraine. Under the DAC rules, these costs could in the first year of a refugee's arrival be counted as ODA. Britain was incurring new expenditure running into several billions of pounds, mostly managed by the Home Office. The costs nearly doubled in 2021, reaching more than £1 billion. They then shot

CHAPTER 13

up to £3.7 billion in 2022.[2] The government did not want to increase total public spending. So the Treasury, under Chancellor Rishi Sunak, decided they would take advantage of the DAC rules and cut the FCDO budget to pay the costs incurred on refugees in the UK. This led not just to a further drastic reduction in aid spent overseas, but also to a complete loss of the FCDO's ability to plan its development spend. The goal was to hit 0.5 per cent each year, and, partly because the Home Office could not predict its own expenditure, the FCDO repeatedly found itself hit with budget changes not just for the future but during the course of each year.

Commentators attacked several other features of the government's approach, going beyond simply the scale and abruptness of the cuts. The lack of transparency was a major beef: NGOs found it impossible to see what was being cut and what was protected. They complained that the government was providing no information, so the only way of working out what was going on was to collect and aggregate information from dozens of the affected organisations.[3] Some alleged that was made more difficult by "gagging clauses" rumoured to be imposed on those still receiving or seeking some money. Suspicions were heightened further by the government's rejection of a freedom of information request from a group of NGOs in February 2021.[4]

Another critique recognised that the cuts were being made but argued there should at least be some sort of strategic rationale over where the axe fell. An obvious option was to close down poorly performing projects. The problem was that there were not many of those, because DFID had managed its portfolio well. Analysts quickly exposed the fact that many good projects were being dropped.[5] What then followed was little better than a free for all. An effort was made to limit the number of formal international agreements that were breached, which meant that previous pledges to, for example, the World Bank's fund for the poorest countries (IDA) were sustained. (Over time, however, cuts were made here too. In 2019 DFID had pledged $2.9 billion to the replenishment of IDA. In the 2021 replenishment that was reduced to less than $2 billion. Similarly, the UK promised £1 billion for the 2022 top up of the Global Fund to Fight AIDS, Tuberculosis and Malaria, a reduction from the previous contribution of £1.46 billion.) But because there were repeated rounds of cuts, it proved impossible to maintain any kind of strategic approach. The FCDO's room for manoeuvre was further limited by a decision to maintain the provision of around £1 billion a year to British International Investments (BII) (the new name Liz Truss – while foreign secretary – gave CDC). That remained attractive to the Treasury. Whether high levels of funding for BII was a priority given cuts everywhere else was not a question they were interested in entertaining. (There was also a shift in BII's focus, away from poorer countries towards more prosperous ones, including in Asia.)

Much of the real ire, however, was directed at the implication of the choices made as they eventually became clear. There was media criticism of cuts of 60 to 70 per cent for humanitarian relief in Yemen and Syria which were announced in March 2021. There were charges of hypocrisy when it emerged that, having said that girls' education would be a priority, the budget for that was being cut by 40 per cent, resulting in an estimated 700,000 fewer girls receiving help to stay in school.[6] The government's claim that it wanted to support women and girls was further undermined by its decision to slash funding for organisations focusing on sexual and reproductive health care. The contribution to the UN's population fund, one of the leading providers, was cut by 85 per cent. They said that the lost money would have helped prevent around 250,000 maternal deaths, nearly 15 million unintended pregnancies, and more than 4 million unsafe abortions.[7] Civil servants warned ministers in advance of the likely effects of the cuts. In 2023 the government provided the parliamentary development committee with an internal assessment prepared earlier that year setting out in excruciating detail the expected impact of that year's cuts. A likely death toll, conservatively estimated but running into many thousands, was calculated for some programmes.[8]

One thing that became increasingly clear as time passed between 2020 and 2023 was that the UK's previous focus on poverty reduction –

CHAPTER 13

which had been sustained for more than 20 years – had quietly and without public acknowledgement been abandoned.

It was not just that aid to the poorest countries was cut severely. The reductions there were significantly larger than elsewhere. The Center for Global Development published analysis on that in February 2023. One finding was that direct funding for least developed and low-income countries was cut by 40 per cent in 2021 alone, compared to between 17 and 29 per cent for middle-income countries. A similar finding was that, as a good number of countries got better off in the decade after 2009, the UK provided them with increasing aid – as opposed to redirecting the money to those countries where incomes were still very low. The conclusion was that there had been a

long-term and significant decline in the poverty focus of the UK's bilateral aid . . . [and] the 2021 aid cuts have exacerbated and accelerated this.[9]

Our calculations show that for the 18 countries in which DFID had focused much of its anti-poverty effort, the volume of direct aid fell (in real terms) from £3.4 billion in 2013/14 to £642 million a decade later. That is a cut of more than 80 per cent. The message of all this was transparent. Britain was no longer interested in making poverty history.

Equally serious was the destruction of the government's capability to manage a development programme. Two sorts of capabilities are needed to do that. The first relates to the analytical skills to identify and design programmes which will have a positive development impact in the context in which they are going to be undertaken. (Some things – like immunisation – work in the same way for everyone who gets them. For many interventions, though, the prospects for success depend on the social, institutional, and economic context in which they take place.) Designing good programmes requires bringing together specialist technical expertise and local contextual knowledge. The second set of capabilities are those required to oversee the implementation of programmes once they have been approved, typically over a period of years. That is again partly about expertise, but it also requires a system: processes which ensure that the finances are managed well, procurement is efficient, progress milestones are tracked, problems are identified promptly, and a feedback loop ensures that issues are widely known and effectively acted on so that the intended results are achieved. An effective project and portfolio management system relies not just on those at the front line for each project, but also others looking independently at what is happening, spotting problems, and getting them resolved. DFID had for many years been praised – by the DAC, by independent reviews commissioned by the Cabinet Office, by the NAO, by parliamentary committees, and by its international peers – for both its systems and its expertise.

The merger simultaneously destroyed the systems and triggered a drastic loss of expertise. Many capable and experienced staff either left completely or moved to other roles in which they thought they would be valued more. (Several of the most capable senior staff quickly took up ambassadorial jobs.) Health, education, and research capacity was hit particularly badly. Many key posts fell vacant from late 2020. More than 200 former DFID staff were reported in 2021 to have left FCDO. Many talented people from the UK and around the world who had previously competed to join DFID were no longer interested. As senior staff still in post told us, attempts to recruit people with the necessary technical skills were still failing in early 2024. That has been compounded by the abolition of supervisory posts overseas. Management staff now in place often do not have the skills and experience to fulfil their responsibilities. Only 60 per cent of senior responsible owners, those officials accountable for major investments, have received training. Only 25 per cent of programme management staff say they want to stay in their roles. Basic processes, like the requirement to get an independent annual review done of every major programme to assess whether it is on track, are simply not being carried out. The FCDO's internal auditors have raised warning flags over the number of core systems which are now either not fit for purpose in the way they are designed or are being systematically ignored.[10]

This fed through also into staff morale. In 2019, before the merger, both DFID and the FCO had staff engagement scores around 70 per cent, at the top end of the Whitehall average. In 2021 and 2022, the combined department's scores fell dramatically, to below the civil service average. The merger was badly received on all sides. The scores among former DFID staff fell into the 40–45 per cent range. A survey of their members in September 2021 by the FDA, the staff union for senior civil servants, found that less than 8 per cent considered the merger to have been positive for international development, with significant concerns among both former DFID and FCO staff.[11]

There has been much commentary on the effect of the abolition of DFID on the UK's international reputation and soft power. Hilary Benn told us of a conversation he had had with Gayle Smith, who had served as the head of the US Agency for International Development in the Obama administration. She had told him that previously:

whenever an issue came up, I picked up the phone and I talked to DFID as a leader in thinking, in policy, in money, and influence.[12]

That was not at all the tone adopted by Smith's successor Samantha Power in a major speech on global food security in July 2022. Having observed the scale of the UK aid cuts, including for emergency relief in Africa, and seen that the UK had recently pushed for rules in the DAC (on COVID-19 vaccines for developing countries) that had the effect of allowing it to claim as ODA expenditure a greater sum than it had in fact spent, she issued a rare public rebuke:

today, when the needs are greatest, assistance budgets are either stagnating or they are being cut. And some countries are rewriting the rules on what counts as development spending, to shield themselves from criticism as they cut funding. Some countries that stepped up before have provided only eight per cent of what they contributed five years ago to the humanitarian response in the Horn [of Africa].[13]

Sarah Champion says that after the merger the UK "went from being a trusted partner to a pariah". She described how during a visit to Geneva in September 2021 with the parliamentary development committee:

we got both barrels from every international organisation we went to ... [there was] real visceral anger. ... it was really bad. ... Not only have we taken the cash away, our reputation has been tarnished.[14]

This view went beyond party politics. In December 2022 the *Daily Telegraph* ran a story describing how Britain was "fading into irrelevance across Africa", with the headline "'The butt of jokes and a model of what not to do': How Britain became the 'used car salesman of Africa'".[15]

Tamsyn Barton, then chief commissioner for the Independent Commission on Aid Impact, synthesised ICAI's findings between 2019 and 2023 in an article published in October 2023 in the newsletter of the DFID alumni association. She commented on the merger and the aid cuts:

The UK's reputation has really suffered. ... We really made huge efforts to dig out any positive impacts. But the gains have been elusive compared to the costs ... The department [was] distracted and inward looking over the period. ... We have seen a falloff in performance ... since 2020.[16]

In early 2024, reviewing what had happened in the UK over the last four years, the DAC issued a commentary. The language was hedged in diplomatic obfuscation, but still got some basic points across. Noting that the 2002 International Development Act mandated a strong

CHAPTER 13

poverty focus they commented that "the merger and capacity constraints has made delivering on this challenging". They warned of the danger that "development is deprioritised in an integrated ministry particularly where resources are stretched", and said a return to "the stable, long-term planning that was previously a hallmark of the United Kingdom's development assistance . . . will be critical". They also made a plea for "rebuilding FCDO's expertise on development" and lamented that the merger had "impacted the United Kingdom's ability to attract and retain talent, with some Posts highly stretched".

None of the results of the merger are surprising. Indeed, they are much as its instigators intended (though perhaps even they would have preferred to have limited the reputational damage). As Douglas Alexander put it to us, the merger was of a piece with the wider politics around Brexit, and it

> *emerged from a reactionary rather than a progressive conception of Britain's place in the world. . . . If you elect politicians who don't fundamentally believe in development . . . it goes very badly.*

Conservative Party ructions

The years after the merger saw continued jostling inside the Conservative Party.[17] Dominic Raab, who remained foreign secretary for the first year after the merger, did little on international development beyond deciding where the aid cuts would fall. The Taliban takeover of Afghanistan, culminating in their capture of Kabul in August 2021, caught Western decision makers on the hop. Raab was criticised for failing to lead an effective response, with the parliamentary foreign affairs committee describing the government as "missing in action". In September 2021 he was moved to the justice department and replaced by Liz Truss.

An aid sceptic, Truss was nevertheless not enamoured of the arrangements she inherited for managing development issues in the FCDO. First, she found there was no one to hold accountable, a problem crystallised in February 2022 when the UK wanted to provide humanitarian and economic assistance alongside its military support for Ukraine in the wake of Putin's invasion. Truss therefore created a new director general post for development and humanitarian issues. Second, she was unhappy about the policy lacuna on development. An intent to produce a new international development strategy had been announced in an "integrated review" of security, defence, development, and foreign policy published in March 2021.[18] The strategy was repeatedly delayed, but Truss finally published it in May 2022. She listed a range of priorities, including investment partnerships, humanitarian relief, women and girls, climate change, and global health. She did not attract rave reviews. Bond, the leading umbrella group for British NGOs, complained that the document

> *is less a strategy than a long-term vision for a whole-of-government approach to development, with little detail and financial commitments. . . . the language promotes British interests, expertise and investment, aimed at a domestic political audience . . . There is little on accountability and transparency – so how will progress be measured and how will the FCDO be held to account?*[19]

A few weeks later, in early July, Boris Johnson was forced to resign. The Conservative Party launched an internal election to succeed him. Truss threw her hat into the ring, and, on 5 September, she was announced as the winner. She brought back the role of development minister, appointed Vicky Ford to the job, and gave her the right to attend Cabinet (though not full Cabinet status). Ford then achieved the dubious record of becoming the UK's shortest serving development minister ever, losing her role when Truss herself resigned in October.

From the middle of 2020, a caucus of backbench Conservative MPs led by Andrew Mitchell conducted a rearguard action against the merger and the aid cuts. They came mostly from the "one nation" wing of the party and had been supporters of the Cameron and May administrations. Mitchell had backed Johnson in the 2019 leadership election, on the basis of a conversation earlier that year. Johnson had said that Mitchell would be "my key adviser on international development". Fully aware that Johnson was slippery, Mitchell had tried to pin him down:

> *"And you'll be keeping DFID as a separate department?"*
> *Boris said, "DFID is safe".*
> *"And no question of going back on the 0.7 per cent promise?"*
> *"Absolutely", he replied.*[20]

The betrayal, as well as the substantive decisions, infuriated Mitchell. He was determined to fight back. As we noted earlier, he and his allies were successful in preventing the abolition of the parliamentary development committee. In June 2021, just before the G7 summit Johnson was hosting in Cornwall, they tried to get a vote in the House of Commons to restore the aid cuts.[21] Mitchell is convinced they would have won at that point. But the vote was not called, and a month later, the government put forward its own motion justifying the cuts, emphasising they would be temporary and buying off some of the Conservative rebels. The government won the vote, though 24 of its own MPs still voted against it.[22]

Mitchell decided that it would not be possible to get DFID reestablished in the immediate future, and that as an interim step he would try to persuade the party leadership that, given the evident failure of the merger and the damage it was doing to the UK's reputation, they should recreate something similar to the Overseas Development Administration established by the Thatcher government. By early 2022, in the wake of the scandal over parties in Downing Street during the COVID-19 pandemic, the skids were under Johnson. Potential successors were circling. When Johnson announced his resignation on 7 July, Mitchell became a leading figure in Jeremy Hunt's leadership campaign. Hunt was a supporter of international development and bought in to Mitchell's plan. When he was knocked out of the leadership election, Mitchell took his proposal to the remaining contenders.

AFTERMATH

Liz Truss seems to have paid attention: her decision when she won to recreate the post of development minister is a reflection of that.

Mitchell also spoke to Rishi Sunak, at an election husting meeting in the Midlands for Conservative Party members. Sunak knew there was a problem. Mitchell was nevertheless surprised when, as the disastrous Truss premiership was brought to a rapid end in October, Sunak, the new prime minister, brought him in as the development minister. Mitchell believed at the time he was appointed that there was an agreement to establish something like the Overseas Development Administration. However, when he arrived in the FCDO, he found that the foreign secretary, James Cleverly, was opposed to that. Knowing he had backing from Number 10, Mitchell forced Cleverly to agree he could review the situation and make proposals for change. From the day he was appointed, he was in touch with four former prime ministers and three previous top-level officials with experience in the Foreign Office, the national security system, and DFID, seeking advice on what to do.

By early 2023 there was agreement to create a second permanent secretary post for development (junior to and reporting through the FCDO permanent secretary), and that about half the staff working on development issues in the FCDO headquarters would be under them. The veteran (and highly regarded) former DFID director general Nick Dyer won an open competition for that role. Late in 2023 there was a further structural change in which most of the remaining headquarters units covering development were also moved under Dyer, who now had two director generals reporting to him. Staff overseas working on development, though, continued to report through the diplomatic chain. That meant there was still a major problem over accountability for aid resources, which Mitchell and his top officials sought to address by centralising quality control and spending decisions.

In his first months in the post, Mitchell had to manage yet another round of cuts to the aid budget, again arising from gushing Home Office spending on newly arrived refugees in the UK. He

CHAPTER 13

did, however, secure a degree of relief from the new chancellor, Jeremy Hunt, who agreed that the FCDO should not bear all the new burden. As a result, UK development spending as a share of national income rose to 0.58 per cent in 2023 (but only 0.35 per cent after accounting for all the Home Office's refugee expenditure in the UK). For the 2024/25 year, the FCDO aid budget was programmed to increase in real terms, regaining a small share of what had been lost since 2020.

Mitchell also got agreement from Number 10 to publish a new White Paper in September 2023. (That was, according to some sources, despite opposition from the foreign secretary.) It attracted positive reviews for reestablishing the reduction of extreme poverty as the core purpose of development efforts, and for striking a new, more collaborative, and partnership-based tone.

Overall, Mitchell has deservedly won plaudits from across the spectrum for the start he made in rebuilding from the rubble. He told friends that he was able to patch things up, but that the reestablishment of a department of state is needed if the UK wants again to play a significant global role on development. The situation he left was also fundamentally unstable. The renewed focus on reducing poverty was not institutionalised, and the delivery system remained broken. Mitchell achieved his successes through determination and force of personality. But what would come next?

Labour considers its options

Keir Starmer, leader of the Labour Party, was clear in his rebuttal of Johnson's announcement of the merger on 16 June 2020. "Abolishing DFID diminishes Britain's place in the world", he told MPs. Asked the same day whether he would undo the merger if elected, he replied:

> *Yes, we introduced DFID for a reason. There was a cross-party consensus for many, many years that DFID did good work. Of course it should be reinstated.*[23]

Labour then watched how the merger played out in practice, frequently lamenting its consequences but saying little more in detail about their own plans.[24] In the summer of 2022, Starmer reconfirmed in an interview with Alastair Campbell and Rory Stewart for their podcast that he would bring back DFID. In February 2023 David Lammy, the shadow foreign secretary, cast doubt on that, telling Cameron and Stewart that the party would have to take account of the state of the world and the country at the time of the next election were they to win, pouring cold water in particular on the immediate prospects for returning to the 0.7 commitment.[25] Labour spokesmen started referring in public to the need for a "new model". In June 2023 Devex, a news website covering development issues, reported that Starmer was backing away from his pledge to reinstate DFID, quoting Labour officials saying they were exploring whether

a development "agency" within the FCDO – with operational independence – could repair the UK's tarnished reputation without the "disruption and cost" of another big institutional shake up.[26]

That attracted a rapid riposte from Sarah Champion, reminding people of Starmer's earlier pledge.[27] It was clear that there was a difference of view between Lammy, who was wary of losing the power that control of the aid budget would give him, and worried about more disruption, and others, particularly in the parliamentary Labour Party, who saw support for development as an important part of Labour's history and values and thought restoring it was a priority.

Behind the scenes, Starmer's office had commissioned confidential papers from recognised experts on how Labour should approach the foreign policy challenges they might inherit. They included papers on what to do about development, covering both policy and organisational arrangements. Labour decision makers wrestled not just with the political considerations, though they were mindful of the party's history and wanted to strike a different pose to the government. They also analysed the substantive merits of different organisational models.

CHAPTER 13

Previous Labour Cabinet ministers with experience of both DFID and the Foreign Office noted that the requirements of a diplomatic service were different to those of a respected development organisation. As one put it,

> *the currency of diplomacy is words, relationships and negotiation, and the time frame is often short term and responsive, while development is about money, technical expertise and project management, and the long term.*

It was noted that the largest providers of development assistance – the US, the European Commission, France, Germany, and Japan, who between them now accounted for 70 per cent of ODA – all had separate institutions, outside their foreign ministries, managing their development programmes, reflecting the belief that they required different expertise and a dedicated approach. The fact that the merger model came from right-wing governments (principally in Australia and Canada) wanting to de-emphasise development was also noted.

In the early summer of 2023, Labour insiders boiled down the choice to three options. The first was to leave things as they were. The second was to create an agency reporting to the FCDO but with operational independence. The third was to re-establish a department of state with its own budget and staffing, but sharing a platform (buildings, IT, and corporate support services) with the Foreign Office and strong coordination in order to minimise unnecessary cost and disruption. Starmer seemed to rule out the first option in meetings in June and September and, partly informed by senior former Labour ministers who he respected, was sceptical about the agency model. He did, however, agree that Labour staffers could do more work on that.

A reshuffle of the Shadow Cabinet in September 2023 brought Lisa Nandy, a high-profile figure with a wide following across the party whose previous jobs had included shadow foreign secretary, into the development portfolio. Over the following months, the party was completely absorbed in handling the fallout of the atrocities perpetrated by Hamas in Israel on 7 October, including the increasingly appalling humanitarian situation in Gaza, which many party members thought required a stronger response from the leadership than they saw. That slowed down thinking on preparing for government.

But in January and February 2024, in the expectation that the election might be called in May and Labour would therefore need a clearer line to include in their manifesto, more internal work was done on the agency model. Some former DFID staff were supportive. But former top mandarins whose views were sought (and who were known to be close to those now responsible for development in the FCDO) were more sceptical. Their advice was that an agency would add significant costs (rough calculations suggested a minimum of an extra £100 million a year, and probably more) and, because it would lead to fragmentation of responsibilities, would undermine effectiveness. The biggest problem though was that creating an agency would be time-consuming and disruptive. They suggested that the alternative of a development department sharing a platform with the Foreign Office could, especially in the light of the organisational changes Andrew Mitchell had managed to achieve, be put in place at negligible cost and with less turmoil from day one of the new government – just as had happened in 1997. Nandy gave a well-received speech at the Overseas Development Institute at the end of February setting out Labour's new vision of a world free from poverty on a planet liveable for all. In answer to questions, she made clear she understood the need for clarity on the organisational arrangements and implied it would be resolved soon.

In fact, the manifesto Labour published for the July 2024 election did little to dampen anxiety among aid agencies that the various progressive straws in the wind in recent years were merely chaff. It was studiously short of detail, going little further than repeating Lisa Nandy's vision of "a world free from poverty on a liveable planet", alongside a stated intent to "rebuild Britain's reputation on international development", "strengthen international development work" and "to lead on this agenda". The reference to the 0.7 target mirrored the Conservatives: that it would be restored as soon as fiscal circumstances allowed. A letter sent by Nandy to the Labour Campaign for International Development shortly afterwards went a little further, recognising the need to rebuild development capabilities and increase the stability of the aid budget. Nevertheless, talking about leadership without distinctive policy ideas, new resources or real organisational improvements will not be admired internationally. And suggesting "development work must be aligned closely with our foreign policy aims" conveys a posture much closer to that of the Johnson government than those of Harold Wilson, Tony Blair, or Gordon Brown, all of whom thought that supporting development was right in its own terms. That said, the outcome of the election means there is plenty of time to prove the doubters wrong.

FOURTEEN

Eliminating World Poverty?

SO, WHAT about making poverty history? As we noted in the Introduction, in 1998 nearly a third of people across the world were below the extreme poverty line defined by the World Bank ("a dollar a day"). At the time of writing, estimates suggest that has fallen to less than 10 per cent.[1] The result was that between 1998 and 2023, the number of people not living in the most extreme poverty grew from about 4 billion people to some 7 billion. As we have explained, DFID made most of its effort, throughout its existence, in 18 poor countries, which between them were home to the majority of the world's extreme poor in 1997 (and still are now). What can we say about progress over the last 25 years in those places? The Human Development Index, which we have referred to throughout the book, shows substantial improvement in the 18 countries between the beginning and the end of the period (see Appendix B). That is corroborated when we look in more detail at some of the key indicators.[2] Average incomes measured in real terms (i.e., after taking account of price increases) increased substantially between 1997 and 2022 in all the countries for which there is data. (The data is not adequate to allow a comparison between the start and the end of the period for Afghanistan or Nigeria). In Bangladesh, Ethiopia, and Rwanda they increased more than four-fold.

It does not necessarily follow that the poverty rate fell commensurately: it may have been, for example, that the gains in higher incomes were scooped by better-off people at the expense of the poorest. From poverty surveys in many of the 18 countries, however, it is clear there was in fact a dramatic reduction in extreme poverty. Bangladesh, Ethiopia, Ghana, India, Nepal, Pakistan, Sierra Leone, Tanzania, and Uganda all saw substantial falls, validated through several surveys across the period. In Bangladesh the poverty headcount fell from 33 per cent to 10 per cent; in India from 40 per cent to 12 per cent; in Uganda from 69 per cent to 42 per cent; and in Sierra Leone from 61 per cent to 26 per cent. The Democratic Republic of Congo and Nigeria may have seen similar reductions too, but the number of surveys is too small to have as much confidence about that as for other countries. Elsewhere there is either inadequate data or, as with Kenya, Malawi, Zambia, and Zimbabwe, large numbers of people appear to have been left behind even while average incomes grew.

It is also worth noting that the total population of these countries grew substantially over the period: in more than half of them, it doubled (on average). In principle one might think that high population growth could make it harder to reduce the poverty rate. In practice, however, the experience in most regions of the world over the past two centuries has been that high population growth has been accompanied by a fall in the poverty rate. That was also the experience for many of the 18 countries from 1997 to 2020. The rising tide lifted not just the great majority of the boats sailing at the beginning of the period, but many news ones too.

Life expectancy (at birth) increased significantly in all the 18 countries. In several of those in which it was lowest in 1997, the improvements were dramatic. In Malawi, for example, it increased by almost 20 years, from about 43 in 1997 to nearly 63 in 2021. Performance was worst in Nigeria, where the increase was less than seven years, and where in 2021, average life expectancy was still only 53, compared to more than 60 in most of the 18 countries and 72 in Bangladesh.

The biggest factor behind this was a dramatic reduction in the number of parents who lost a child (or several children) before they reached their fifth birthday. The infant mortality rate fell by more than 35 per cent in every country, and by more than 60 per cent in many. This can be attributed directly to many of the things DFID (and some other development organisations) prioritised, in particular immunisation, malaria control, tackling HIV/AIDS, and other support to improve primary health care.

Similarly, there was a substantial increase in the number of children who went to school. There is a shortage of data in some countries. But there were large gains in most of those where data was consistently collected, including Ethiopia, Ghana, India, Kenya, Mozambique, Nepal, Pakistan, Tanzania, and Zambia. In Ethiopia the primary school enrolment rate increased from 34 per cent in 1998 to 85 per cent in 2015. In Mozambique it went from 50 per cent to 94 per cent; in Tanzania from 50 per cent to more than 80 per cent. In some countries (like Malawi, Rwanda, and Zimbabwe) reported enrolment was already high in the late 1990s and was sustained.

Taking all this together, it is clear that the years 1997–2020 saw dramatic progress in reducing poverty. There were other life improvements too, in particular more clean water, better sanitation, and the spread of electricity. Billions of people also gained access to a lot more information, through the arrival of mobile phones. Much of this was consistent with the vision set out in the MDGs. In truth, however, the proponents of the MDGs in the late 1990s had not expected so much progress. Most of them saw the goals as aspirational targets, and would have settled for much less than what transpired. In the event, what was achieved in this period eclipsed any previous quarter century in human history.

We have analysed DFID's contribution throughout the book. As Masood Ahmed has said, the department's creation in 1997 coincided with

> *the unipolar moment when the West was feeling confident and generous after the collapse of the Soviet Union and there was a peace dividend to be deployed. Development provided the new global project and the technicians of development asserted that they had the technology to deliver results. That attracted the support of the*

CHAPTER 14

leaders of government. Clare Short had the genius to understand the moment and seize the initiative in ways that established development agencies could not.

DFID had by 2003 become one of the world's most influential organisations in international development. That was brought about through the combination of effective political leadership, wider government backing, the setting and retention of clear objectives behind which growing resources were rigorously deployed, the employment of large numbers of capable and motivated staff, and the effective use of analysis and evidence in advocacy and partnerships with others. This period was one in which conditions were favourable for global development, and while not all of DFID's efforts were successful, it brought energy and dynamism. The department's overall role in improving the living conditions and life experiences of people in many of the world's poorest countries in the years up to 2003 cannot be quantified, but its contribution was distinctive and influential.

DFID's impact in reducing global poverty grew further between 2003 and 2010, particularly in the 18 countries we have looked at. The global context in this era was conducive for progress in poorer countries, until the environment deteriorated in the wake of the 2008 financial crisis. DFID's growing budget, influence, capability, focus, and political support from the highest levels of the UK government allowed it to make a substantial direct contribution towards the achievement of the MDGs. These years also saw the emergence for the first time of a cross-party political consensus that the UK should aim to play a leading role in international development, creating a platform for a further decade of strong British commitment towards the reduction of global poverty.

Even though by 2010 there were signs of choppier waters ahead, with some features of the previous DFID approach beginning to fray, the period from then until 2016 probably saw DFID's largest direct impact in reducing poverty, simply because the resources at its disposal then were at a peak, and the available evidence shows that the department spent them well. The UK's influence over the international development system and what other donors were doing may have been ebbing by this time, but the department's staff were still globally respected, and Britain was still able on occasion to convene Western countries to agree collective action (for example in summits on immunisation, improving the status of women and girls, and large-scale humanitarian crises). And even in the years from 2016 to 2020, characterised as they were by all the turmoil around Brexit and the souring of the UK's global reputation, the department was still operating at a scale sufficient to make a worthwhile difference in reducing poverty. It was not until 2020 that it all fell apart.

Lessons

What lessons can we draw from the story of DFID? The first is about the power of a clear, credible, ambitious long-term vision. If the goal is too vacuous, or lacks precision, or does not appear plausible in the prevailing context, vision statements are frequently a waste of space. And to be useful, they have to be backed with precise, durable objectives, and a persuasive theory of change describing the way in which they will be achieved. The MDGs hit the sweet spot. The time frame was realistic. The context, both in terms of the geopolitics of the late 1990s and evidence of rapid development in some key developing countries (most notably China), was conducive. The nature of the MDG goals – increasing incomes, reducing infant deaths, getting more children into school – and the fact that there were not too many of them meant they were easy to communicate and intrinsically attractive to many people. It was nevertheless courageous for Clare Short to bet the farm on the endeavour: her ambition and energy mattered.

Second, building an organisation dedicated for an extended period to the achievement of the vision was crucial. Many public organisations suffer from objectives that are too complex or conflict with each other, or where priorities frequently chop and change. The Overseas

CHAPTER 14

Development Administration contained many able and committed people, and was a competent project manager. It provided a valuable foundation. But DFID was a completely different beast. It benefitted hugely from having Short at its head for six long years. Thousands of people came into the department over that period, and Short and her top managers were successful in ensuring that all were imbued with the mantra of poverty reduction. It was constantly reinforced and became the dominant feature of the culture. It was not a hard sell, because people came to and stayed in the department because they believed in the mission. That was true for its political leaders, too, for much of DFID's life. It was lucky to have had many ministers who wanted the role and had the skills for it, several of whom had time to prepare before taking office and stayed in post long enough to make a difference.

Just as important as the people was the creation – and continuous updating and adjusting – of systems and processes, and a way of doing things, that supported the achievement of the department's goals. Deep expertise, evidence, analysis, and knowledge was valued and invested in. Much of the department's global influence stemmed from that. Good systems – project appraisal, monitoring, risk management, review – meant that money was spent in a way that ensured that goals were achieved. In the second half of its life, DFID upgraded its approach to value for money, transparency, and accountability, so that the target its critics had to aim at remained as small and well defended as possible. At the same time, the department pulled off the competing trick of retaining sufficient flexibility and risk appetite to enable it to innovate successfully (though that became increasingly difficult towards the end). It was genuinely a thought leader in many areas, though it sometimes irritated allies by too much tell and not enough show.

Third, a credible, appealing vision and a capable organisation could have achieved little without generous resourcing. DFID was well funded because of personal choices made at the top of government, above all by Gordon Brown and David Cameron. There is an argument to be made that ultimately the 0.7 per cent commitment became an albatross. Would the later attacks have been more muted had the Conservative government decided in 2012 to slow down the journey to 0.7 given wider austerity? It is impossible to know. But what is clear is that having a continuously growing and – after the early period – substantial budget for more than 20 years was essential for both DFID's direct contribution to reducing poverty and its international influence.

A fourth lesson relates to partnerships. DFID did not always get that right. The department understood, intellectually, that it was only through collaboration with others – inside government, with other donors, and with decision makers in developing countries – that it could make poverty history. After the early years in which battles had to be fought and won to secure its position, it worked hard to coordinate well with others in Whitehall. It also built and invested in international partnerships with other donors, influential foundations, multilateral bodies, and developing country leaders and opinion formers. In particular, it devoted huge effort to creating and sustaining a consensus on the key priorities for international development and how to focus on them. Sometimes all this was done well, on occasion less so. Ultimately, it was overwhelmed by the aid scepticism of the right wing of the Conservative Party. Once they assumed positions of power, there was little to be done.

That exposes a fundamental truth about the role Britain plays in international development. Unlike other areas of public policy – defence, the welfare state, the NHS – development is discretionary. That means the choices made by governing parties are not forced upon them by electoral necessity. Rather, they reveal genuine values and priorities. From 1997 to 2020, the choices were in one direction. The last four years have seen a volte face. The decisions taken by the new government, elected in July 2024, especially what they do in their first year, will expose their values and their world view, and how – if at all – they want to help shape the global future.

CHAPTER 14

What next?

So what about the future? How should the UK think about its role in the period ahead? Global poverty increased again in the wake of COVID-19: getting it falling once more at the rate it did at the start of the century requires a concerted international policy response which is currently lacking. As of now, many developing countries are in the midst or on the cusp of a debt crisis redolent of the 1980s and 1990s. Alongside all this, human rights are in too many places now being eroded – as, in some countries, is the position of women and girls.

Many African countries think Britain and the rest of the West is relegating support for their development behind the mitigation of climate change (for which collaboration with better-off Asian and South American countries matters more than Africa) and global health priorities like pandemic risk, which are not the main cause of death and illness in their countries. The simple truth is that many of those countries have lost confidence in the West, including prominently the UK. They don't like – and many feel threatened by – China and Russia, but they see little in much Western policy which reflects their concerns or interests. The Gaza crisis has exposed that in a particularly painful way. There is concern among Western policymakers that many countries in Africa, Asia, the Middle East, and elsewhere are at best lukewarm in their support for Ukraine and their criticism of Russia. Many poor countries would like to see Britain back playing the role on development they saw in the years from 1997. When they think the UK is genuinely committed to supporting and promoting their development, they are more likely to be sympathetic to the British perspective on other issues – from Ukraine to climate to human rights, gender equality, organised crime, and beyond.

Developing countries are very diverse. Some of those prominent in current international debate have average incomes higher than several EU countries, and 20 times those of the poorest African nations. Different countries accordingly need different sorts of support. Broadly, better-off developing countries mostly want assistance with the green energy and climate transition, while low-income countries (and some which have recently graduated from the low-income to lower-middle-income category) need help with debt relief and money for development to reduce poverty and cope with the impact of climate change.

Many people in developing countries, especially in Africa, are entirely reliant on small scale, rain-fed agriculture for their livelihoods. Global warming is an existential threat to them: the central development challenge for these countries in the decades ahead is how they can diversify and modernise their economies to create alternative livelihoods. That has profound implications not just for agriculture and the rural economy but also for health, education, social protection, infrastructure, the development of the private sector, and far beyond. Separately, many better-off but still emerging economies do not have the resources or capacity to transition their economies towards net zero. Most are currently not major polluters, but they need targeted help to transition towards low-carbon solutions for their energy needs, housing, transport, and wider infrastructure.

There remains scope for the UK to play a distinctive role on global development. This is an arena in which Britain could quickly restore its international reputation. But the policy focus for the remainder of the 2020s and beyond will not be the same as for the last 25 years. The underlying aspirations – the creation of human freedoms as envisaged after the Second World War by the founders of the United Nations, including freedom from material deprivation and freedom of expression – are perpetual. But today's circumstances, with climate change, conflict, communications technology, globalisation, and new geopolitical realities, mean that a new approach is now needed.

The way development happens in future will bear similarities with the past. National action will determine more than the international environment. But much will be driven by scientific and technological innovation and the spread of knowledge. That is what has happened since the agricultural and industrial revolutions in eighteenth- and nineteenth-century Britain spread through Europe and North America; over time, greater connectivity has dramatically increased the speed at which new technologies created in one place are adopted in others. Much, too, will arise from the workings of the market economy, which became the universal global system with the collapse of state planning models following the death of Mao Zedong and the dissolution of the Soviet Union.

In the past few generations, aid has contributed to global development in two main ways. First, simply through the transfer of resources accompanied by policy advice (especially in the sphere of economic management) – starting prominently with the US Marshall Plan in Europe after the Second World War. And second, through the way aid has been used to develop new technology and ensure universal access to existing knowledge – as through the green revolution from the 1960s and cheap health technologies like vaccines from the 1990s.

In the period ahead governments in the UK and other Western countries are unlikely to play as prominent a role on large-scale resource transfer as they did in the 15 years from the late 1990s. Their role in spreading and supporting the application of new technology, however, may be greater, given the extraordinary breadth and rate of change and their continuing scientific pre-eminence.

The UK will need to be selective. It cannot move the dial everywhere. It should support multilateral organisations and collaborate in reforms to make them more effective. But in the directly managed bilateral aid programme it should concentrate on a limited number of topics in a defined set of countries. Three things need resolving – policy priorities, resources, and structures.

Some people might argue that poverty is no longer the priority, and the focus needs to shift in particular to deal with geopolitical and environmental threats. The MDGs were substantially achieved, after all, so why keep banging on about that agenda?

That is wrong, for three reasons. First, what about the remaining (roughly) 700 million people, nearly 10 per cent of humanity, still sentenced to the grinding misery and extreme suffering that subsisting on two dollars a day implies? Lifting those people a rung or two up the ladder should be the primary obligation. Second, there are 2.5 billion people, nearly a third of humanity who have barely escaped the extreme poverty threshold and are still living on less than $3.50 a day. These people can easily fall back, and they all have lives still characterised by barely tolerable suffering. Helping that large group is the next priority. Third, geopolitical and environmental threats, in particular climate change, cannot in any case be met without helping that vast population a bit further up the ladder. The choice is therefore not between reducing poverty and saving the environment. The environment cannot be safeguarded without reducing poverty.[3]

By dint of its history, relationships, and expertise, the UK is still well placed to act as a champion for these issues, especially for low-income countries in Africa. In doing that, the goal should be to build an international approach in which the burden is better shared across all the financiers. None of this is to speak against the urgent imperative of action on global environmental and health issues. It is about Britain playing an international role that helps the world as a whole strike a good balance, and ensuring that action on global issues does not fail because the voice of the most vulnerable and needy is not properly listened to.

On resources, there is no prospect of the UK returning to 0.7 per cent in the foreseeable future. Nor would that be wise: the current machine is not capable of spending a lot more money well enough. The first period of the new government's tenure would be better spent remedying that – just as was done from 1997 to 2000, when DFID's capabilities were strengthened to equip it to spend the budget that then grew rapidly. That does not mean there is nothing to be done on resources now. The funding system for the aid budget needs cleaning up by the Treasury. The budget needs to be less volatile and more predictable in the medium term. Next, the recent practice of using a large slice of the development budget for financial transactions (in particular ever more capitalisation of BII) needs to be phased out. It distorts choices, taking money away from other activities that would generate greater gain for the poorest people and countries. In addition, the government should return to the system that prevailed for 50 years up to 2010, where the bulk of the aid budget is managed by a single department, rather than being sprayed across Whitehall, which, as a slew of parliamentary and NAO reports have shown, has not made aid more effective. And finally, the spending plans the government has inherited – some of which run several years into the future – will need to be reviewed to see how far they contribute to its top priorities. A root and branch review is needed, just as in 1997 and (to a degree) 2010, both to identify and clear out sub-optimal activities on which the ODA budget is currently being spent and in order to ensure that new priorities are not merely rhetorical, but backed with real money too.

The government's organisational arrangements will also need to be fixed. As currently structured, the FCDO is unable to rebuild the development expertise that was lost with the merger, or to manage its ODA budget with the kind of rigorous, long-term focus necessary to make a real impact. The quickest, easiest, and cheapest solution would be to bring the FCDO's development staff and ODA resources into a dedicated department of state alongside – and sharing a platform with – the Foreign Office. That would also facilitate a resurrection of patient, sustained but clear-eyed partnerships which, as Barbara Castle in the 1960s and Clare Short in the 1990s understood, is the only basis on which development cooperation can ultimately succeed.

ACKNOWLEDGEMENTS

OUR FIRST thanks are to the Gates Foundation and the Open Society Foundations, who generously supported this work. We are in particular grateful to Joe Cerrell, Mark Malloch Brown, Andrew Mace, and Russell Pickard.

No one helped us more than Bernat Camps Adrogue, our research associate at the Center for Global Development between 2022 and 2024. He gathered and organised a vast amount of documentary material and analysed a huge volume of data, both on DFID and on trends in poverty and other development outcomes in the countries in which the department worked. He also arranged a series of workshops and produced transcripts for dozens of structured interviews which we conducted.

Many people agreed to be interviewed during the course of 2022 and 2023. In some cases we have quoted them; in others, including for a significant number still serving in government, we have drawn on the information they provided without naming them.

A number of people provided us with original written material. We are particularly grateful to Carew Treffgarne, a long-serving education adviser in DFID who in 2012 and 2013 conducted more than 180 detailed structured interviews with senior and mid-level DFID staff and ministers on their experiences in the department (as well as with civil servants in the Treasury). She kindly allowed us access to her records. These are referenced in footnotes throughout the book as "Treffgarne interviews". We are also indebted to Gavin McGilli-

ACKNOWLEDGEMENTS

vray for a series of valuable notes on DFID's involvement in private sector development.

Several anonymous peer reviewers read and offered important comments and correctives on three papers we published in 2022 and 2023 which form the basis for Parts I and II.

Many other people who worked in or were associated with the department have also provided invaluable assistance. We particularly want to thank Masood Ahmed, Michael Anderson, Douglas Alexander, Hilary Benn, Owen Barder, Jonathan Beynon, Richard Calvert, Eamon Cassidy, Suma Chakrabarti, Sarah Champion, Stefan Dercon, Nick Dyer, Martin Dinham, Jim Drummond, Mick Foster, Peter Freeman, Annabel Gerry, Peter Gill, Peter Grant, Romilly Greenhill, Pauline Hayes, John Holmes, Joy Hutcheon, Tim Lankester, Laurie Lee, Richard Manning, Malcolm Smart, Marcus Manuel, Simon Maxwell, David Miliband, Andrew Mitchell, Chris Mullin, Jonathan Powell, Caroline Rickatson, Peter Ricketts, Matthew Rycroft, Sam Sharpe, Clare Short, Rory Stewart, Gareth Thomas, Minouche Shafik, John Vereker, Myles Wickstead, and Alan Winters.

A number of colleagues at the Center for Global Development have, in a variety of direct and indirect ways, helped too, notably Rachael Calleja, Tom Drake, Mikaela Gavas, Sam Hughes, Ian Mitchell, Catarina Santos, Emily Schabacker, Maya Verber, and Edward Wickstead.

Our thanks to Julie Willis at Westchester Publishing Services UK for overseeing the production of the book, and to Adam Bell for copy editing the manuscript. Thanks to Steve Kress for the cover design.

During the course of its life, we estimate that some 10,000 people from more than 50 countries worked in or very close to DFID. They all contributed, in a myriad of different ways and sometimes over many decades, to improving the life experience of countless numbers of the world's poorest and most deprived people.

Inevitably, we will have got some things wrong; and for that we are responsible.

APPENDIX A

Secretaries of State and Permanent Secretaries 1997–2020

Secretaries of state

May 1997–May 2003	Clare Short
May 2003–October 2003	Valerie Amos
October 2003–June 2007	Hilary Benn
June 2007–May 2010	Douglas Alexander
May 2010–September 2012	Andrew Mitchell
September 2012–July 2016	Justine Greening
July 2016–November 2017	Priti Patel
November 2017–May 2019	Penny Mordaunt
May 2019–July 2019	Rory Stewart
July 2019–February 2020	Alok Sharma
February 2020–September 2020	Anne-Marie Trevelyan

Permanent secretaries

May 1997–February 2002	John Vereker
February 2002–November 2007	Suma Chakrabarti
November 2007–March 2008	Sue Owen (acting)
March 2008–March 2011	Minouche Shafik
March 2011–July 2017	Mark Lowcock
July 2017–January 2018	Nick Dyer (acting)
January 2018–March 2020	Matthew Rycroft
March 2020–September 2020	Nick Dyer (acting)

APPENDIX B

Trends in Global Development Indicators

Figure A.1. GNI per capita (current US$) for focus countries, 2000–20

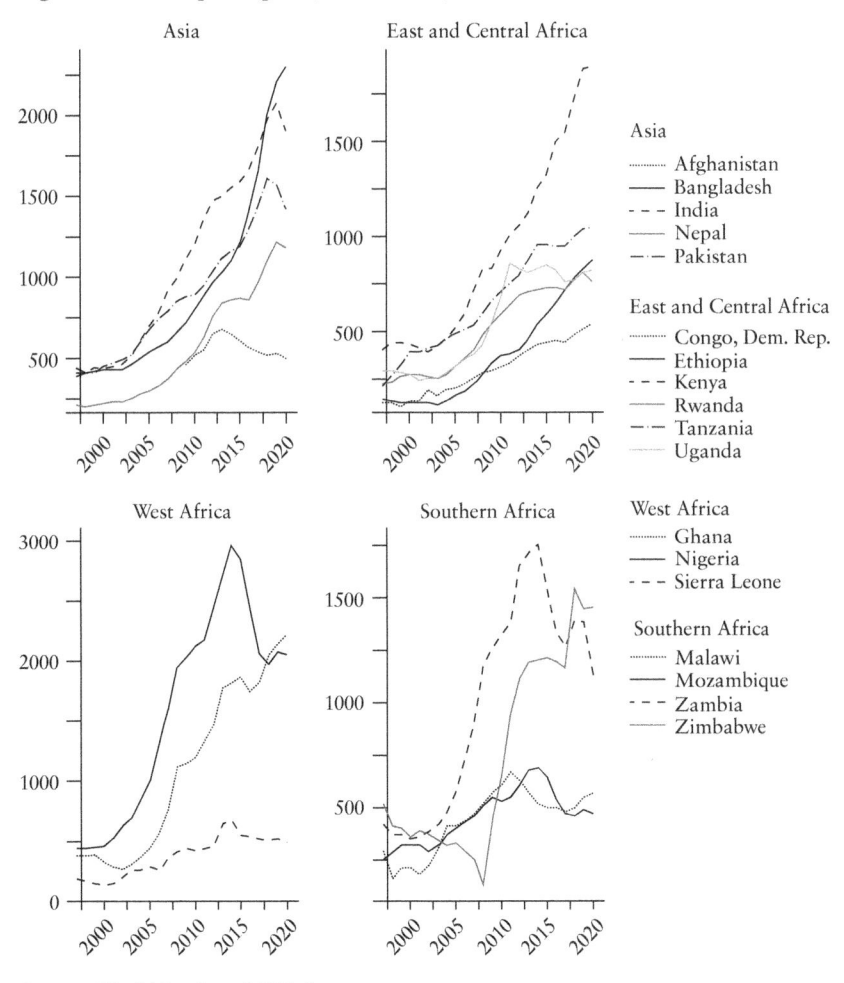

Asia
- Afghanistan
- Bangladesh
- India
- Nepal
- Pakistan

East and Central Africa
- Congo, Dem. Rep.
- Ethiopia
- Kenya
- Rwanda
- Tanzania
- Uganda

West Africa
- Ghana
- Nigeria
- Sierra Leone

Southern Africa
- Malawi
- Mozambique
- Zambia
- Zimbabwe

Source: World Bank and UN data.

Figure A.2. Life expectancy at birth for focus countries, 2000–20

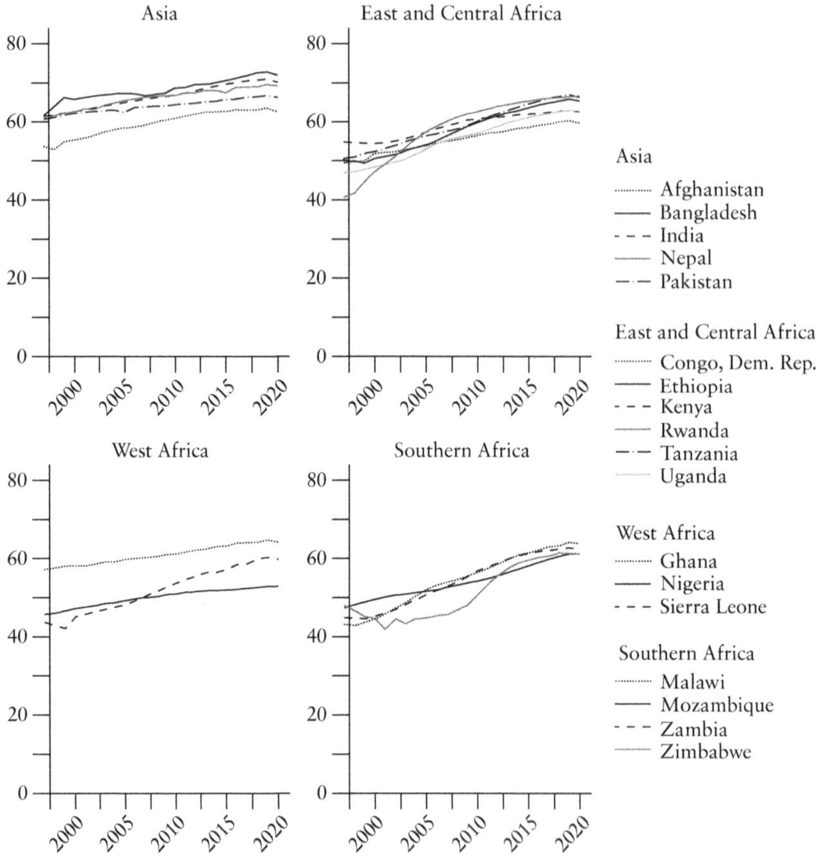
Asia
East and Central Africa
West Africa
Southern Africa
80
60
40
20
0
2000
2005
2010
2015
2020
Asia
Afghanistan
Bangladesh
India
Nepal
Pakistan
East and Central Africa
Congo, Dem. Rep.
Ethiopia
Kenya
Rwanda
Tanzania
Uganda
West Africa
Ghana
Nigeria
Sierra Leone
Southern Africa
Malawi
Mozambique
Zambia
Zimbabwe

Source: World Bank and UN data.

Figure A.3. Mortality rate, under five (per 1,000 live births) for focus countries, 2000–20

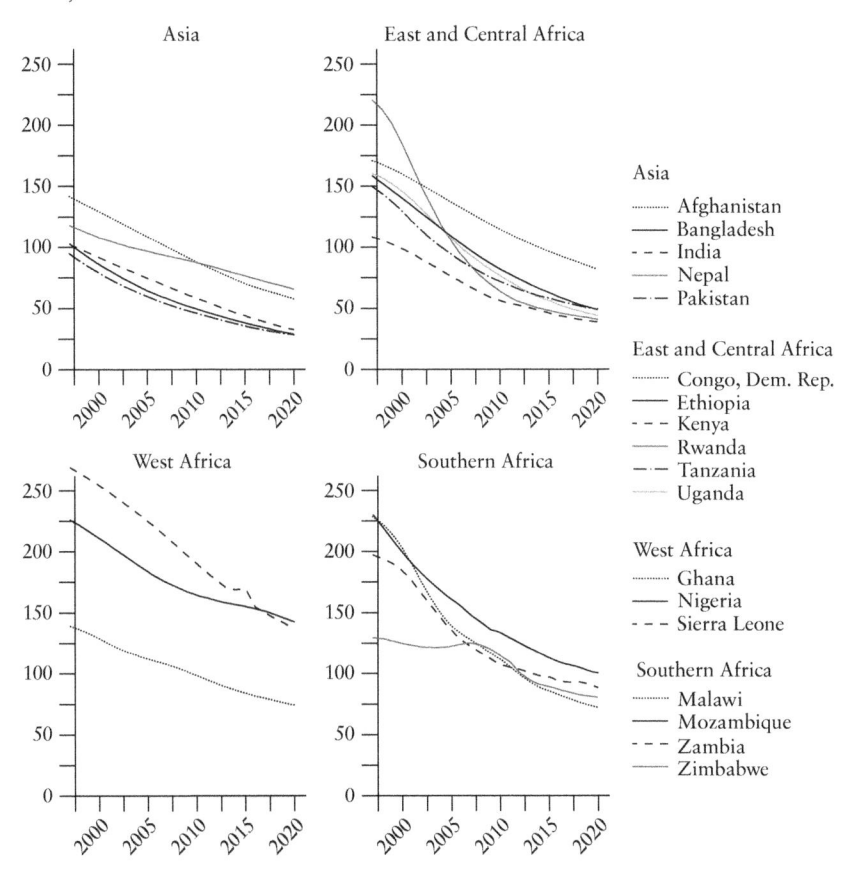

Source: World Bank and UN data.

Figure A.4. Human Development Index 1997–2020

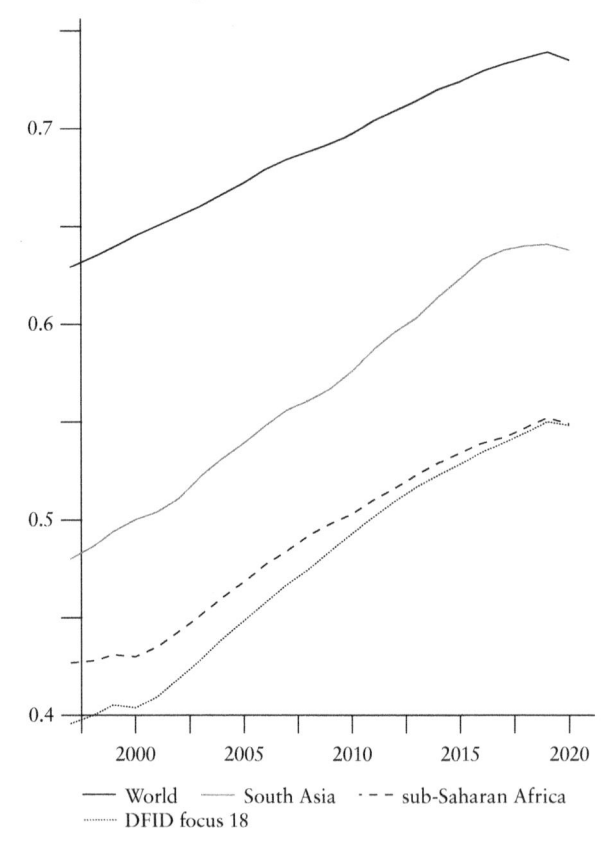

Source: World Bank World Development Indicators, accessed through the R Package "WDI".

APPENDIX C

UK ODA and DFID Spending 1997–2020

The monetary figures in the following tables are all presented in £million in 2022 prices, i.e., adjusted for inflation to show how spending changed in real terms over the period. The underlying data comes from DFID Annual Reports and the FCDO Annual Report for 2020/21.

Table A.1. 1997/98–2002/03

	97/98	98/99	99/00	00/01	01/02	02/03
Afghanistan	0.2	0.3	0.1	0.2	0.4	56.6
Bangladesh	63.3	111.7	107.0	118.5	99.8	123.5
DRC	–	–	–	5.2	9.2	21.1
Ethiopia	5.9	8.5	10.8	25.9	18.8	65.9
Ghana	26.1	79.1	71.9	116.4	85.4	86.4
India	130.5	143.5	161.7	176.4	298.6	254.8
Kenya	44.6	52.0	40.9	79.3	41.2	69.2
Malawi	42.1	79.2	77.1	93.8	69.6	84.5
Mozambique	33.8	41.1	35.3	50.1	63.8	49.9
Nepal	28.4	27.1	25.5	28.8	33.9	43.8
Nigeria	12.1	16.4	22.4	26.5	32.6	47.8
Pakistan	40.6	34.0	33.6	21.4	70.6	62.0
Rwanda	–	22.7	24.3	54.9	44.5	57.6
Sierra Leone	5.1	15.0	50.0	58.7	56.9	53.9
Tanzania	69.4	82.1	104.5	112.3	104.6	123.3
Uganda	78.9	85.5	87.6	139.5	110.3	86.9

(*continued*)

Table A.1. 1997/98–2002/03 (continued)

	97/98	98/99	99/00	00/01	01/02	02/03
Zambia	21.1	18.9	17.7	87.2	64.7	61.6
Zimbabwe	18.7	17.2	19.6	17.7	24.3	50.3
Total 18 countries	620.9	834.2	889.8	1,212.8	1,229.0	1,399.1
18 countries as per cent of regional programmes	49	57	61	66	65	64
Total-DFID regional programmes	1,278.4	1,456.7	1,457.6	1,835.0	1,887.7	2,189.8
18 countries as per cent of total DFID	18	22	21	27	26	26
Total DFID	3,437.6	3,828.3	4,200.6	4,527.5	4,649.2	5,291.7
Total bilateral UK ODA	2,794.5	2,680.3	3,563.6	3,672.7	3,861.5	3,862.4
Total multilateral UK ODA	1,255.5	941.7	1,455.5	1,650.0	1,563.9	2,421.4
18 countries per cent of total ODA	15	23	18	23	23	22
Total ODA	4,050.1	3,622.0	5,019.1	5,322.7	5,426.6	6,283.6

Source: DFID Annual Reports.

Table A.2. 2003/04–2009/10

	03/04	04/05	05/06	06/07	07/08	08/09	09/10
Afghanistan	110.6	130.3	153.5	150.3	159.2	186.5	199.0
Bangladesh	92.3	199.3	183.2	171.2	173.6	176.4	188.7
DRC	21.2	61.6	80.8	134.2	115.8	118.9	151.3
Ethiopia	65.1	105.3	96.6	135.0	208.6	223.4	309.2
Ghana	93.5	113.5	133.0	104.5	112.2	136.5	120.9

(*continued*)

Table A.2. 2003/04–2009/10 (continued)

	03/04	04/05	05/06	06/07	07/08	08/09	09/10
India	345.5	389.5	389.4	366.6	395.9	410.6	401.1
Kenya	41.9	62.7	100.1	93.3	75.7	99.3	80.4
Malawi	85.6	99.5	109.1	92.8	104.2	93.8	116.8
Mozambique	59.0	76.8	87.6	82.4	96.7	99.8	95.8
Nepal	44.8	51.2	52.2	52.3	64.0	75.6	80.5
Nigeria	51.4	71.7	126.1	124.1	150.6	142.6	165.0
Pakistan	106.7	39.7	111.6	136.0	135.4	172.3	54.4
Rwanda	45.3	70.5	106.1	25.8	68.9	73.3	72.6
Sierra Leone	56.7	56.4	50.0	55.1	60.6	68.7	61.8
Tanzania	128.6	150.5	170.1	167.1	179.4	187.0	197.4
Uganda	87.8	96.3	104.9	112.7	106.6	105.2	95.7
Zambia	39.7	42.6	73.4	60.8	62.8	63.8	68.9
Zimbabwe	53.4	37.7	58.2	48.8	67.3	72.8	85.3
Total 18 countries	1,529.1	1,855.2	2,186.1	2,112.9	2,337.5	2,506.5	2,544.8
18 countries as per cent of regional programmes	58	67	68	71	70	74	68
Total-DFID regional programmes	2,616.0	2,787.0	3,213.5	2,995.6	3,343.0	3,409.0	3,747.1
18 countries as per cent of total DFID	27	32	33	28	32	32	27
Total DFID	5,685.1	5,845.6	6,628.3	7,610.2	7,353.0	7,946.7	9,262.9
Total bilateral UK ODA	4,694.7	7,141.1	7,380.6	4,261.7	6,023.4	6,869.8	7,363.3

(*continued*)

Table A.2. 2003/04–2009/10 (continued)

	03/04	04/05	05/06	06/07	07/08	08/09	09/10
Total multilateral UK ODA	2,237.1	2,277.0	3,167.6	3,230.9	3,434.3	3,616.4	4,625.6
18 countries per cent of total ODA	22	20	21	28	25	24	21
Total ODA	6,932.4	9,422.8	10,547.8	7,492.6	9,457.7	10,486.2	11,988.9

Source: DFID Annual Reports.

Table A.3. 2010/11–2016/17

	10/11	11/12	12/13	13/14	14/15	15/16	16/17
Afghanistan	137.6	211.7	243.1	239.1	219.6	160.9	204.7
Bangladesh	240.5	267.8	252.1	328.2	219.9	180.9	182.7
DRC	185.3	191.1	177.6	206.6	181.1	165.6	150.0
Ethiopia	329.2	426.1	335.5	356.2	409.5	409.4	396.6
Ghana	116.5	104.8	63.1	114.8	64.6	71.7	70.3
India	385.4	356.3	255.9	214.3	193.0	164.4	55.1
Kenya	97.6	127.8	120.0	172.1	116.8	167.3	158.6
Malawi	97.6	92.2	151.5	107.7	75.3	96.4	105.0
Mozambique	117.3	116.6	85.5	99.0	83.7	57.4	73.6
Nepal	81.8	84.1	74.0	132.6	102.9	103.6	116.6
Nigeria	199.4	229.9	258.8	339.4	291.5	260.3	361.0
Pakistan	279.8	287.4	264.5	320.6	303.1	409.3	510.3
Rwanda	101.8	99.8	78.9	108.8	82.2	93.4	85.3
Sierra Leona	85.7	85.6	84.5	99.1	54.4	58.7	161.6
Tanzania	201.5	186.1	194.2	220.9	167.2	224.7	218.7

(*continued*)

Table A.3. 2010/11–2016/17 (continued)

	10/11	11/12	12/13	13/14	14/15	15/16	16/17
Uganda	130.8	100.7	110.7	120.3	122.3	115.9	133.1
Zambia	73.0	59.0	70.9	85.2	73.0	60.8	59.2
Zimbabwe	95.5	117.1	107.2	134.2	83.5	104.4	126.8
Total 18 countries	**2,956.3**	**3,144.1**	**2,928.1**	**3,399.0**	**2,843.7**	**2,905.2**	**3,169.3**
18 countries as per cent of regional regional programmes	68%	71%	68%	61%	70%	60%	59%
Total-DFID regional programmes	**4,324.0**	**4,450.1**	**4,329.5**	**5,572.2**	**4,047.1**	**4,879.8**	**5,389.0**
18 countries as per cent of total DFID	29%	31%	30%	28%	25%	25%	26%
Total DFID	10,276.4	10,050.7	9,691.7	12,255.1	11,461.9	11,535.2	12,105.3
Total bilateral UK ODA	7,158.0	7,242.7	8,514.6	8,426.7	9,327.9	10,385.8	10,642.9
Total multilateral UK ODA	4,584.7	4,223.2	5,936.5	6,025.4	5,445.6	5,893.9	6,354.6
18 countries per cent of total ODA	25%	27%	20%	24%	19%	18%	19%
Total ODA	11,742.2	11,465.8	14,450.9	14,452.7	14,774.2	16,279.8	16,997.6

Source: DFID Annual Reports.

Table A.4. 2017/18–2020/21

	17/18	18/19	19/20	20/21
Afghanistan	173.7	203.0	213.8	159.2
Bangladesh	203.6	205.9	271.5	196.4
DRC	204.6	217.4	156.6	125.4
Ethiopia	380.0	349.7	330.2	248.9
Ghana	59.4	47.3	38.4	21.6
India	52.6	49.1	29.6	43.0
Kenya	153.6	112.4	108.4	69.6
Malawi	87.7	85.7	73.5	54.2
Mozambique	57.5	71.1	93.3	52.8
Nepal	113.5	101.7	91.3	82.6
Nigeria	332.4	301.8	264.8	216.7
Pakistan	432.3	312.2	290.5	165.6
Rwanda	69.3	70.9	59.1	42.2
Sierra Leona	128.6	93.9	84.3	65.4
Tanzania	194.6	175.6	143.6	92.3
Uganda	146.9	117.8	141.6	71.7
Zambia	59.8	30.5	42.8	35.5
Zimbabwe	110.4	110.9	115.0	81.9
Total 18 countries	**2,960.5**	**2,656.7**	**2,548.3**	**1,825.1**
18 countries as per cent of regional programmes	59%	57%	55%	52%
Total DFID regional programmes	5,027.1	4,675.0	4,666.1	3,507.6
18 countries as per cent of total DFID	24%	22%	21%	16%
Total DFID	12,217.9	12,295.5	12,032.7	11,603.4

(*continued*)

Table A.4. 2017/18–2020/21 (continued)

	17/18	18/19	19/20	20/21
Total bilateral UK ODA	10,905.9	11,619.1	10,759.6	7,396.1
Total multilateral UK ODA	6,227.1	5,814.7	5,581.3	4,426.7
18 countries per cent of total ODA	17%	15%	16%	15%
Total ODA	17,132.8	17,434.3	16,332.9	11,822.8

Source: DFID Annual Reports and FCDO Annual Report 2020/21.

ABBREVIATIONS

BII	British International Investments
CDC	Commonwealth Development Corporation
CERF	Central Emergency Response Fund
DAC	Development Assistance Committee
DFID	Department for International Development
EBA	"Everything But Arms"
ECHO	European Commission Humanitarian Office
FCDO	Foreign, Commonwealth and Development Office
FCO	Foreign and Commonwealth Office
FGM	female genital mutilation
FTI	Fast Track Initiative
Gavi	Global Alliance on Vaccines and Immunization
GBS	general budget support
GDP	gross domestic product
HDI	Human Development Index
HIPC	Heavily Indebted Poor Countries
HIV/AIDS	human immunodeficiency virus / acquired immune deficiency syndrome
ICAI	Independent Commission on Aid Impact
IDA	International Development Association
IFFIm	International Finance Facility for Immunisation
IMF	International Monetary Fund
MAR	multilateral aid review
MDG	Millennium Development Goals

MDRI	Multilateral Debt Relief Initiative
MEFF	multilateral effectiveness framework
NAO	National Audit Office
NGO	non-governmental organisation
NHS	National Health Service
ODA	official development assistance
ODI	Overseas Development Institute
OECD	Organisation for Economic Co-operation and Development
PPP	purchasing power parity
SDG	Sustainable Development Goals
TMSA	Trade Mark Southern Africa
UN	United Nations
UNICEF	United Nations Children's Fund
VSO	Voluntary Service Overseas

NOTES

Introduction
1. In 'purchasing power parity' (PPP) terms, based on 1990 prices. A purchasing power parity dollar is one that can buy the same resources anywhere in the world. A purchasing power parity dollar in India buys the same amount of food or nutritional value as a purchasing power dollar in, say, Zambia. The current definition (reflecting changes in purchasing power since then) is a daily income below $2.15 in 2017 prices.
2. The World Bank's Poverty and Inequality Database and the 2022 Poverty and Shared Prosperity report. www.worldbank.org/en/publication/poverty-and-shared-prosperity

1. Why Labour Created DFID
1. In the end, she would tally 28,134 votes, nearly 75 per cent of the total cast in the constituency. See: en.wikipedia.org/wiki/Birmingham_Ladywood_(UK_Parliament_constituency)#Elections_in_the_1990s
2. Short, 2004, 55.
3. Since in the British convention "of" is not included in the abbreviation of a name, a Department of International Development would be D-I-D, or DID (which was the acronym used in a 1996 Labour Party policy document setting out the intent to create a new department). "For" is included, and with D-F-I-D being cumbersome Vereker worried people would pronounce the department's name like a word. For the record, one of the authors of this book pronounces the department's name in the style of the Welsh region; the other tends to spell out the letters ("D.F.I.D.").
4. White Papers are presented to Parliament to promulgate government policy, and sometimes then get embedded in legislation. In this case, the

1997 White Paper made eliminating global poverty the overarching goal of Britain's contribution to development.
5. Lankester, 2013, 13.
6. There were less than five years between 1964 and 1997 when the minister with day-to-day responsibility for development was either a member of, or attended, Cabinet (all under Labour administrations), in the periods 1964–67 and 1975–76.
7. Thomas-Symonds, 2022, 121.
8. Though Barbara Castle was to become an influential figure in Harold Wilson's Cabinet from 1974 to 1976.
9. Barder, 2005.
10. Vereker, 2020.
11. We are grateful to Peter Freeman, a senior official in the department for many years, for material on Judith Hart, including the following vignette: "She aroused strong emotions, even among civil servants. Her Private Secretary in 1969 took to putting romantic poems at the top of her box before closing it and eventually had to be sent home from a trip to India after harassing her while drunk. Amazingly he was still a Head of Department in the Overseas Development Ministry when she returned five years later and her office had to ensure that they didn't meet."
12. Reeves, 2019, 143–4; Vereker, 2020.
13. While aid tended to increase in nominal terms, for most of the Thatcher years it declined or stagnated when adjusted for inflation, and failed to keep pace with economic growth, resulting in a steady, gentle decline in the official development assistance-to-GNI ratio away from the UN's 0.7 per cent target, according to the UK's Statistics on International Development.
14. Vereker, 2020.
15. See Ireton, 2013, esp. 18–39.
16. Ireton, 2013, 185–210.
17. The preceding two paragraphs draw extensively on Ireton, 2013, and Barder, 2005.
18. Interviews with authors.
19. This later meant that official development assistance as a percentage of GNI would hit historical lows in 1997–99, falling to 0.24 per cent.
20. Hamilton subsequently lost his seat in 1997 to an independent candidate, Martin Bell. This signals the depth of feeling about the issue: independents rarely win parliamentary seats in the UK.
21. Formally, *Regina v. Secretary of State for Foreign and Commonwealth Affairs, ex parte World Development Movement Ltd.*

NOTES

22. The best account is in Lankester, 2013. Pergau is the best-known abuse of the UK aid programme because it became a very public scandal. But it was not the worst. In 1987 the UK supplied 21 Westland helicopters to India for £65 million, effectively paying for them from the aid programme. They barely flew; after crashes in 1988 and 1989, in which a number of people were killed, they were sold for less than £1 million in 1993. At least Malaysia got a viable dam generating electricity.
23. Hurd was foreign secretary in the Thatcher and Major governments. His son, Nick, was later a minister in DFID.
24. Indeed, Tim Lankester, then ODA's permanent secretary, requested a ministerial direction from Hurd in order to proceed with the project. These were very rare at the time, demonstrating how controversial the project was.
25. Between October 1993 and July 1994 there was rarely a week in which the Pergau story was not in the news. *The Times*, not known for its support for aid, printed over 50 articles, editorials, and letters. It called the project "a monstrous exception to the generally taut, targeted and well monitored British overseas aid programme". Lankester, 2013, 117.
26. Then Tony Blair's head of policy, and later an MP and foreign secretary. He is now the head of the International Rescue Committee.
27. In its first term, Labour both introduced new legislation clarifying the acceptable uses of British aid and abolished the Aid and Trade Provision, through which Pergau had been funded. See Chapter 2.
28. Robin Cook's famous speech setting out the new government's "ethical foreign policy" on 12 May 1997 was a manifestation of how that intent was brought into government.
29. Labour Party, 1996. Several interviewees credit David Mepham, an adviser working in Labour HQ, who worked on the document and later became Short's special adviser in government, for ensuring the reference to establishing a department was included. It was, however, signed off by Cook, who had an eagle eye for detail and is unlikely to have allowed something substantial he had reservations about to slip through (interviews with authors).
30. Labour Party, 1997. Consistent with the emphasis on fiscal prudence, the 1997 manifesto notably did not repeat a 1992 pledge to reach the UN target within the term of a single parliament.
31. The main posts in the Labour Shadow Cabinet at that time were filled following elections among Labour MPs. Meacher had the shadow development role from 1992 to 1993; Clarke from 1993 to 1994; Lestor from 1994 to 1996.

NOTES

32. She was unwell, with motor neurone disease. She died in March 1998.
33. Short, 2004, 47–9.
34. Short, 2004, 50.
35. Election result: web.archive.org/web/20100714134916/http://www.election.demon.co.uk/shadow.html
36. She resigned from Neil Kinnock's front bench team over the first Gulf War. Short, 2004, 21–34.
37. OECD, 1996. At just 20 pages, it was one of the DAC's shorter contributions. Few of its others have achieved a higher ratio of influence per page. Much of the report found its way into the UN Millennium Development Goals, arguably the most successful collaborative international initiative in history to improve the average human life experience.
38. Short, 2004, 53.
39. OECD, 1996, 9.
40. Facilitated by new World Bank work on poverty measurement, applying a clearly defined, universal standard for the first time – the "dollar a day" poverty line.
41. Short, 2004, 53–4.
42. Fabian Society Working Papers, May and July 1964, cited in Ireton, 2013, 31.
43. Hansard, 3 February 1964 (Second Reading of International Development Association Bill).
44. His father was a naval commander, his brother a diplomat and a distant ancestor a viscount. But Vereker, as well as being clever and ambitious, had an independent streak. After school at Marlborough College, he spurned Oxbridge for a scholarship at the new university in Keele. He enjoyed challenging orthodoxies.
45. Short, 2004, 54.
46. Short, 2004, 54, and private interviews.
47. As John Vereker has put it, this provided the embryo from which DFID was later able to flourish.
48. This is not to say that Overseas Development Administration had absolutely no strategic influence beyond the transactional: it worked constructively on issues ranging from the end of apartheid in South Africa to economic reform in the former Soviet Union.
49. There are countless examples of this. Lowcock recalls an unedifying saga in which the Overseas Development Administration was prevailed upon to finance the construction of a road through the Mau Forest in Kenya, a reservoir of valuable biodiversity and Kenya's single most

NOTES

important water catchment area. The Overseas Development Administration's environment advisers were against the proposal, fearing the effect would be accelerating deforestation. They were overruled because Kenya's President Moi wanted the road and the UK's high commissioner in Nairobi thought it would damage relations to decline to pay for it.

50. Interviews with authors.
51. Interviews with authors.
52. Short, 2004, 51.
53. Short, 2004, 52, and private interviews. It is perhaps surprising that there was not more consideration of what Labour could learn from other countries' systems, but Short did at least look into the issue.
54. Short, 2004, 51. We have seen no evidence that Gordon Brown, later such a strong advocate for international development, was drawn into this discussion.
55. Kampfner, 2003, 64. Kampfner was a journalist at the time, and is now an executive director at Chatham House.
56. Interviews with authors. Strictly, Coles was senior to Vereker. Coles was a full permanent secretary, and Vereker at this point a second (i.e., junior) permanent secretary (so graded because the Overseas Development Administration job was smaller than that at the FCO).
57. Kampfner, 2003, 64.
58. Interviews with authors.
59. Since 1986 she had campaigned against their practice of publishing large photos of topless young women on page three of each morning's paper. Years later, she won: the practice was finally discontinued in 2015. Short described it as "a victory for public dignity".
60. Andrew Mitchell is perhaps the closest.
61. In 1997, 3 May was a Sunday and 4 May a public holiday. Number 94 Victoria Street was the site of what was, until that day, the Overseas Development Administration.
62. The BBC clearly believed that Short would be appointed, which was why they were willing to spend money in advance preparing the documentary, the plan for which Gill agreed with Short's team before the election.
63. Interviews with authors.

2. Policy, Money, and Organisation
1. Short, 2004, gives a full account from her perspective. For a flavour of how it felt from the Number 10 end, see Campbell, 2007 (for example

NOTES

672–4). The tone towards Short throughout occupies a range between (at best) snippy and (more often) excoriating.
2. All these quotes are from Barder, 2005, 3 (and, for his sources, 33).
3. This paragraph draws on data from the IMF's World Economic Outlook (2023) database.
4. Data taken from the World Development Indicators. In Malawi GDP per capita PPP in constant 2017 international dollars declined from $937 in 1990 to $875 in 1994 before recovering; in Zambia from $2,290 in 1990 to low of $1,991 in 1994 and had still not recovered by the end of the decade; and in Nigeria from $3,260 in 1990 to a low of $2,895 in 1995 and had still not recovered by the end of the decade.
5. It would not be until 2005 that the Multilateral Debt Relief Initiative (MDRI), extending the terms of forgiveness to loans from the IMF, the International Development Association (IDA) loans from the World Bank, and those from the African Development Bank, was agreed.
6. See, for example, Our World In Data for a summary of the extent of poverty over time. ourworldindata.org/poverty?insight=global-extreme-poverty-declined-substantially-over-the-last-generation#key-insights
7. In economic terms, the "marginal utility" of income declines as income increases. This logic provides the rationale for focusing support on the very poorest people in the world, as argued by (for example) Kenny, 2021.
8. Data taken from the World Development Indicators.
9. Interviews with authors.
10. John Vereker and Richard Manning, the director general responsible for policy, also played important roles.
11. "Together you and I will begin to build the new society. . . . and we will give back to our children what they deserve – a heritage of hope." DFID, 1997.
12. UK aid was lower in real terms in 1997 than it had been in 1979 and had halved as a proportion of national income. DFID, 1997, 35.
13. "This is not just a White Paper about aid. It is a White Paper about sustainable development." DFID, 1997, 16.
14. In 2022 Liz Truss, then foreign secretary, renamed it British International Investments (BII). See Chapter 13.
15. DFID, 1997, 50–76.
16. Interviews with authors.
17. The record of the parliamentary discussion at the launch of the White Paper is here hansard.parliament.uk/commons/1997-11-05/debates/921ac

772-af68-4f25-a417-90ba0c5afefd/InternationalDevelopment#contribution-779385b1-ff32-454f-8d94-4c9b0f995fd5
18. International Development Committee report on *The Development White Paper*, 1997/98 Parliamentary session.
19. OECD DAC Development Cooperation Review of United Kingdom, 1998, www.oecd-ilibrary.org/development/development-co-operation-reviews-united-kingdom-1998_9789264162778-en
20. Olivié and Perez, 2020, 76.
21. Barder, 2005, 16.
22. *Journal of International Development*, 1998, 151–276. The cavils irritated Short, who pointed out that she had never said the DAC goals were the only thing that mattered, just that they did matter, and that it was unfair to criticise her at the moment of the White Paper's publication for not being able to prove that in the years ahead it would be implemented. Of course, the fact that the *Journal of International Development* devoted a special issue to it showed they thought the White Paper was a big deal (interviews with authors).
23. DFID, 1997, 19.
24. Treffgarne interviews.
25. Vereker, 2002, 137.
26. In a rare if not unique step for a White Paper, summary versions were given away in supermarkets. Short wanted to engage the public.
27. For a detailed assessment of DFID's approach, see Valters and Whitty, 2017.
28. These linkages were strengthened when Suma Chakrabarti was appointed director general in DFID in 2001.
29. Treffgarne interviews.
30. Treffgarne interviews.
31. Short, 2004, 89–90.
32. DFID, 2000, 7. DFID used the words goals and targets interchangeably when describing the DAC framework.
33. As Richard Manning put it in an interview with us: "Clare Short was brilliant at giving very consistent messaging from the top. . . . she would repeat the same thing ad nauseum. Very effectively. And you could go anywhere in the DFID universe, and they all had the same story." Every one of Short's forewords in the five annual Departmental Reports during her tenure repeated the mantra that the department's raison d'être was the achievement of the International/Millennium Development Goals.

NOTES

34. Interviews with authors.
35. *The Economist*, 14 December 2000. Some of the detail in the article annoyed Short, who wrote a reply complaining it contained "snide comments on my political views.... The White Paper rejects the market fundamentalism of the 1980s for which *The Economist* was such an apologist." "Ouch", said *The Economist* in a follow-up article. (*The Economist*, 4 January 2001). From today's perspective, the exchange looks like one where each side is a bit embarrassed to be told they agree with the other.
36. *The DAC Journal*, 2001, I–13.
37. *The DAC Journal*, 2001.
38. Specifically, General Government Gross Debt was declining as a percentage of GDP during this period, according to the IMF's World Economic Outlook database.
39. Short, 2004, 90–1.
40. All these examples were mentioned in our private interviews or the Treffgarne interviews.
41. In 1996/97 the cost amounted to £614 million; by 2002/03 it was £928 million. DFID's contribution to the EU budget remained substantial thereafter, but it fell significantly as a share of DFID's growing total budget.
42. DFID, 1997, 38–9.
43. Barder, 2005, 17. One of the architects of the DFID model was Nick Dyer, who later became the permanent secretary responsible for development in the merged Foreign, Commonwealth and Development Office.
44. Lowcock recalls discussing this with him and Short in 11 Downing Street in the final stage of one Spending Review.
45. Others took a different approach: the US then – as now – provided very little money direct to governments (sometimes just 3–4 per cent of the US Agency for International Development's budget). Instead, they largely operated through American technical assistance contractors, meaning that the lion's share of the budget never left the US.
46. We are grateful to Mick Foster for material we are drawing on in the following paragraphs.
47. He died prematurely in his fifties.
48. This is a compressed summary: there were a lot of complex technical issues addressed in this evolution, including in the accounting arrangements, and in how to maximise the likelihood that additional foreign exchange provided through central banks to governments did in practice flow through into higher spending on programmes that would contribute to the MDGs.

NOTES

49. Ghana, Malawi, Mozambique, Rwanda, Sierra Leone, Tanzania, Uganda, and Zambia were among the countries benefitting.
50. That was often a time-consuming and bureaucratically complex process, for which the expertise, negotiating skills, and professional reputation of DFID staff were well suited. In the EU (which was to become one of the leading budget support donors), it involved persuading the Court of Auditors to adjust their approach.
51. Material provided by Richard Manning.
52. In addition there was as time passed an increasing use of sector budget support, which drew the eye to how well resources were used by line ministries, though in fact many of the same risks arose there.
53. Ireton, 2013, 85 and 131.
54. See, for example, Table A3.1 in the Joint Evaluation of General Budget Support 1994–2004: Malawi, available online at assets.publishing.service.gov.uk/media/5a79841240f0b63d72fc675c/gbs-malawi.pdf. General Budget Support alone approached one-third of the Government Budget in at least one year in this period, and often exceeded one-fifth.
55. It is sometimes thought that all the UK's aid is governed by this legislation (and the 2002 Act that replaced it). That is mistaken: other government departments may spend money in a way which complies with the OECD rules on official development assistance (ODA), and so is part of what the UK reports annually as its aid level, but they did (and do) that under their own legislation.
56. For a fuller description, see Ireton, 2013, 53–4. It is noteworthy that the Section 2 of the Act removes the poverty reduction requirement in respect of British overseas territories.
57. There is another power created by the Act, which was initially rarely used, but became more important later, allowing the department to issue loans, provide guarantees, or acquire securities of a company (as well as authorising the core business of making grants).
58. This interpretation is corroborated in DFID's 2003 Departmental Report (Cm 5914, May 2003, 13). Incidentally, the Act does not preclude the purchase of weapons. Short wanted, in the wake of a crisis in Sierra Leone in which armed gangs tried to replace the legitimate government, to have the authority if necessary to do that. Arms purchases do not, though, count as official development assistance (aid) under the OECD rules, so if it were done under the 2002 Act (and so far as we are aware, it never has been), that would not count towards the 0.7 per cent target.

NOTES

59. Barder, 2005, 21. (Barder cites Short and the BBC as sources.)
60. In the UK system, main departments are generally headed by secretaries of states, who are Cabinet members. They are supported by junior ministers, most of whom are MPs but who also include appointees from the House of Lords. There is a hierarchy: below Cabinet members, there are ministers of state, and below them parliamentary under secretaries of state. All Short's deputies were parliamentary under secretaries of state. (Hilary Benn was unique in serving in all three ministerial roles in DFID). In practice, the influence of junior ministers depends less on rank and more on what their secretary of state decides to delegate to them and how effective they are.
61. George Foulkes from 1997–2001; Chris Mullin for a few months from January 2001; Hilary Benn from mid-2001 to mid-2002; and Sally Keeble from then until shortly after Clare Short's departure in 2003.
62. In his diary for 30 January 2001 he says this: "I begin to realise what a formidable politician Clare is. Everyone speaks well of her. There is a real sense of loyalty. In three years she has transformed DFID from a backwater, firmly in the grip of the Foreign Office, to an independent department, with its own (expanding) budget, pursuing its own agenda firmly focused on the poorest people in the poorest countries." And on 3 April, recording a discussion with John Vereker on Short's plan for a third minister, he said "there barely seemed enough work for two, let alone three. . . . He [Vereker] agreed." Mullin, 2009, 163, 191. Later, when a minister at the Foreign Office, Mullin described DFID as "a happy Department".
63. Treffgarne interviews.
64. See Chapter 5.
65. While head of the DFID regional office for East Africa from 1999 to 2001, Lowcock conducted the review that proposed these new arrangements.
66. Ministers did, though, see short concept notes at the beginning of the project design phase so were able to satisfy themselves that what was planned was in line with their wishes. (Material provided by Richard Manning.) The levels of delegated authority were later increased and remained high up to 2012.
67. *The DAC Journal*, 2001, I–17.
68. Short, 2004, 260.
69. www.nao.org.uk/reports/department-for-international-development-performance-management-helping-to-reduce-world-poverty/
70. Riddell, 2007, 182.

71. Cassells and Watson, 2001.
72. Having previously been written but kept secret, mostly for fear that candid assessments might offend partner governments.
73. DFID annual Departmental Reports contain information on staffing. The figures are, however, somewhat opaque and can be confusing: staff in scientific units that were contracted out earlier in the 1990s are included in early reports, inflating the figures; conversely staff hired locally into country offices are often not included. We are drawing here and in what follows on that data, and detailed information collected through the Treffgarne interviews.
74. According to Suma Chakrabarti, among other government departments, only the Treasury and Department of Transport at that time had a comparable economic capability.
75. Eyben, 2003.
76. *The DAC Journal*, 2001, I–17.
77. DFID Departmental Report 2002, Cm 5414, April 2002, 90.
78. Interviews with authors and Treffgarne interviews.
79. Some former senior officials go further than this, criticising the professional groups for tending to proselytise for their sectors, with damaging consequences.
80. Interviews with authors and Treffgarne interviews. Short joked that she had needed to get a larger table in her office to accommodate all the people she wanted in discussions. Short, 2004, 80.

3. Whitehall and the International System

1. Short herself contributed to this impression. See for example Short, 2004, 78–9. Senior officials from the time also told us they spent more hours than they would have preferred resolving and de-escalating quarrels.
2. Barder, 2005, 20. Reinforcing this, one thing that comes out of the Treffgarne interviews is that relations with the Treasury were particularly strong: each side valued the other's respect for evidence, data, and analysis.
3. Hill, 2001, 346.
4. Pedley, 2003. assets.publishing.service.gov.uk/government/uploads/system/uploads/attachment_data/file/67939/ev644.pdf
5. These rules essentially set the criteria which must be satisfied for a good to qualify as "from" a country. It requires that the materials constituting a good have been "sufficiently transformed" in a country before the good can benefit from the trade preferences afforded to that country. They aim to prevent a good from a high-income country being routed through a

NOTES

low-income country with little change in order to benefit from tariff or quota-free status.
6. See, for example, Page and Hewitt, 2002. Their primary – fair – criticism was that the "LDC" category was too expansive and included relatively well-off countries, since it is not determined solely by income. Since poor countries mainly compete with each other in trade, extending benefits to relatively rich ones would divert trade from the poorest to the less poor.
7. See Ireton, 2013, 99–116, for a fuller description.
8. See Lowcock, 2022, 4–8.
9. Lowcock bears part of the responsibility. In mid-August he was at home on holiday while waiting for his next assignment, having just returned from three years in southern Africa. He was called one evening and asked to come to work for a few days to design a compensation scheme for the victims of the volcano. Arriving at the office in the middle of the following morning, he was told that he would be presenting his proposals to the secretary of state that lunchtime, so she could announce them the same afternoon. The scheme devised was not sophisticated.
10. Short, 2004, 91–102.
11. Seldon, 2004, 392–407.
12. Barder, 2005, 16–17.
13. publications.parliament.uk/pa/cm200607/cmselect/cmquad/117/117we08.htm
14. See Chanaa, 2005, for an academic treatment of this problem.
15. A good summary of the situation can be found here: sites.tufts.edu/corruptarmsdeals/tanzanias-air-traffic-control-system/
16. Poverty figures taken from the World Bank World Development Indicators. The suitability of the system was questioned directly by the UN's International Civil Aviation Organization; even in 2002, when the deal was approved, it was noted that a top-class civil aviation system could be purchased for as little as £3.5 million. See: news.bbc.co.uk/1/hi/uk_politics/2044206.stm
17. See: www.theguardian.com/world/2010/feb/06/bae-tanzania-arms-deal and www.theguardian.com/world/2007/jan/15/bae.armstrade
18. Short, 2004, 119–22.
19. See: www.theguardian.com/world/2010/feb/05/bae-systems-arms-deal-corruption
20. As an aside, this report was ahead of its time. Its analysis and findings presage influential academic work published a decade or two later, and

the cast of witnesses and those who submitted written evidence was impressive, including future DFID Chief Economist L. Alan Winters.
21. IDC, 2004, 11. publications.parliament.uk/pa/cm200304/cmselect/cmintdev/79/79.pdf
22. Owen, 2010. www.ippr.org/files/images/media/files/publication/2011/05/Immigration%20under%20Labour%20Nov2010_1812.pdf. Owen had been Jack Straw's special adviser from 1993 to 2005, covering the period (1997–2001) that Straw was home secretary.
23. www.theguardian.com/commentisfree/2015/mar/24/labour-immigration-90s-my-one-regret-host-communities
24. one.oecd.org/document/DCD/DAC(2000)22/En/pdf. As we shall see, the UK's stance on that was overturned in 2021, with ruinous consequences for the aid budget.
25. See, for example, publications.parliament.uk/pa/cm200607/cmselect/cmenvaud/77/7710.htm
26. The 2004 CDI, which assessed aid given in 2003, included a more expansive "security" component, and the UK was an extremely high performer on this new metric, pushing it up the rankings.
27. See, for example, Hulme, 2009, and Richard Manning, 2009.
28. Myles Wickstead, then UK alternate director on the board of the World Bank, recalls an occasion in 1998 when at a board meeting chaired by Mark Malloch Brown (then a vice president at the World Bank, and shortly to become administrator of the UN Development Programme), he was invited to take the floor with the introduction: "Next on my list is Mr Wickstead, who will no doubt tell us yet again about the international development goals." But DFID officials were shrewd as well as relentless in the way they pursued the campaign.
29. Meyer, 2005, 77–8.
30. Birmingham 1998 G7 Communique, quoted in Manning, 2009, 87. On one account, Brian Atwood threatened to resign if the US did not agree (interview with authors).
31. Hilde Johnson became the Norwegian development minister in October 1997; Eveline Herfkens (who had been a director on the World Bank board) the Dutch minister in August 1998; and Heidemarie Wieczorek-Zeul the German minister in October 1998.
32. A full account of the impact of the Utstein group is in Michalopoulos, 2020.
33. See for example Michalopoulos, 2020, 35–7.

34. Quoted in Michalopoulos, 2020, 36. Wieczorek-Zeul called her "stubborn" and "some stubbornness can go a long way". Short herself said the Utstein group "enjoyed our battles in the international system" (Short, 2004, 83).
35. The joint document itself was, however, as Richard Manning recalls, controversial, with NGOs claiming the secretary-general had sold out to the Bretton Woods institutions.
36. Fourteen of the targets were quantifiable.
37. Short, 2004, 89.
38. Interview with authors.
39. Manning, 2009, 96–7. This paper also includes a more detailed comparison between the International Development Goals and the Millennium Development Goals. Manning was from 1997 to 2003 a DFID director general and then became chair of the DAC.
40. Hulme, 2009, 24.
41. Short, 2004, 82. She explicitly credits DFID officials with developing the analysis and arguments she relied on.
42. Short, 2004, 84.
43. DFID 2001 Departmental Report, Cm 5111, March 2001, 37–8; DFID 2003 Departmental Report, Cm 5914, May 2003, 24–5.
44. Treffgarne interviews. It is mentioned almost as often as the MDGs.
45. Aid provided as a proportion of donor countries' GNI was at historically low levels during the 1980s, having been higher in the 1960s and 1970s.
46. Without Johnson, because Norway was (and is) not in the EU.
47. Brown's idea was for an international financing facility, which would borrow on the capital markets against future aid flows to provide an extra $50 billion a year in the short term. This did not fly, but the idea led to the creation of the International Finance Facility for Immunisation, and a few years later (as we will see) Brown set a timetable for the UK to reach 0.7 per cent.
48. At least that was the DFID assessment in early 2003 (DFID 2003 Departmental Report, Cm 5914, May 2003, 24). Ex post, the increases seem to have been larger. Note: these figures are in cash (nominal terms); in Figure 3.2 they have been converted to 2021 prices, which inflates them.
49. Michalopoulos, 2020, 126.
50. Riddell, 2007, 100–1.
51. On which there is a good account in Michalopoulos, 2020, 151–4.
52. www.clareshort.org/speeches/protectionism-in-aid-procurement

NOTES

53. Interviews with authors.
54. Richard Manning recalls being woken up early one morning in London by a British negotiator in Japan, being told "it's not going very well", and replying that the prime minister wants a result, so keep going and they'll agree.
55. That, however, did not include technical assistance or food aid – which explains why in the years around 2005 (and subsequently) 70 per cent of US aid remained tied.
56. Riddell, 2007, 99.
57. And the practical impact of UK untying has frayed in recent years, with UK firms winning a noticeably high proportion of tenders.
58. As described in Chapter 2.
59. We are grateful to Peter Grant, who held senior roles in DFID with responsibility for multilateral aid between 1996 and 2005, for material we are drawing on in this section.
60. The heads of the agencies were not all best pleased. Jim Wolfensohn, president of the World Bank, was reported to have suggested to his staff that they produce a similar report on DFID (private interviews).
61. DANIDA, 2008.
62. Treffgarne interviews.
63. They weren't alone: see, for example, Sandefur, 2023.
64. This section relies heavily on invaluable material provided by Gavin McGillivray, a senior private sector specialist in DFID for many years up to 2021.
65. See eaif.com.
66. Including, as Richard Manning recalls, enthusiastic advocacy from Tony Blair at the Johannesburg summit on sustainable development in 2002, who then tasked DFID with leading the follow-up.

4. "Clare's New World"? The Verdict on the Short Years

1. *Clare's New World* was the title of the 1997 BBC documentary we mentioned at the end of Chapter 1.
2. fred.stlouisfed.org/series/MCOILWTICO
3. Sustained, moderate real economic growth is, almost always, associated with eventual improvements in human development indicators and poverty. See: lantpritchett.org/wp-content/uploads/2022/05/Basics-legatum-paper_short.pdf
4. DFID's annual Departmental Reports all contain detailed analysis and data on its contribution to the millennium goals in the countries it

focused its work on. See, for example, pages 23–7 of the 2001 Departmental Report and 178 and 183 of the 2004 report.
5. Quoted in Barder, 2005, 30.
6. Brown, 2017, 136–7.
7. Seldon, 2004, 406.
8. Seldon, 2007, 322–3.
9. Labour Party, 2001, 40.
10. "Time for common sense" was the curious strap line, and it was fronted by then leader William Hague, who in a later guise as foreign secretary from 2010 was notably supportive of DFID and its first Conservative secretary of state, Andrew Mitchell.
11. House of Commons International Development Committee, 2002.
12. House of Commons International Development Committee, 2003.
13. As Lowcock discovered around 2004, when his young son brought home a geography textbook explaining how DFID's compensation scheme for the victims of the 1997 eruption of the Montserrat volcano, which Lowcock senior had designed one morning that August, had been so miserly that it led to widespread protests by the islanders.

5. The Policy Evolves, the Budget Grows, and DFID's Reputation Blossoms
1. Again, excepting a relatively brief interruption occasioned by the global financial crisis. Source: IMF Primary Commodity Price Index data.
2. All of the growth data in this section is taken from the World Bank's Databank.
3. That is, excluding high income countries in Africa, and including the many developing countries in the rest of the world.
4. It is telling that the main exception to this trend in Africa, South Africa, was the country most integrated into the global economy.
5. DFID, 2006.
6. Sue Unsworth, who from the 1980s had been the most senior woman in the department's management team, was particularly influential. She was widely credited as the person who did most to bring political economy analysis to the heart of thinking in DFID – and to make it less prone to wishful thinking. She died young, sadly, in 2016.
7. hansard.parliament.uk/Commons/2006-10-26/debates/06102646000002/InternationalDevelopment?highlight=2006%20white%20paper%20making%20governance%20work%20poor#contribution-06102646001156. The minister referred to was Gareth Thomas, Benn's deputy.

NOTES

8. For example, DFID, 2005a; DFID, 2005b; DFID, 2010a.
9. Interview with authors.
10. Interview with authors. Anderson worked for the department for nearly a decade from 2003, reaching the rank of director general. He then moved to a senior role in 10 Downing Street.
11. The World Bank did, including through its system for allocating resources to poorer countries, focus on the importance of institutional capacity for development, but it was slow to address conflict and insecurity.
12. See OECD DAC, 2005.
13. *The OECD Journal on Development*, 2006, 10.
14. DFID, 2009.
15. By then prime minister.
16. hansard.parliament.uk/Lords/2009-07-06/debates/0907064000458/InternationalDevelopment?highlight=international%20development%20white%20paper#contribution-0907064000132
17. Michalopoulos, 2020, 172–3.
18. DFID, 2006.
19. DFID, 2009.
20. DFID, 2010b, 73.
21. DFID, 2006; DFID, 2009.
22. DFID thought quite hard about aid allocation within low-income countries, and updated its evidence-based aid allocation model to guide political decisions. This was the focus of debates about whether to allocate money to the countries with the strongest policy environments, or with the greatest needs (often conflict and fragile states); and also about whether DFID wanted to compensate for higher or lower levels of aid from other donors.
23. Interview with authors.
24. Colenso, 2012. (Colenso had previously been head of profession for education in DFID.)
25. Gulrajani, 2010.
26. DFID, 2007, 173.
27. Valters and Whitty, 2017.
28. Appointed to the House of Lords by Tony Blair in 1997, she was a junior minister in the Foreign Office before joining DFID. She was later the UN under-secretary-general for humanitarian affairs.
29. He continues to endear himself to many of them by regularly attending the parties of the DFID Alumni Association.

NOTES

30. Guha and Callan, 2007.
31. Lowcock, the senior DFID official covering the World Bank at the time, was on the call.
32. Interview with authors.
33. Interview with authors.
34. Seldon and Lodge, 2010, 9.
35. Interview with authors.
36. Interview with authors.
37. Interviews with authors.
38. Mitchell, 2021, 156.
39. It's also worth noting that all those we have spoken to found their time at DFID professionally fulfilling, and matched by few other things in their careers. When we asked Hilary Benn which of the many important roles in his now long and distinguished career he had found more fulfilling or enjoyable than being development secretary, he paused for several seconds. "None", he said.
40. Though CDC, a company owned by the department, did that, as covered below.
41. DFID did though sometimes second UK civil servants to work in government departments in developing countries.
42. He also wanted a new challenge. He became governor of Bermuda. (Interview with authors.)
43. Interview with authors.
44. Later, departmental boards in Whitehall were often chaired by ministers; frequently (including in DFID) an executive board chaired by the permanent secretary and operating more like corporate boards slotted in below them.
45. A third director general post was also created on the management board, to which Lowcock was appointed in 2003.
46. Interview with authors.
47. In DFID terminology, senior civil servants were graded as permanent secretary, director general, director, or deputy director. A director headed a division. A deputy director reported to a director, and (confusingly) headed a department. Where we use the word department, though, we are talking about DFID as a whole.
48. Interview with authors.
49. Devanny and Berry, 2021.
50. Valters and Whitty, 2017.

NOTES

51. Treffgarne interviews.
52. Interview with authors.
53. As Richard Manning has pointed out to us, Chakrabarti's reforms went with the thrust of the model that had been championed for much of the 1990s by Bob Ainscow, then the Overseas Development Administration's only director general. (Email correspondence, November 2023.)
54. When Lowcock joined as a graduate trainee in 1985, these Office Instructions ran to three large bound files. The naïve new entrant astonished his colleagues by reading them.
55. *The OECD Journal on Development*, 2006, 69.
56. Interview with authors.
57. *The Guardian*, 4 December 2009.
58. *The OECD Journal on Development*, 2006, 34.
59. In the summer of 2001 Lowcock returned from Africa to become DFID's finance director. One sunny day in August, in his first week in the role, he was visited by the director in the NAO who was responsible for DFID's accounts. The message was that the test version of the accounts prepared in the new format was so bad that they would, if issued for real, be disclaimed – a technical term meaning that they were too inaccurate even to be fit to be qualified. It transpired that no one involved in their preparation and approval, from the lowliest cash book clerk to the permanent secretary, was a qualified accountant. Lowcock signed himself up for years of exams to become a member of the Chartered Institute of Public Finance and Accountancy, encouraged other colleagues to get qualified, too, and hired a number of finance professionals from outside.
60. Interviews with authors.
61. publications.parliament.uk/pa/cm200809/cmselect/cmpubacc/618/618.pdf
62. *DFID Annual Report and Accounts, 2008–09,* July 2009, HC 867-I, 56. The lobby group Stonewall included DFID in its list of the top 100 employers for lesbian, gay, bisexual, and transgender staff.
63. *The OECD Journal on Development*, 2006, 72. This applied to staff across the whole department. In its 2002/03 annual report, the department profiled by way of example George Otto, a junior official in the procurement team based in DFID's headquarters near Glasgow. He described in vivid terms how what he was doing was ending world poverty (*DFID Departmental Report 2002/03*, Cm 5914, 16).
64. The UK's most senior civil servant.

NOTES

65. The mean score was substantially lower, because engagement was weaker in departments with huge numbers of relatively junior staff (like the Department for Work and Pensions, and HM Revenue and Customs).
66. assets.publishing.service.gov.uk/government/uploads/system/uploads/attachment_data/file/867298/Civil-Service-People-Survey-Main-Department-Scores-2009-to-2019.pdf
67. publications.parliament.uk/pa/cm200809/cmselect/cmpubacc/618/618.pdf
68. Interview with authors.
69. Quoted in Valters and Whitty, 2017.
70. *The OECD Journal on Development*, 2006, 71.
71. Dissanayake and Lowcock, 2023. See also Chapter 2.
72. The 2006 International Development (Reporting and Transparency) Act. www.legislation.gov.uk/ukpga/2006/31/pdfs/ukpga_20060031_en.pdf#:~:text=An%20Act%20to%20require%20the%20Secretary%20of%20State,aid%3B%20and%20for%20connected%20purposes.%20%5B25th%20July%202006%5D
73. This sort of data took increasing space in annual departmental reports from 2004 (when the document included an estimate that the department was lifting 2 million people a year out of poverty).
74. Interview with authors.
75. Quoted in Valters and Whitty, 2017.
76. This had also long been a practice of the US Agency for International Development (and still is).
77. Lowcock recalls visiting a hospital in southern Nigeria around this time, and being taken to see its broken diesel generator which was emblazoned with a dusty Union Jack sticker. The generator had stopped working because it was not maintained properly. The sticker and the conversation it provoked inadvertently sent the message that Britain was to blame.
78. odi.org/en/insights/is-dfid-any-good-or-isnt-it-and-whos-asking/
79. Maxwell observed that, by contrast, the Foreign Office was scored in the bottom two categories in six out of the ten criteria.
80. *DFID Annual Report and Resource Accounts 2008–09*, July 2009, HC 867-I, 51.

6. Crises and Summits
1. Though the US spent many tens of billions of dollars over nearly a decade trying to disprove that.
2. See, for example, Brown, 2017, 291–3.

NOTES

3. Interviews with authors.
4. reliefweb.int/report/world/reform-international-humanitarian-system-hilary-benn-dfid-uk (Accessible on relief web: posted 15 December 2004).
5. Interviews with authors.
6. They included a number of DFID staff and their families.
7. Ireton, 2013, 100.
8. See Lowcock, 2022, in particular 5–8, 143–9, 150–77.
9. A 2008 evaluation by Martin Barber and others of the CERF described its faster responses and greater focus on neglected emergencies as "a remarkable achievement". cerf.un.org/sites/default/files/resources/CERF_Two_Year_Evaluation.pdf
10. Interview with authors.
11. Seldon, 2007, 323. Seldon provides a good account of the whole G8 process.
12. Seldon, 2007, 369.
13. Stewart, 2013, 2.
14. Seldon, 2007, 324.
15. And it is noteworthy that they were signed off despite Blair's absence for much of 7 July, when he had to return to London following terrorist attacks in the capital that day.
16. Rawnsley, 2010, 335.
17. Seldon and Lodge, 2010, 154–5.
18. Interview with authors.
19. There is a gripping account of the summit preparations and its conduct in Rawnsley, 2010. See the chapter titled "Trillion Dollar Man" (617–36).
20. Brown, 2017, 323–36.
21. Interviews with authors.
22. Dissanayake, then working for the government of Malawi, saw the benefit of this there.
23. committees.parliament.uk/work/140/effectiveness-of-uk-aid/publications/. Some of these studies tie themselves up in abstruse methodological issues from which they never escape.
24. *DFID Annual Report and Resource Accounts 2008–09*, July 2009, HC 867-I, 40.
25. Valters and Whitty, 2017.
26. Michalopoulos, 2020, 183–5. Things then got worse. Michalopoulos concludes that bilateral donors essentially abandoned the Paris aid effectiveness agenda in the decade after 2010.

NOTES

7. Lives Getting Better: How DFID Made a Difference

1. A number of readers of papers we published in 2023 pointed out additional topics we could have covered, including gender policy, infrastructure, rural and urban livelihoods, a variety of governance issues, financial services, water and sanitation, and a range of environmental challenges. There is much of interest to be said on all of these. They are covered in, for example, the department's annual reports and publications by others (including the parliamentary development committee).
2. Interviews with authors. It was recognised that capable institutions came in a variety of different forms.
3. *DFID in 2009–10: Response to the International Development (Reporting and Transparency) Act 2006*, 70.
4. In the case of Afghanistan, the money was channelled via the World Bank through a dedicated trust fund supported by many donors. This was, in effect, budget support, though it was not reported as that but as a grant to the World Bank.
5. *DFID in 2009–10: Response to the International Development (Reporting and Transparency) Act 2006*, 68–9.
6. Interview in *Finance & Development*, September 2023.
7. Unpublished research for authors by Bernat Camps Adrogue.
8. That is one of the under-discussed dimensions of the current debt crisis in poorer countries.
9. Beynon and Dusu, 2010. Beynon now works for the Center for Global Development.
10. Quoted in Michalopoulos, 2020, 206.
11. Michalopoulos, 2020, 206–7.
12. Interview with authors.
13. www.bbc.co.uk/news/education-18836618
14. Brown, 2017, 391.
15. Lowcock, who thought he followed the issues closely, was impressed with Brown's detailed knowledge when briefing him on the plane from London to the Commonwealth Heads of Government Meeting in Uganda in late 2007, a moment at which Brown had quite a lot else on his mind.
16. Benn also had a background in education, having worked as a special adviser to Education Secretary David Blunkett from 1997 to 1999. At the outset of the Mozambique event Mandela announced he was coming out of retirement to support this cause. At the end of it he re-announced his retirement (Brown, 2017, 191).

17. As time passed, the department provided ever greater detail on its activities through its annual reports. See Volume 1 of the 2009–10 report, pages 21–65, for a detailed (though still summary) description of its contribution to each of the MDGs (including education) across all focus countries. The following paragraphs draw on that material and other annual reports from 2003–10. (Note that the department's own definition of its focus countries changed over time, and includes more than we have examined.)
18. That had also historically been the case in rich countries, including the UK. See Lowcock, 2021, 105 and 111–2.
19. Lowcock was in Malawi when, on the first day of the new school year after the election, a million children (not far short of 10 per cent of the population, and many of them teenagers) showed up in class for the first time.
20. Interviews with authors.
21. Colenso, 2012, 57.
22. This and the following paragraph draw heavily on Treffgarne, 2019.
23. This and subsequent paragraphs draw on Volume 1 of the 2009/10 DFID annual report, pages 21–65, as well as earlier annual reports.
24. Interview with authors.
25. The rationale was compelling: the economic case for immunisation was strong, and borrowing more than may otherwise have been possible could therefore be justified. The EU statistical agency's ruling did, however, raise eyebrows. And the government's accounting for its contribution to IFFIm created a precedent in controversial tinkering with the UK's fiscal rules which was later extended to more dubious propositions, as we will explain in Part III.
26. Pearson et al., 2011.
27. Authors interview with Michael Anderson.
28. Making markets for vaccines. Ideas to action. Washington, DC, Center for Global Development, 2005 (www.vaccineamc.org/files/markets4vaccines.pdf).
29. Advance Market Commitment for Pneumococcal Vaccines Annual Report 2009–10 (www.gavi.org/sites/default/files/document/2009-2010-pneumococcal-amc-annual-reportpdf.pdf).
30. Kremer, Levin, and Snyder, 2020.
31. This section draws on interviews with Minouche Shafik and others and Treffgarne interviews.
32. See for example Hanlon, Barrientos, and Hulme, 2010.

NOTES

33. Some useful early summaries were produced: Davies, 2009; Kabeer, 2009. These papers also document and distil many of the underlying studies.
34. *DFID Annual Report and Accounts 2008/09*, HC867-I, July 2009, 15.
35. We are heavily indebted to Gavin McGillivray for material in this section.
36. *Working with the Private Sector to Eliminate Poverty*, DFID, 2005, web.archive.org/web/20240709091713/https:/healthmarketlinks.org/sites/default/files/resources/2809_file_dfid_private_sector.pdf
37. www.fsdkenya.org/themes/digital-finance/an-overview-of-m-pesa/
38. Wolf, 2024. www.ft.com/content/9d2a98dc-16f9-11d9-bbe8-00000e2511c8
39. CDC Group plc 2010 Annual Report and Accounts. assets.bii.co.uk/wp-content/uploads/2010/06/25150810/Annual-Report-and-Accounts-2010.pdf
40. CDC's returns from 2004 to 2008 were higher than those enjoyed by investors in the MSCI emerging markets index. Of course, these returns also called into question whether CDC was doing more than replacing private sector investors.
41. Harvard Business School, October 2015, "The Impact of Funds – An Evaluation of CDC 2004–12", Josh Lerner, Ann Leamon, Dong Ik Lee. www.hbs.edu/ris/Publication%20Files/Impact%20of%20Funds-Final.ver2_bc4bc8d2-1496-41e2-975c-ea3de9fb57a7.pdf
42. NAO, 2008.
43. Whitty later became a nationally renowned figure as the UK's chief medical officer during the COVID-19 pandemic. One economist commented to Dissanayake shortly after he joined the department that "you can tell Chris is clever because he can make jokes that economists find funny as well as jokes the scientists find funny".
44. Young Lives has produced a number of well-cited research reports.
45. *DFID in 2009–10 Response to the International Development (Reporting and Transparency) Act 2006*, The Stationery Office, 2010, 75. The remainder of the DFID money going to the World Bank went in contributions to their main funds, on which the bank itself took the decisions on which countries and which projects to support. Some of the money going through the UN was for humanitarian response, where governments were sometimes the problem and so could not be the channel for money.
46. *The OECD Journal on Development*, 2006.
47. Our World in Data: ourworldindata.org/extreme-poverty-in-brief
48. For reasons we explained in Chapter 4.

49. See Table 5.2 in Chapter 5.
50. It generally vied for the top spot with the US, most of whose money was provided outside government budgets, limiting its influence on national policy, and the EU – of which the UK was part, and which typically worked in lockstep with DFID. (Analysis of OECD data for authors by Bernat Camps Adrogue. In Afghanistan four of the top ten donors were US government departments, each tending to do their own thing with limited coordination among them.)
51. Douglas Alexander told us that among the few politicians at his wedding were Gordon Brown, Des Browne (defence secretary from 2007), and David Miliband (foreign secretary). They were determined their departments would work well together (interview with authors).
52. Interview with authors.
53. hansard.parliament.uk/Commons/2007-05-09/debates/07050989000009 /IndependentAdvisoryCommitteeOnDevelopmentImpact(IACDI). Its members were impressive, including Rachel Glennerster who later became the DFID chief economist and, in 2024, president of the Center for Global Development. In particular they tried to improve the quality of DFID's own evaluation work, which was later lost sight of somewhat.
54. Conservative Party, 2005.
55. See Mitchell, 2021, 155–91.
56. Owen, 2023.
57. They could also poke fun at their own naivety. Michael Anderson recalls a joke they all enjoyed: "How many DFID advisers does it take to change a light bulb? None. If you supply enough energy at the right voltage and the right price, the light bulb will change itself" (interview with authors).
58. Interview with authors.
59. DAC Peer Review, quoted in *DFID Annual Report and Resource Accounts 2008–09,* July 2009, 10.

8. The Problem Gets Harder

1. Patel, Sandefur, and Subramanian, 2021.
2. According to data accessed from the World Bank databank.
3. Mihalyi and Trebesch, 2023.
4. It is important to be even-handed here. Increased Chinese lending was welcomed by developing countries; they needed the finance. And for the most part, while the deals were untransparent, they were not necessarily predatory. The terms many Chinese entities lent on were fairly similar to

NOTES

the terms China itself received from countries like Japan during its own rapid take-off.
5. Lowcock, 2022, 180–1.
6. See, for example, Pritchett and Kenny, 2013.
7. This section draws heavily on Our World In Data's excellent summary, by Hannah Ritchie and Max Roser: ourworldindata.org/millennium-development-goals
8. ourworldindata.org/millennium-development-goals
9. Shafik remained permanent secretary until March 2011. Following an international competition, the prime minister (David Cameron) appointed Lowcock as her successor. He held the post until July 2017; as the principal adviser to DFID ministers, and the person with whom the buck stopped in implementing their decisions, he is therefore heavily implicated in what the department did in this period.
10. Interviews with authors.
11. According to Martin Dinham's contemporaneous notes, the figure was around 60 per cent.
12. Quotes drawn from Martin Dinham's private records.
13. Mitchell 2021, 157.
14. Umubano, which means "partnership' or "relationship' also operated in Sierra Leone for part of its existence.
15. Collier, 2007.
16. Mitchell, 2021, 187.
17. Mitchell, 2021, 156.
18. Mitchell, 2021, 168.
19. Mitchell, 2021, 190.
20. See, for example, this tweet by Sam Coates, from *The Times*, on X, the platform formerly known as Twitter: twitter.com/SamCoatesSky/status/243968932933943296
21. See, for example: www.independent.co.uk/news/uk/politics/tories-overseas-aid-cut-rishi-sunak-b1761089.html
22. Seldon and Snowdon, 2015, 479–81.
23. Seldon and Snowdon, 2015, 481.
24. Quoted in Barder, 2012, David Cameron's "golden thread" theory of development is a little too convenient, *The Guardian* Online 27 August 2012. www.theguardian.com/global-development/poverty-matters/2012/aug/27/david-cameron-development-theory-convenient
25. Seldon and Snowdon, 2015, Chapters 9 and 27.

NOTES

26. The World Bank's World Development Report in 2011 was on the topic of Conflict, Security and Development, recognising their increasingly intertwined nature: documents1.worldbank.org/curated/en/806531468161369474/pdf/622550PUB0WDR0000public00BOX361476B.pdf
27. A play on the famous first lines of Anna Karenina: "All happy families are alike; each unhappy family is unhappy in its own way."
28. "Inclusive" growth because the department's focus on poverty remained strong, and its increasing focus on girls and women under Justine Greening meant that work to support economic growth needed to also contribute to gender equality.
29. It is not the case that poverty is entirely a phenomenon of fragility, but it is certainly the case that fragile countries are making slower progress against poverty than poor but stable ones. See: www.cgdev.org/blog/do-half-worlds-poor-really-live-fragile-states

9. Old Wine, New Bottles

1. There was some relabelling of things created under Labour (including the system of Public Service Agreements), but the substance of much of what we described in Chapters 2 and 5 was kept and built on.
2. DFID Annual Reports.
3. Valters and Whitty, 2017. Valters and Whitty's paper is the best survey of these issues for the 1997–2017 period.
4. Hughes and Mitchell, 2023. www.cgdev.org/blog/how-did-uks-assessments-multilateral-value-money-affect-aid-allocations; note that the overall message of this blog is that DFID's funding was not fully responsive to *changes* in the multilateral aid review (MAR) score between 2011 and 2016, when it was next undertaken; but the most important indicator is the relationship between scores and allocations, which is strong.
5. *DFID Annual Report 2010–11*, HC989-I, 2
6. *DFID Annual Report and Accounts 2012–13*, HC 12, 27 June 2013.
7. That was part of a wider reduction in the proportion of the UK's bilateral aid (a much broader category than DFID's country programmes) channelled through organisations based in developing countries. Analysis by Sam Hughes of data reported to the OECD CRS shows that in 2010, 22 per cent of UK bilateral ODA (excluding in-donor spend on refugees, students, admin, research, and development awareness) was channelled through organisations based in recipient countries

NOTES

(governments, NGOs, and private firms), whilst 10 per cent was channelled through the equivalent UK-based organisations. By 2020 their positions had reversed with 7 per cent channelled through recipient-based organisations and 35 per cent through UK-based organisations. (Much of the bilateral aid channelled neither through organisations in developing countries nor ones in the UK went though multilateral agencies, in the multi-bi category. It was classified by the DAC as bilateral because the choice over the countries and programmes supported was with the donor, not the agency.)

8. The statement was made in the aid strategy published that November. assets.publishing.service.gov.uk/media/5a81adae40f0b623026989a0/ODA_strategy_final_web_0905.pdf. In fact, the UK continued to provide substantial volumes of general budget support indirectly, because the World Bank and the European Development Fund (among others), for which Britain was among the largest financiers, both continued the practice.
9. Other bilateral donors too increasingly contracted multilateral agencies, NGOs, and private companies for the delivery of specified results and outputs.
10. Honig, 2015.
11. See Chapter 7.
12. icai.independent.gov.uk/review/dfids-trade-development-work-southern-africa/review/
13. Whether that had the effect of increasing public confidence in the quality of UK aid spending is questionable.
14. www.publishwhatyoufund.org/app/uploads/2016/12/2010-Aid-Transparency-Assessment.pdf
15. www.publishwhatyoufund.org/files/2012-Aid-Transparency-Index_web-singles.pdf
16. Quoted in Valters and Whitty, 2017, 30.
17. Dissanayake and Ritchie, 2022.
18. Valters and Whitty, 2017, 30.
19. www.nao.org.uk/reports/investigation-into-the-departments-approach-to-tackling-fraud/
20. An internal review in 2013 called for a stripping back of bureaucratic processes and an improvement of DFID's ability to commission and implement flexible and adaptive programmes (Valters and Whitty, 2017, 30).
21. Correspondence with authors in 2023.

308

NOTES

22. www.cgdev.org/blog/which-government-departments-spend-uk-aid-most-effectively
23. icai.independent.gov.uk/html-version/prosperity-fund/
24. A few other uses were found, of which capital for the Private Infrastructure Development Group, which we discussed in Chapter 3, was the most important, but they were small beer compared to the money for CDC.
25. Mitchell, 2021, 188.
26. Many of these arguments are made convincingly by Moss and Clemens, 2005. They pointed out that the logic used to derive the original target would, by 2005, have implied levels of aid to the poorest countries of just 0.01 per cent of GNI, and negative aid to many developing countries, both absurd.
27. Dissanayake's first job in DFID involved, among other things, copy and pasting responses to hundreds of such letters.
28. Bone was a long-standing Tory MP, though he eventually had the whip withdrawn and was recalled from Parliament in 2023.
29. Heppell, Crines, and Jeffery, 2017.

10. Better Lives: Reprise

1. It is important to emphasise that, as for earlier in the department's life, it is impossible to do justice in the space available here to the scale and breadth of its contribution to the MDGs in this period. What follows is purely illustrative.
2. Though the size of the India programme fell, and it was reshaped to focus on private sector development, reflecting rapid progress there.
3. That did not, however, mean the overseas territories were out of the public eye. In late December 2016 the department hit the headlines over a £285 million airport it had built in St Helena. It was completed on time and within the final budget, but it then transpired that air turbulence around the island – located in the middle of the Atlantic Ocean – meant that the original plan to fly in Boeing 737s was not viable. It looked like DFID had created a white elephant. In fact, other aircraft were found which could use the runway successfully and a weekly air service was set up. A legal case was brought against the consultants who had recommended the 737s. It was settled out of court, with the consultants both denying any wrongdoing and making a seven-figure payment to the department. Had the problem been identified at the outset, the airport would probably never have been built – so the error benefitted the Saints.

NOTES

4. Over this period, the UK was much the most poverty-focused of the five largest bilateral donors. See: www.cgdev.org/publication/assessing-uks-oda-focus-poverty-and-africa
5. www.gov.uk/government/news/family-planning-london-summit-11-july-2012
6. IACI Report *Assessing DFID's Results in Nutrition*, 2020, icai.independent.gov.uk/html-version/assessing-dfids-results-in-nutrition/
7. www.gov.uk/government/news/uk-to-protect-140-million-people-from-tropical-diseases
8. www.cartercenter.org/resources/pdfs/news/health_publications/guinea_worm/DFID-Guinea-worm-02032016.pdf. Carter was not the only former US president to engage with DFID. Bill Clinton did so too, visiting the department's London headquarters.
9. www.gov.uk/government/news/uk-and-gates-foundation-commit-to-polio-eradication
10. www.gov.uk/government/news/uk-leads-final-push-to-make-polio-history
11. We are grateful to Susannah Hares at the Center for Global Development for material on this.
12. Barber published books on "Deliverology", and, in 2013, a detailed account of his work in Punjab. rtepakistan.org/wp-content/uploads/2013/03/The_good_news_from_Pakistan_final.pdf
13. www.pearson.com/content/dam/corporate/global/pearson-dot-com/files/michael-barber/The-Punjab-Education-Roadmap.pdf
14. icai.independent.gov.uk/review/icai-report-department-international-developments-bilateral-aid-pakistan/. Recent work has questioned the impact of the programme on learning outcomes. See https://reproducibility.worldbank.org/index.php/catalog/102
15. icai.independent.gov.uk/review/assessing-uk-aids-results-in-education/
16. For example, in this assessment by ICAI on emergency response in the Horn of Africa: icai.independent.gov.uk/wp-content/uploads/ICAI-report-FINAL-DFIDs-humanitarian-emergency-response-in-the-Horn-of-Africa11.pdf
17. *DFID Annual Report and Accounts 2014–15*, HC223, July 2015, 5.
18. Seldon and Snowdon, 2015, 482.
19. web.archive.org/web/20240331230443/https:/www.cdc.gov/vhf/ebola/history/2014-2016-outbreak/index.html
20. For a comprehensive account of the Syria crisis and its humanitarian dimensions, see Lowcock, 2022, 55–88.

NOTES

21. www.gov.uk/government/topical-events/supporting-syria-conference-2016/about
22. *DFID Annual Report & Accounts 2010–11*, foreword by Secretary of State Andrew Mitchell. assets.publishing.service.gov.uk/media/5a7963a140f0b642860d7b55/Annual-report-2011-vol1.pdf
23. DFID, 2010, "The Engine of Development: The Private Sector and Prosperity for Poor people". www.gov.uk/government/publications/the-engine-of-development-the-private-sector-and-prosperity-for-poor-people
24. See, for example, Banerjee, Duflo, Glennerster, and Kinnan, 2015. Note that some nuance is required here: micro-savings schemes may have larger welfare impacts than microcredit schemes, and there are doubtless some situations in which microfinance can be valuable. Nevertheless, the balance of the evidence suggests it should not be a major plank of an economic development portfolio.
25. See Chapter 7.
26. The full text of the speech is here: www.gov.uk/government/speeches/andrew-mitchell-on-the-reform-of-cdc-group-plc
27. For India, for example, in only the eight poorest states.
28. As discussed in Chapter 9, this was the best idea the department could come up with for using the new non-fiscal capital the Treasury had invented.
29. NAO, 2016, 9.
30. The review was completed in 2019 but will have covered investments and deals that were begun during the early post-reforms period, that is from around 2012. icai.independent.gov.uk/review/cdc/review/
31. *DFID Annual Report and Accounts 2015–16*, HC329, July 2016, 5
32. assets.publishing.service.gov.uk/media/5a79dbc840f0b670a8025f24/StrategicVision-OneYearOn.pdf
33. icai.independent.gov.uk/review/vawg/review/
34. It stood outside DFID's small coffee shop, often used for meetings, and through which virtually every staff member in London passed once or twice a day.
35. DFID, 2011.
36. www.economist.com/international/2016/05/12/what-david-camerons-anti-corruption-summit-did-and-didnt-achieve
37. www.gov.uk/government/speeches/stephen-obrien-transparency-accountability-and-good-governance
38. assets.publishing.service.gov.uk/media/5a7cba9eed915d6822362304/GOSAC1.pdf

39. icai.independent.gov.uk/review/dfids-approach-anti-corruption-impact-poor/review/
40. www.theguardian.com/politics/2016/may/11/david-cameron-corporate-money-laundering-offence-anti-corruption-summit
41. thepolicypractice.com/sites/default/files/2020-05/is-dfid-getting-real-about-politics-final-report-march-2016.pdf
42. thepolicypractice.com/sites/default/files/2020-05/is-dfid-getting-real-about-politics-final-report-march-2016.pdf
43. *DFID Annual Report 2010/11*, 9.
44. The parliamentary development committee singled this project out for praise in their 2019 report.
45. www.greenclimate.fund/news/united-kingdom-pledges-double-contribution-green-climate-fund
46. icai.independent.gov.uk/review/uks-international-climate-fund/our-approach/
47. publications.parliament.uk/pa/cm201719/cmselect/cmintdev/1432/1432.pdf
48. assets.publishing.service.gov.uk/government/uploads/system/uploads/attachment_data/file/553402/2016-UK-Climate-Finance-Results2.pdf
49. Interviews with authors.
50. www.un.org/sg/en/management/hlppost2015.shtml
51. Indeed, Lant Pritchett, a well-known development economist, once told a seminar Dissanayake attended that "the only good thing about the SDGs is that there are so many of them that no-one cares".
52. Michalopoulos, 2020, 230.
53. www.gov.uk/government/publications/uk-aid-tackling-global-challenges-in-the-national-interest
54. Even when, as in the case of Bangladesh, the development path was carved out with tolerance rather than active support from the state.
55. See final sections of Chapters 4 and 7.

11. The Last Gasp
1. A full list of all the ministers who held office in the department from 2016–20 is contained in the DFID Annual Reports and Accounts published in July each year from 2017 to 2020 (HC8, HC1215, HC2390, and HC517).
2. Seldon and Newell, 2019, 363.
3. Mullin, 2020.
4. Rory Stewart was the only person other than Hilary Benn who was both secretary of state and a junior minister in DFID.

NOTES

5. *DFID Annual Report and Accounts 2019–20*, HC517, July 2020.
6. general-election-2010.co.uk/conservative-manifesto-2017-a-strong-and-united-nation-in-a-changing-world/
7. *DFID Annual Report and Accounts 2016–17*, HC 8, July 2017, 7.
8. bbc.co.uk/news/uk-politics-37758164
9. *The Daily Mail* provides one example: www.dailymail.co.uk/news/article-4095882/Britain-scraps-5million-foreign-aid-Ethiopia-s-Spice-Girls-Mail-revealed-blood-boiling-waste-taxpayers-money.html
10. *DFID Annual Report and Accounts 2017–18*, HC1215, July 2018, 7.
11. Lowcock, 2022, 203–5.
12. *DFID Annual Report and Accounts 2018–19*, HC2390, July 2019, 7.
13. www.conservatives.com/our-plan/conservative-party-manifesto-2019, 52, 55.
14. *DFID Annual Report and Accounts 2019–20*, HC517, July 2020, 6–7.
15. *DFID Annual Report and Accounts 2019–20*, HC517, July 2020, 29–60.
16. *DFID's Work on Education*, HC 367, Session 2017–19, November 2017.
17. *Definition and administration of oda*, HC 547 June 2018, 3–4.
18. *Definition and administration of oda*, HC 547 June 2018, 4.
19. Seldon and Newell, 2019.
20. For an account of that, see Lowcock, 2022, x–xv.
21. We are much indebted to Gavin McGillivray for detailed information on the DFID's oversight of CDC in this period.
22. *DFID Annual Report and Accounts 2019–20*, HC517, July 2020, 31.
23. www.nao.org.uk/reports/the-effectiveness-of-official-development-assistance-spending/
24. Devanny and Berry, 2021, 100.
25. For a full analysis of the global humanitarian scene from 2016 to 2020, see Lowcock, 2022.
26. *DFID Annual Report and Accounts 2019–20*, HC517 July 2020, 172. (This includes spending in Lebanon and Jordan primarily for Syrians who had fled to those countries to escape the war at home.)
27. World Bank data quoted by Wolf, 2023.

12. **"The Writing Is on the Wall"**
1. Devanny and Berry, 2021. There is an excellent summary of the arguments of the aid sceptics at 97.
2. Devanny and Berry, 2021, 98.
3. www.ft.com/content/03bb726a-157d-11e9-a581-4ff78404524e
4. Seely and Rogers, 2019.

NOTES

5. www.theguardian.com/global-development/2019/dec/19/aid-groups-warn-boris-johnson-against-combining-dfid-with-foreign-office
6. www.bbc.co.uk/news/uk-51507273
7. Mullin, 2020.
8. *Effectiveness of UK aid: Interim Report*, HC215, 9 June 2020.
9. Devanny and Berry, 2021, 87, quoting from Johnson's statement in Parliament on 16 June 2020.
10. Devanny and Berry, 2021, 105.
11. Devanny and Berry, 2021, 108.
12. Nicholas Westcott, *The Death of DFID*, quoted in Devanny and Berry, 109.
13. Quoted in Devanny and Berry, 2021, 110.
14. Quoted in Devanny and Berry, 2021, 108.
15. *Report on potential impact of merger*, HC596, 16 July 2020.
16. Mitchell, 2021, 350–53.
17. Interview with authors.
18. Interview with authors.
19. Interview with authors. The committee remained active, producing reports on, for example, Afghanistan, nutrition, COVID-19, debt relief, extreme poverty and the SDGs, climate, humanitarian crises, Ghana, Tigray, and Pakistan. The government similarly attempted to clip the wings of ICAI, including, when it became clear that ICAI would survive, an effort to control what and when it published, which would have destroyed the body's independence. That was also seen off.
20. Devanny and Berry, 2021, 86–112.
21. WhatsApp messages, released by the COVID Inquiry in 2023, between Sedwill and Simon Case, then a senior official at Number 10 and soon to be Sedwill's successor as Cabinet secretary, reveal a concern that the process was being rushed at a time when the relevant civil servants were already under huge pressure from the pandemic.

13. Aftermath

1. icai.independent.gov.uk/review/management-of-the-0-7-oda-spending-target-in-2020/
2. devinit-prod-static.ams3.cdn.digitaloceanspaces.com/media/documents/three-years-of-uk-aid-cuts-where-has-ODA-been-hit-hardest-factsheet-1.pdf
3. www.bond.org.uk/news/2021/05/uk-aid-cuts-little-information-but-devastating-consequences/

NOTES

4. www.publishwhatyoufund.org/2021/05/untangling-the-uk-aid-cuts-a-transparency-journey-timeline/
5. www.cgdev.org/blog/survival-fittest-or-missing-random-how-fcdos-cuts-have-fallen-across-portfolio
6. www.bond.org.uk/news/2021/05/uk-aid-cuts-little-information-but-devastating-consequences/
7. blogs.lse.ac.uk/politicsandpolicy/uk-oda-cuts/
8. www.bbc.co.uk/news/uk-politics-66378364
9. www.cgdev.org/publication/how-reverse-decline-poverty-focus-uk-aid
10. Interviews with authors.
11. www.civilserviceworld.com/news/article/fco-and-dfid-merger-seen-as-failure-survey-of-officials-finds
12. Interview with authors.
13. www.usaid.gov/news-information/speeches/jul-18-2022-administrator-power-speech-line-between-crisis-and-catastrophe. Power announced an additional $5 billion in US emergency assistance to help countries combatting a growing hunger problem when Russia's invasion of Ukraine led to a spike in global food prices.
14. Interview with authors.
15. www.telegraph.co.uk/global-health/terror-and-security/butt-jokes-model-what-not-do-how-britain-became-used-car-salesman/
16. *The Four Corners*, Issue 64, October 2023.
17. The following pages draw *inter alia* on private interviews with several people then or at the time of writing serving in government.
18. www.gov.uk/government/collections/the-integrated-review-2021
19. www.bond.org.uk/news/2022/05/the-international-development-strategy-a-rapid-assessment/
20. Mitchell, 2021, 260.
21. www.theguardian.com/politics/2021/jun/08/not-democracy-deny-mps-vote-aid-cuts-andrew-mitchell-says
22. www.theguardian.com/politics/live/2021/jul/13/uk-covid-live-news-sage-cases-nhs-coronavirus-aid-debate
23. www.bbc.co.uk/news/uk-politics-53062858
24. The following paragraphs draw on discussions and private correspondence with several current and previous members of the Cabinet and Shadow Cabinet as well as with Labour Party staff, and on papers commissioned by the Labour Party from a variety of experts from 2021 to 2024.
25. The Rest Is Politics Podcast, July 2022 and February 2023.

NOTES

26. www.devex.com/news/uk-labour-leader-starmer-backs-off-pledge-to-restore-aid-department-105657
27. www.devex.com/news/senior-uk-labour-mp-says-party-must-set-up-aid-department-on-day-one-105684

14. Eliminating World Poverty?
1. World Bank data quoted by Wolf, 2023.
2. Figures in the following paragraphs are drawn from published UN, IMF, and World Bank data analysed for the authors by Bernat Camps Adrogue.
3. Lee Crawfurd has recently published useful new analysis of global poverty: Crawfurd, 2024.

BIBLIOGRAPHY

A note on sources
In the writing of *Rise and Fall* we were fortunate in the rich sources available to us. We drew heavily on material put into the public domain by DFID, in particular the annual reports published throughout the department's life.

From 2011, DFID uploaded detailed information on virtually every programme it approved and funded to DevTracker, including project documents (such as Business Cases, Annual Reviews, and Project Completion Reviews) and detailed spending and expenditure data. The database now also includes some (but not all) projects paid for by UK ODA but run by other departments. It is an invaluable reference for those seeking to understand the detail of how DFID sought to achieve its objectives. devtracker.fcdo.gov.uk/

We also conducted structured interviews and drew on interview records given to us by others, as described in the Acknowledgements.

Other primary data we consulted includes:

- DFID Workforce Management Information 2011–2020: www.gov.uk/government/collections/dfid-workforce-management-information-public-body. DFID's staffing numbers and other information is collected here. Note that staffing numbers in this database may, for technical reasons, vary from those presented in annual reports. Where they do, we prefer data from Annual Reports, which better reflect operational reality.
- Our World in Data: ourworldindata.org/. For virtually any question of importance in international development, Our World in

Data has collated the available information and often published useful analyses.
- World Bank, Databank: databank.worldbank.org/. Probably the most comprehensive dataset pertaining to international development available.
- IMF World Economic Outlook Databases: www.imf.org/en/Publications/SPROLLs/world-economic-outlook-databases#sort=%40imfdate%20descending. Again, an invaluable source of data for global economic conditions.
- FRED: Economic Data: fred.stlouisfed.org/. The Federal Reserve's Economic Data.

Relevant published material (which in many cases are cited in footnotes) is set out below.

Baldoumas, Abigael. "UK aid cuts: Little information, but devastating consequences." *Bond*, 20 May 2021. www.bond.org.uk/news/2021/05/uk-aid-cuts-little-information-but-devastating-consequences/

Banerjee, Abhijit, Esther Duflo, Rachel Glennerster, and Cynthia Kinnan. "The miracle of microfinance? Evidence from a randomized evaluation." *American Economic Journal: Applied Economics*, 7(1), 22–53, 2015. www.jstor.org/stable/43189512

Barber, Martin, Abhijit Bhattacharjee, Roberta M. Lossio, and Lewis Sida. "Central Emergency Response Fund: Two year evaluation." CERF, United Nations, July 2008. cerf.un.org/sites/default/files/resources/CERF_Two_Year_Evaluation.pdf

Barber, Michael. "The good news from Pakistan: How a revolutionary new approach to education reform in Punjab shows the way forward for Pakistan and development aid everywhere." London: Reform, 2013.

Barber, Michael and Katelyn Donnelly. "The Punjab education roadmap: Transforming opportunity for 20 million children." *Education Today*, 64(2), 9–12, 2014.

Barder, Owen. "Reforming development assistance: Lessons from the UK experience." CGD working paper 70. Washington, DC: Center for Global Development, 2005. www.cgdev.org/publication/reforming-development-assistance-lessons-uk-experience-working-paper-70

Barder, Owen. "David Cameron's "golden thread" theory of development is a little too convenient." *The Guardian Online*, 27 August 2012. www.theguardian.com/global-development/poverty-matters/2012/aug/27/david-cameron-development-theory-convenient

BBC. "Tanzania radar sale 'waste of cash'." 14 June 2002. news.bbc.co.uk/1/hi/uk_politics/2044206.stm

BBC. "Gordon Brown given UN education role." 14 July 2012. www.bbc.co.uk/news/education-18836618

BBC. "Aid to be cut unless it is value for money, says Patel." 25 October 2016. www.bbc.co.uk/news/uk-politics-37758164

BBC. "Cabinet reshuffle: International development and Foreign Office merger?" 14 February 2020. www.bbc.com/news/uk-51507273

BBC. "International development and Foreign Office to merge." 16 June 2022. www.bbc.co.uk/news/uk-politics-53062858

BBC. "UK foreign aid cuts: Thousands will die as a result, says report." 2 August 2023. www.bbc.co.uk/news/uk-politics-66378364

Beynon, Jonathan and Andra Dusu. "Budget support and MDG performance." Development Paper Number 2010/01, European Commission, March 2010. www.eerstekamer.nl/eu/publicatie/20100330/budget_support_and_mdg_performance/document

Bond. "The international development strategy: A rapid assessment." 16 May 2022. www.bond.org.uk/news/2022/05/the-international-development-strategy-a-rapid-assessment/

Brown, Gordon. *My Life, Our Times*. London: The Bodley Head, 2017.

Brown, Will. "'The butt of jokes and a model of what not to do': How Britain became the 'used car salesman' of Africa." *The Daily Telegraph*, 19 December 2022. www.telegraph.co.uk/global-health/terror-and-security/butt-jokes-model-what-not-do-how-britain-became-used-car-salesman/

Cabinet Office. "Civil service people survey summary of main department scores 2009 to 2019." London: Cabinet Office, 2020.

Cable, Vince. *Money and Power: The 16 World Leaders Who Changed Economics*. London: Atlantic Books, 2022.

Campbell, Alastair. *The Blair Years: Extracts from the Alastair Campbell Diaries*. London: Hutchinson, 2007.

Cassells, Andrew and Julia Watson. "ODA/DFID support to health sector reform and health sector management: Synthesis study." Evaluation Report EV594. London: DFID, 2001.

CDC. Annual Report and Accounts 2009–10. London: CDC Group plc, 2010.

Center for Global Development. *Making Markets for Vaccines: Ideas to Action*. Report of the Center for Global Development Advance Market Commitment Working Group. Washington, DC: Center for Global Development, 2005. www.cgdev.org/publication/9781933286020-making-markets-vaccines-ideas-action

Chanaa, Jane. "Arms sales and development: Making the critical connection." *Development in Practice*, 15(5), 710–16. August 2005. www.jstor.org/stable/4030151

Claussen, Jens, Philip Amis, Simon Delay, and John McGrath. "Malawi Country Report." *Joint Evaluation of General Budget Support 1994–2004*, 2006. assets.publishing.service.gov.uk/media/5a79841240f0b63d72fc675c/gbs-malawi.pdf

Colenso, Peter. "Donor policies: The evolution and development of DFID's commitment to education in fragile states 2000–10" in Zuki Karpinska (ed.), *Education, Aid and Aid Agencies*. London: Continuum, 2012.

Collier, Paul. *The Bottom Billion: Why the Poorest Countries Are Failing and What Can Be Done about It*. Oxford: Oxford University Press, 2007.

Conservative Party. *It's Time for Action: Conservative Election Manifesto 2004*, Conservative Party, 2005.

Conservative Party. *Conservative Manifesto 2017: A Strong and United Nation in a Changing World*, Conservative Party, 2017.

Conservative Party. *Get Brexit Done. Unleash Britain's Potential: The Conservative and Unionist Party Manifesto 2019*, Conservative Party, 2019.

Cook, Robin. *The Point of Departure*. London: Simon and Schuster, 2003.

Crawfurd, Lee. "Do half the world's poor really live in fragile states?" Center for Global Development blog, 9 February 2024. www.cgdev.org/blog/do-half-worlds-poor-really-live-fragile-states

The DAC Journal. "Development cooperation review of the United Kingdom." 2(4), I6-I100, 2001. www.oecd-ilibrary.org/development/the-dac-journal_journal_dev-v2-4-en

The Daily Mail. "Britain scraps £9million foreign aid for Ethiopia's Spice Girls after Mail revealed 'blood boiling' waste of taxpayers' money." 6 January 2017. www.dailymail.co.uk/news/article

BIBLIOGRAPHY

-4095882/Britain-scraps-5million-foreign-aid-Ethiopia-s-Spice-Girls-Mail-revealed-blood-boiling-waste-taxpayers-money.html

DANIDA. "Assessing multilateral organisation effectiveness." Evaluation Study 2008/3, Ministry of Foreign Affairs of Denmark, 2008. web.archive.org/web/20210311132606/http:/www.oecd.org/derec/denmark/42211723.pdf

Davies, Mark. *DFID Social Transfers Evaluation Summary Report*. DFID Evaluation Department Working Paper 31, July 2009. assets.publishing.service.gov.uk/media/5a79e9aee5274a684690cfee/dfid-soc-trsfrs-summ-rpt-wp-31.pdf

Delong, J. Bradford. *Slouching Towards Utopia: An Economic History of the Twentieth Century*. New York: Basic Books, 2022.

Dercon, Stefan. *Gambling on Development: Why Some Countries Win and Others Lose*. London: Hurst and Company, 2022.

Devanny, Joe and Philip A. Berry. "The Conservative Party and DFID: Party statecraft and development policy since 1997." *Contemporary British History*, 36(1), 86–123, 2021.

Development Initiatives. "Three years of UK aid cuts: Where has ODA been hit hardest?" Bristol: Development Initiatives, 2023.

DFID. *Eliminating World Poverty: A Challenge for the 21st Century*. White Paper on International Development, Presented to Parliament by the Secretary of State for International Development by Command of Her Majesty, Cm 3789, November 1997.

DFID. *Eliminating World Poverty: Making Globalization Work for the Poor*. White Paper on International Development, Presented to Parliament by the Secretary of State for International Development by Command of Her Majesty, Cm 5006, December 2000.

DFID. *Fighting Poverty to Build a Safer World: A Strategy for Security and Development*. London: DFID, 2005a.

DFID. *Why We Need to Work More Effectively in Fragile States*. London: DFID, 2005b.

DFID. *Working with the Private Sector to Eliminate Poverty*. London: DFID, 2005c.

DFID. *Eliminating World Poverty: Making Governance Work for the Poor*. White Paper on International Development, Presented to Parliament by the Secretary of State for International Development by Command of Her Majesty, Cm 6876, July 2006.

DFID. *DFID Annual Report 2007*. London: The Stationery Office, May 2007.

DFID. *Eliminating World Poverty: Building Our Common Future.* White Paper on International Development, Presented to Parliament by the Secretary of State for International Development by Command of Her Majesty, Cm 7656, July 2009.

DFID. *Building the State and Securing the Peace.* London: DFID, 2010a.

DFID. *DFID in 2009–10.* London: The Stationery Office, July 2010b.

DFID. *The Engine of Development: The Private Sector and Prosperity for Poor People.* London: DFID, 2010c.

DFID. *Governance Portfolio Review Summary.* London: DFID, 2011.

DFID. *The Strategic Vision for Girls and Women: One Year On.* London: DFID, 2012.

DFID. *Operational Plan 2011–2015: Governance, Open Societies and Anti-Corruption Department, Update.* London: DFID, June 2013.

DFID. *Is DFID Getting Real About Politics?* London: DFID, 2016.

Dissanayake, Ranil and Mark Lowcock. "Setting the Compass for Eliminating World Poverty: The Department for International Development 1997–2003." CGD Policy Paper 311. Washington, DC: Center for Global Development, 2023. www.cgdev.org/publication/setting-compass-eliminating-world-poverty-department-international-development-1997

Dissanayake, Ranil and Euan Ritchie. "A Higher Bar or an Obstacle Course? Peer Review and Organizational Decision-Making in an International Development Bureaucracy." CGD working paper 615, Washington, DC: Center for Global Development, 2022. www.cgdev.org/publication/higher-bar-or-obstacle-course-peer-review-and-organizational-decision-making

Dorling, Danny. *Slowdown: The End of the Great Acceleration – and Why It's a Good Thing.* New Haven: Yale University Press, 2020.

Duncan, Alan. *In the Thick of It: The Private Diaries of a Minister.* London: William Collins, 2021.

Dunt, Ian. *How Westminster Works . . . and Why It Doesn't.* London: Weidenfeld and Nicholson, 2023.

Dunton, Jim. "FCO and DfID merger seen as failure, survey of officials finds." Civil Service World, 29 September 2021. www.civilserviceworld.com/news/article/fco-and-dfid-merger-seen-as-failure-survey-of-officials-finds

The Economist. "A Short treatise on globalisation." 14 December 2000.

The Economist. "No praise, please, I'm Labour." 4 January 2001.

The Economist. "What David Cameron's anti-corruption summit did and didn't achieve." 12 May 2016.

Elliott, Francis and James Hanning. *Cameron: The Rise of the New Conservative*. London: Fourth Estate, 2007.

Eyben, Rosalind. "Mainstreaming the social dimension into the Overseas Development Administration: A partial history." *Journal of International Development*, 15, 879–92, 2003. doi.org/10.1002/jid.1041

The Financial Times. "Boris Johnson calls for UK's aid department to be closed." 11 January 2019.

Gavi. "Advance market commitment for pneumococcal vaccines annual report 2009–10." 2010.

The Guardian. "BAE's secret $12m payout in African deal." 15 January 2007.

The Guardian. "BAE admits guilt over corrupt arms deals." 6 February 2010a.

The Guardian. "BAE deal with Tanzania: Military air traffic control – for country with no airforce." 6 February 2010b.

The Guardian. "Civil servants face axe as Brown acts to cut deficit." 4 December 2009.

The Guardian. "I stand by Labour's immigration policy in the 90s. But I do have one regret." 24 March 2015.

The Guardian. "David Cameron to introduce new corporate money-laundering offence." 12 May 2016.

The Guardian. "Aid groups warn Boris Johnson against combining DfID with Foreign Office." 19 December 2019.

The Guardian. "'Not democracy' to deny MPs a vote on overseas aid cuts." 8 June 2021.

The Guardian. "MPs vote to approve £4bn foreign aid cut amid claims it could last for years – as it happened." 13 July 2021.

Guha, Krishna and Eoin Callan. "Wolfowitz laid out terms for partner's pay package." *The Financial Times*, 12 April 2007. www.ft.com/cms/s/42f29804-e8ae-11db-b2c3-000b5df10621.html

Gulrajani, Nilima. *Re-imagining Canadian Development Cooperation: A Comparative Examination of Norway and the UK*. Toronto: Walter and Duncan Gordon Foundation, 2010.

Hanlon, Joseph, Armando Barrientos, and David Hulme. *Just Give Money to the Poor: The Development Revolution from the Global South*. Boulder: Kumarian Press, 2010.

Heppell, Timothy, Andrew Crines, and David Jeffery. "The UK government and the 0.7% international aid target: Opinion among conservative parliamentarians." *British Journal of Politics and International Relations*, 19(4), 895–909, ISSN 1369–1481, 2017. doi.org/10.1177/1369148117726247

Hill, Christopher. "Foreign Policy" in Anthony Seldon (ed.), *The Blair Effect*. London: Little, Brown, 2001.

HM Government. 2016 UK Climate Finance Results, 2016.

HM Government. *Global Britain in a Competitive Age: The Integrated Review of Security, Defence, Development and Foreign Policy*, CP 403. London: Her Majesty's Stationery Office, 2021.

HM Treasury and DFID. UK aid: Tackling global challenges in the national interest, Cm 9163. London: Her Majesty's Stationery Office, 2015.

Honig, Daniel. "Navigating by Judgment: Organizational Structure, Autonomy, and Country Context in Delivering Foreign Aid." Doctoral dissertation, Harvard University, Graduate School of Arts & Sciences, 2015.

House of Commons International Development Committee. *Financing for Development: Finding the Money to Eliminate World Poverty*, HC785-I, July 2002.

House of Commons International Development Committee, DFID Departmental Report 2003, HC825, October 2003.

House of Commons Public Accounts Committee. Assessment of the Capability Review programme, Forty-fifth Report of Session 2008–09, HC 618. London: The Stationery Office Limited, 2009.

Hughes, Sam and Ian Mitchell. "How did the UK's assessments of multilateral value for money affect aid allocations?" Center for Global Development blog, 11 December 2023. www.cgdev.org/blog/how-did-uks-assessments-multilateral-value-money-affect-aid-allocations

Hughes, Sam and Ian Mitchell. "How to reverse the decline in the poverty focus of UK aid." CGD Note. Washington, DC: Center for Global Development, 2023. www.cgdev.org/publication/how-reverse-decline-poverty-focus-uk-aid

Hulme, David. "The Millennium Development Goals (MDGs): A short history of the world's biggest promise." Brooks World Poverty Institute Working Paper 100, 2009.

ICAI. Report: DFID's Humanitarian emergency response in the Horn of Africa, ICAI Review. London: ICAI, 2012.

ICAI. Report: Evaluation of DFID's bilateral aid to Pakistan, ICAI Review. London: ICAI, 2012.

ICAI. Report: DFID's approach to anti-corruption and its impact on the poor, ICAI Review. ICAI: London, 2014.

ICAI. Report: The UK's International Climate Fund, ICAI Review. London: ICAI, 2014.

ICAI. Report: The cross-government Prosperity Fund, ICAI Rapid Review. London: ICAI, 2015.

ICAI. Report: DFID's efforts to eliminate violence against women and girls. ICAI Review. London: ICAI, 2016.

ICAI. Report: CDC's investments in low-income and fragile states, ICAI Review. London: ICAI, 2019.

ICAI. Report: Assessing DFID's results in nutrition, ICAI Results Review. London: ICAI, 2020.

ICAI. Report: Management of the 0.7% ODA spending target in 2020, ICAI Review. London: ICAI, 2021.

ICAI. Report: Assessing UK aid's results in education, ICAI Review. London: ICAI, 2022.

IDC. Migration and Development: How to make migration work for poverty reduction, House of Commons Library, 2004.

IDC. DFID's work on education: Leaving no one behind? First Report of Session 2017–19, HC 367, House of Commons Library, 2017.

IDC. UK aid for combating climate change Eleventh Report of Session 2017–19. HC 1432, House of Commons Library, 2019a.

IDC. Definition and administration of ODA Fifth Report of Session 2017–19, HC 547, House of Commons Library, 2019b.

IDC. Effectiveness of UK Aid: Interim Report and Effectiveness of UK Aid: potential impact of FCO/DFID merger: Government Response to the Second & Fourth Reports of the Committee Fourth Special Report of Session 2019–21, HC820, House of Commons Library, 2020a.

IDC. Effectiveness of UK aid: Potential impact of FCO/DFID merger Fourth Report of Session 2019–2. HC 215, House of Commons Library, 2020b.

The International Development (Reporting and Transparency) Act 2006. www.legislation.gov.uk/ukpga/2006/31/pdfs/ukpga_20060031_en.pdf

Ireton, Barrie. *Britain's International Development Policies: A History of DFID and Overseas Aid*. London: Palgrave Macmillan, 2013.

Jenkins, Elma. "Untangling the UK aid cuts – a transparency journey timeline." Publish What You Fund blog, 12 May 2021. www.publishwhatyoufund.org/2021/05/untangling-the-uk-aid-cuts-a-transparency-journey-timeline/

Journal of International Development. "Special issue: The United Kingdom white paper on international development." March/April 1998, 151–276. onlinelibrary.wiley.com/toc/10991328/1998/10/2

Kabeer, Naila. "Scoping Study on Social Protection Evidence on impacts and future research directions." London: DFID, 2009.

Kampfner, John. *Blair's Wars.* London: The Free Press, 2003.

Kenny, Charles. "We should be spending more of available aid in poorer countries, not less." CGD Working Paper 564. Washington, DC: Center for Global Development, 2021. www.cgdev.org/publication/we-should-be-spending-more-available-aid-poorer-countries-not-less

Kenny, Charles. *Getting Better: Why Global Development Is Succeeding – And How We Can Improve the World Even More.* London: Basic Books, 2011.

Kremer, Michael, Jonathan D. Levin, and Christopher M. Snyder. "Advance market commitments: Insights from theory and experience." NBER Working Paper No. 26775, February 2020.

Labour Party. *Britain in the World.* Labour Party, 1996.

Labour Party. *Labour Party Manifesto.* Labour Party, 1997.

Labour Party. *Ambitions for Britain: Labour's Manifesto for 2001.* Labour Party, 2001.

Lankester, Tim. *The Politics and Economics of Britain's Foreign Aid.* New York: Routledge, 2013.

Lerner, Josh, Ann Leamon, and Dong Ik Lee. "The impact of funds: An evaluation of CDC 2004–12." Harvard Business School, 2015. www.hbs.edu/ris/Publication%20Files/Impact%20of%20Funds-Final.ver2_bc4bc8d2-1496-41e2-975c-ea3de9fb57a7.pdf

Lowcock, Mark. *Ten Generations: A Family Story from Rags to Riches.* London: Matador, 2021.

Lowcock, Mark. *Relief Chief: A Manifesto for Saving Lives in Dire Times.* Washington, DC: Center for Global Development, 2022.

Manning, Richard. "Using Indicators to Encourage Development: Lessons from the Millennium Development Goals." Danish Institute for International Studies, 2009.

Maxwell, Simon. "Is DFID any good or isn't it? And who's asking?" ODI, 2007. odi.org/en/insights/is-dfid-any-good-or-isnt-it-and-whos-asking/
Merrick, Rob. "Senior UK Labour MP says party must set up aid department 'on day one'." *Devex*, 8 June 2023. www.devex.com/news/senior-uk-labour-mp-says-party-must-set-up-aid-department-on-day-one-105684
Merrick, Rob. "UK Labour leader Starmer backs off pledge to restore aid department." *Devex*, 2 June 2023. www.devex.com/news/uk-labour-leader-starmer-backs-off-pledge-to-restore-aid-department-105657
Meyer, Christopher. *DC Confidential: The Controversial Memoirs of Britain's Ambassador to the U.S. at the Time of 9/11 and the Run-Up to the Iraq War*. London: Weidenfeld and Nicholson, 2005.
Michalopoulos, Constantine. *Ending World Poverty: Four Women's Noble Conspiracy*. Oxford: Oxford University Press, 2020.
Mihalyi, David and Christoph Trebesch. "Who lends to Africa and how? Introducing the Africa debt database." Kiel Institute for the World Economy Working Paper 2117, ISSN 1862–1155, 2023. www.ifw-kiel.de/publications/who-lends-to-africa-and-how-introducing-the-africa-debt-database-20876/
Mitchell, Andrew. *Beyond a Fringe: Tales from a Reformed Establishment Lackey*. London: Biteback, 2021.
Mitchell, Ian and Sam Hughes. "Which government departments spend UK aid most effectively?" Center for Global Development blog, 7 December 2020. www.cgdev.org/blog/which-government-departments-spend-uk-aid-most-effectively
Moss, Todd and Michael Clemens. "Ghost of 0.7%: Origins and relevance of the international aid target." CGD Working Paper 68, Washington, DC: Center for Global Development, 2005. www.cgdev.org/publication/ghost-07-origins-and-relevance-international-aid-target-working-paper-68
Mullin, Chris. "At DFID." *London Review of Books*, 19 March 2020.
Mullin, Chris. *A View from the Foothills*. London: Profile Books, 2009.
Nandagiri, Rishita, Joe Strong, Tiziana Leone, and Ernestina Coast. "Recent UK cuts to global health funding will cause irrevocable damage under the guise of 'tough but necessary decisions.'" LSE British Politics and Policy blog, 26 May 2021. blogs.lse.ac.uk/politicsandpolicy/uk-oda-cuts/

NAO. Investing for development: the Department for International Development's oversight of CDC Group plc. www.nao.org.uk/wp-content/uploads/2008/12/080918.pdf, 2008.

NAO. Department for International Development: investing through CDC, Report by the Comptroller and Auditor General. HC 784, National Audit Office, 2016.

NAO. Investigation into the Department for International Development's approach to tackling fraud: Report by the Comptroller and Auditor General, HC1012, 2017.

NAO. The effectiveness of Official Development Assistance expenditure, HC2218. London: National Audit Office, 2019.

OECD. *Shaping the 21st Century: The Contribution of Development Cooperation*. OECD, May 1996.

OECD DAC. United Kingdom, Development Co-Operation Review Series, No. 25, Development Assistance Committee, read.oecd-ilibrary.org/development/development-co-operation-reviews-united-kingdom-1998_9789264162778-en#page2, 1997.

OECD DAC. Review of ODA Reporting of the Costs of Refugees in Donor Countries, Development Co-Operation Directorate, DCD/DAC (2000)22, one.oecd.org/document/DCD/DAC(2000)22/En/pdf, 2000.

OECD DAC. *Principles for Good International Engagement in Fragile States*. Paris: OECD DAC, 2005.

The OECD Journal on Development. 7(3), OECD, 2006.

Olivié, Iliana and Aitor Perez (eds.), *Aid Power and Politics*. New York: Routledge, 2020.

Owen, Ed. "Reactive, defensive and weak" in Tim Finch and David Goodhart (eds.), *Immigration under Labour*. IPPR, 2010.

Owen, Nicholas. "Minouche Shafik: The everywhere economist." *Finance and Development*, 1 September 2023. Washington, DC: IMF. www.imf.org/en/Publications/fandd/issues/2023/09/PIE-the-everywhere-economist-minouche-shafik

Page, Sheila and Adrian Hewitt. "The new European trade preferences: Does 'everything but arms' (EBA) help the poor?" *Development Policy Review*, 20(1), 91–102, 2002. doi.org/10.1111/1467-7679.00159

Patel, Dev, Justin Sandefur, and Arvind Subramanian. "The new era of unconditional convergence." *Journal of Development Econom-

ics, 152, ISSN 0304–3878, 2021. doi.org/10.1016/j.jdeveco.2021.102687

Pearson, Mark, Jeremy Clarke, Laird Ward, Cheri Grace, Daniel Harris, and Matthew Cooper. "Evaluation of the international finance facility for immunisation (IFFIm)." HSLP, 2011. iffim.org/sites/default/files/evaluations/IFFIm-Evaluation-Main-Report-HLSP-21-June-2011.pdf

Pedley, David. "Changes in strategic influence: DFID's contribution to trade policy." Evaluation Report EV644. London: DFID, 2003.

Perlo-Freeman, Samuel. "Tanzania's air traffic control system." Tufts University Fletcher School, 2017. sites.tufts.edu/corruptarmsdeals/tanzanias-air-traffic-control-system/

Piketty, Thomas. *Capital in the Twenty-First Century*. Cambridge: Belknap Press of Harvard University, 2014.

Pinker, Steven. *Enlightenment Now: The Case for Reason, Science, Humanism, and Progress*. Viking, 2018.

Pritchett, Lant and Charles Kenny. "Promoting millennium development ideals: The risks of defining development down." CGD Working Paper 338. Washington, DC: Center for Global Development, 2013. www.cgdev.org/publication/promoting-millennium-development-ideals-risks-defining-development-down-working-paper

Pritchett, Lant with Addison Lewis. "Economic growth *is* enough and only economic growth is enough." Mimeo, 2022. lantpritchett.org/wp-content/uploads/2022/05/Basics-legatum-paper_short.pdf

Publish What You Fund. Aid Transparency Assessment, 2010. www.publishwhatyoufund.org/app/uploads/2016/12/2010-Aid-Transparency-Assessment.pdf

Publish What You Fund. Aid Transparency Assessment, 2012. www.publishwhatyoufund.org/files/2012-Aid-Transparency-Index_web-singles.pdf

Rawnsley, Andrew. *Servants of the People: The Inside Story of New Labour*. London: Penguin, 2000.

Rawnsley, Andrew. *The End of the Party: The Rise and Fall of New Labour*. London: Viking, 2010.

Reeves, Rachel. *Women of Westminster: The MPs Who Changed Politics*. London: I. B. Taurus, 2019.

Report by the Comptroller and Auditor General. *Department for International Development: Performance Management: Helping to Reduce World Poverty*. London: The Stationery Office, 2002.

Ricketts, Peter. *Hard Choices: What Britian Does Next*. London: Atlantic Books, 2021.

Riddell, Roger. *Does Foreign Aid Really Work?* Oxford: Oxford University Press, 2007.

Ridley, Matt. *The Rational Optimist*. London: Fourth Estate, 2010.

Ritchie, Euan and Ranil Dissanayake. "Survival of the fittest or missing at random? How FCDO's cuts have fallen across the portfolio." Center for Global Development blog, 5 August 2021. www.cgdev.org/blog/survival-fittest-or-missing-random-how-fcdos-cuts-have-fallen-across-portfolio

Ritchie, Euan, Ian Mitchell, and Sam Hughes. "Assessing the UK's ODA focus on poverty and Africa." Center for Global Development Note. Washington, DC: Center for Global Development, 2021. www.cgdev.org/publication/assessing-uks-oda-focus-poverty-and-africa

Ritchie, Hannah and Max Roser. "Now it is possible to take stock: Did the world achieve the Millennium Development Goals?" Published online at OurWorldInData.org, 2018, ourworldindata.org/millennium-development-goals

Robert Cassen and Associates. *Does Aid Work?* Oxford: Oxford University Press, 1986.

Sabin, Paul. *The Bet: Paul Ehrlich, Julian Simon, and Our Gamble over Earth's Future*. New Haven: Yale University Press, 2013.

Sandefur, Justin. "How economists got Africa's aid epidemic wrong." Center for Global Development blog, 31 May 2023. www.cgdev.org/blog/how-economists-got-africas-aids-epidemic-wrong

Seely, Bob and James Rogers. "Global Britain: A twenty-first century vision." Henry Jackson Society, 2019.

Seldon, Anthony (ed). *The Blair Effect: The Blair Government 1997–2001*. London: Little, Brown, 2001.

Seldon, Anthony. *Blair*. London: Free Press, 2004.

Seldon, Anthony. *Blair Unbound*. London: Simon and Schuster, 2007.

Seldon, Anthony and Guy Lodge. *Brown at 10*. London: Biteback, 2010.

Seldon, Anthony and Raymond Newell. *May at 10*. London: Biteback, 2019.

Seldon, Anthony and Peter Snowdon, *Cameron at 10*. London: William Collins, 2015.

Sen, Amartya. *Development as Freedom*. Oxford: Oxford University Press, 1999.
Sen, Amartya. *The Idea of Justice*. London: Allen Lane, 2009.
Sharma, Ruchir. *Breakout Nations*. London: Allen Lane, 2012.
Short, Clare. *An Honourable Deception?* London: Free Press, 2004.
Smil, Vaclav. *Numbers Don't Lie: 71 Things You Need to Know About the World*. London: Viking, 2020.
Stewart, Graham. *Bang! A History of Britain in the 1980s*. London: Atlantic Books, 2013.
Stewart, Rory. *Politics on the Edge: A Memoir from Within*. London: Jonathan Cape, 2023.
Sunstein, Cass. *Simpler: The Future of Government*. Simon and Schuster, 2013.
Thomas-Symonds, Nick. *Harold Wilson: The Winner*. London: Weidenfeld & Nicholson, 2022.
Treffgarne, Carew B.W. "Joined-up government? Insights from education during DFID's first decade." *International Journal of Educational Development*, 68, 45–55, ISSN 0738–0593, 2019. doi.org/10.1016/j.ijedudev.2019.04.009
Valters, Craig and Brendan Whitty. *The Politics of the Results Agenda in DFID 1997–2017*. London: Overseas Development Institute, 2017.
Vereker, John. "Blazing the trail: Eight years of change in handling international development." *Development Policy Review*, 20, 133–140, 2002. doi.org/10.1111/1467-7679.00161
Vereker, John. "The search for the silver bullet." *Commonwealth Journal of International Affairs*, 109(1), 42–51, 2020. doi.org/10.1080/00358533.2020.1717092
Wallace-Wells, David. *The Uninhabitable Earth: Life After Warming*. Tim Duggan Books, 2019.
Wolf, Martin, "Sweep away the barriers to growth." *Financial Times*, 5 October 2004.
Wolf, Martin, "Poor countries debt is fuelling destitution." *Financial Times*, 20 December 2023.
Woods, Ngaire. *The Globalisers: The IMF, the World Bank and Their Borrowers*. Ithaca: Cornell University Press, 2006.

INDEX

Page numbers in **bold** indicate tables; page numbers in *italics* indicate figures.

abortion services, 139
Actis, 80, 146–147
Afghanistan, 95, 102, 120–121, 235, 242
Africa, 27–29, 32, 43, 46–47, 159; asylum seekers, 48; country offices, 50; debt levels, 28; Ebola outbreak, 193–194; economic growth, 96, 196; G8 commitments, 123–125; inflation and GDP per capita growth, 28, *83*; private enterprise, 80
Africa Conflict Prevention Pool, 60
Ahmed, Masood, 109, 253
aid:
    budget, 41, 90, 116, 164, 181–188, **182**, **221**; budget cuts, 228, 231, 235–236; changing priorities, 217–218; versus development, 20–21; effectiveness, 76, 116, 118, 127–129, 153; and foreign policy, 228; general budget support (GBS), 130–134, 153; increases, 101–103, **103**; levels, 72–74, *73*; misuse of funds, 15–16, 225; as moral necessity, 13; one-off projects, 45; resistance to, 11, 225–226; tied aid, 48, 74–76
Aid and Trade Provision, 11, 32, 33–34, 41
Alexander, Douglas, 98, 99–100, 120, 156, 232, 242; as Secretary of State for International Development, 105–108, 128
Amos, Valerie, 105
Anderson, Michael, 98, 205
Annan, Kofi, 68
Arab Spring, 161, 168
arms sales, 15, 57–58, 60–63
Ashdown, Paddy, 171
asylum seekers, 48, 63–64, 235
Atwood, Brian, 66

BAE Systems, 62–63
Balkan wars, 58, 60
Banda, Hastings, 135

INDEX

Bangladesh, 136, 252
Barber, Michael, 192
Barder, Owen, 56–57
Barrientos, Armando, 142
Barton, Tamsyn, 241
Benn, Hilary, 50, 97, 100, 101, 114–116, 140, 150, 175, 232, 240;
   as Secretary of State for International Development, 105–106, 121–122, 134
Beynon, Jonathan, 133
bilateral programmes, 44–45, 131, 171–172
Bill and Melinda Gates Foundation, 78, 138, 141–142, 190
Black Wednesday 1992, 14
Blair, Tony:
   commitment to development, 23–24, 32, 39, 89, 119, 123–124; first Cabinet, 7, 24; humanitarian response, 60; private enterprise, 80; record on aid and development, 26
Blue Book, 111–112, 179
Blunkett, David, 64
Bone, Peter, 186
Bottomley, Arthur, 10, 12
Bourn, John, 51–52
branding, 117
Bretton Woods institutions, 68, 71
Brexit, 213, 220, 242, 255
bribery, 81. *See also* corruption
Britain in the World, 17, 18, 23–24
British International Investments (BII), 237. *See also* Commonwealth Development Corporation (CDC)

Brown, Gordon, 14, 27, 36, 40–41, 44, 62, 67, 71, 72, 89, 98–99, 128, 150;
   commitment to development, 119, 124; on education, 134–135, 137; health initiatives, 140; impact on financial crisis, 126–127; as Prime Minister, 105–106, 112
budget allocations, 36–38, 40–47, **42**, 58, 71, 72, 79–80, 101–104, **101**, 170, 174, 180, **271–277**
budget cuts, 228, 231, 235–236
budget support *See* general budget support (GBS)
Buhari, Muhammadu, 202
Burt, Alistair, 214
Bush, George W., 72, 105, 123–124

Calvert, Richard, 7
Camdessus, Michael, 67, 71
Cameron, David, 3, 97, 155, 167, 230;
   approach to development, 167–168; on corruption, 201–202; health initiatives, 188–190
Campbell, Alastair, 7–8, 25, 247
Carter, Jimmy, 189–190
cash transfers, 142–143
Cassidy, Eamon, 112
Castle, Barbara, 10, 12, 20–21
Center for Global Development, 65, 141, 183, 238
Central Emergency Response Fund (CERF), 122–123
Chakrabarti, Suma, 50, 108–111, 115, 134, 154
Chalker, Lynda, 14, 165
Champion, Sarah, 227, 232, 241, 247
charities, 90, 137

334

INDEX

Chevening Scholarship programme, 41
China, 83, 160
Clare's New World, 25
Clarke, Tom, 17
Clegg, Nick, 167
Cleverly, James, 245
climate change, 33, 65, 100, 123, 127, 161, 203–205, 217, 223, 258
coalition government, 164
Coles, John, 24
Commonwealth Development Corporation (CDC), 32, 79–80, 146–147, 184, 196–197, 222, 237
Commonwealth Education Fund, 137
conflicts, responses and prevention, 58–61, 120–121, 194–195, 243. *See also* Iraq War
Conservative party:
  approach to development, 8–13, 90, 97, 106, 155, 217–220; coalition government, 164; election 2010, 164; political problems 1997, 14–16
Cook, Robin, 16, 17, 24, 30, 62
corruption, 62–63, 81, 100, 117, 179, 201–203
country offices, 111–112, 149
Coverdale, Alan, 45
COVID-19 pandemic, 217, 223–224, 240, 244, 258
Criterion 8, 61
cross-party consensus, 155–156
culture of department, 54–55, 111, 114–115

Daily Express, 225
Daily Mail, 225
Daily Telegraph, 225–226, 241
Darfur crisis, 122
deaths by conflicts, 59
debt relief, 28, 67, 70–72, 102, 124, 126
Democratic Republic of Congo, 30, 179, 223
Department for International Trade, 226
Department for the Environment, 104
Department of Trade and Industry, 22, 33, 75
Dercon, Stefan, 168–169
Development Assistance Committee (DAC), 18–22, 34, 40, 51, 54, 64, 76, 98, 150–151, 156, 197, 235, 241–242;
  Development Goals, **19**, 32–33, 36–38, 41, 66–69
Dinham, Martin, 163–164
disasters, major, 30, 58–60, 90, 122–124. *See also* conflicts, responses and prevention; humanitarian response
Doha Development Round, 58
donor flags, 117
donors, 45–47, 74, 78, 98, 128–129, 134, 139–141, 153, 160, 185, 190
Duncan, Alan, 155, 166, 231
Dusu, Andra, 133
Dyer, Nick, 227, 245

East Kilbride office, 110
Ebola outbreak, 193–194, 223
economic improvement, 82–84, 96, 159–160, 195–198
Economist, The, 27, 39–40

INDEX

education, 134–137, 153, 172–173, 191–193, 237, 253
Emerging Africa Infrastructure Fund, 80
Enhanced Structural Adjustment Facility, 71
Environmental Audit Committee, 65
environmental policy, 33, 65. *See also* climate change
equality, 19, 199–200, 206, 258
Ethiopia, 30, 58, 124, 131, 153
European Commission Humanitarian Office (ECHO), 122
European Exchange Rate Mechanism, 14
European Union (EU), 2, 57–58, 72–73, 90
Everything But Arms (EBA) scheme, 57–58
Extractive Industries Transparency Initiative, 81
Eyben, Ros, 53

Fabian Society, 20
family planning, 189
famine, 30, 58, 124, 193
Featherstone, Lynne, 166, 199
financial crisis, 96, 98, 106, 126
Financial Times, 105, 226
flag branding, 117
Ford, Vicky, 243
Foreign, Commonwealth and Development Office (FCDO), 227, 234, 236–237, 239–240, 242–243, 245, 262
Foreign Office, 7–11, 22–23, 24, 41, 49, 56, 60, 104, 183, 226
Forsyth, James, 228
Foster, Mick, 46

Foster, Mike, 107
Foulkes, George, 49–50
fragile states, 101–103, 113, 136, 168
fraud losses, 180. *See also* corruption

Gaddafi, Muammar, 168
gagging clauses, 236
Gates, Bill, 140, 181. *See also* Bill and Melinda Gates Foundation
Gaza, 249, 258
gender equality, 19, 199–200, 206, 258
general budget support (GBS), 130–134, 153
genocide, 30
Ghani, Ashraf, 202
Gill, Peter, 25
girls *See* women and girls
Global Alliance on Vaccines and Immunization (Gavi), 78, 141, 188
Global Conflict Prevention Pool, 60
globalisation, 38, 39, 259
global warming, 161, 259
governance, quality of, 33, 201–203
Green Climate Fund, 204
Greenhill, Robert, 88
Greening, Justine, 166, 170, 173, 177–179, 181, 198, 199–200, 213–214
Greenstock, Jeremy, 69
Greenwood, Anthony, 10, 12
Guardian, The, 112, 226
Guinea Worm disease, 189–190
Gulrajani, Nilima, 102

Hague, William, 166
Hamilton, Neil, 15

336

INDEX

Hart, Judith, 10–11
health initiatives, 78–79, 138–142, 153, 188–190
Heavily Indebted Poor Countries (HIPC) framework, 28
Herfkens, Eveline, 73
Hill, Christopher, 57
HIV/AIDS, 78–79, 139–140, 190
Home Office, 64
Hughes, Sam, 183
Hulme, David, 70
Human Development Index (HDI), 84, 85, 133, 152, *152*, 208, 223–224, 251, *270*
humanitarian responses, 58–60, 90, 121–124, 161, 193–195, 199, 223–224, 237, 243. *See also* conflicts, responses and prevention; disasters, major
hung Parliament, 164
Hunt, Jeremy, 244, 246
Hurd, Douglas, 15, 23
Hussein, Saddam, 90, 95
Hutcheon, Joy, 199
hydrocarbons, 81
hysteresis, 220

Imfundo, 136
immigration, 63–64
immunisation programmes, 78, 115, 139–141, 188–190
Independent Commission on Aid Impact (ICAI), 175–177, 183, 192, 197, 200, 202, 204, 227, 235, 241
India, 41, 50, 252
Indian Ocean tsunami 2004, 122–123

inequality, 199–200. *See also* equality
infant mortality, 140, 142, 223, 252–253, *269*
inflation, 27–28, *28*, 82–83, *83*, 126
International Aid Transparency Initiative, 177
International Development (Gender Equality) Act 2014, 199–200
International Development Act 1980, 32
International Development Act 2002, 48, 64, 183, 221, 241
International Development Association, 42
International Environmental Transformation Fund, 104
International Finance Facility for Immunisation (IFFIm), 140–141
International Monetary Fund (IMF), 11, 23, 67, 70–71, 127
International Women's Day, 199
Investor in People benchmark, 54
Iraq War, 24, 26, 61, 89–90, 95, 101, 105, 120
Ireton, Barrie, 79
Israel, 249

Johnson, Boris, 2, 214, 217, 226–228, 243–244
Joint Aid Policy Committee, 22
Journal of International Development, 34
Judd, Frank, 10–11

Kampfner, John, 24
Ki-moon, Ban, 126, 205
Kosovo crisis, 60, 89

INDEX

Labour party:
  approach to development, 8–13, 89–90, 249; election 2010, 164; immigration policy, 64; internal politics, 16–18; landslide win 1997, 14
Lammy, David, 247
Lestor, Joan, 17, 25
Lewis, Ivan, 107
Liberal Democrats, 34;
  coalition government, 164; election 2010, 164
Libya, 168
life expectancy, 3, 29, 84, 140, 152, 190, 208, 223–224, 252, 268
Live Aid, 124, 155
'long peace,' 160

Maastricht Treaty 1993, 15
Macdonald, Simon, 231
Major, John, 14–15, 70
Make Poverty History campaign, 124, 154
malaria, 78–79, 139, 141, 190
Malik, Moazzam, 97
Malik, Shahid, 107
Malloch Brown, Mark, 69
malnourishment, 29
Mandela, Nelson, 134
Manning, Richard, 47, 69, 109, 116, 180
Maxwell, Simon, 118
May, Theresa, 199, 213, 215, 220
McVey, Esther, 225–226
Meacher, Michael, 17
Merron, Gillian, 107
Michalopoulos, Costas, 74, 206
Middle East, 48, 101, 109, 159, 168

migration, 33, 63
Miliband, David, 16
Millennium Development Goals (MDGs), 66–69, 72, 84, 86, 95, 99, 115, 126, 132–133, 135, 137–139, 153–154, 161–163, 172, 205–206, 253
Ministry of Defence, 60–61
Mitchell, Andrew, 97, 99, 108, 155, 230–231, 243–246;
  as Secretary of State for International Development, 164–167, 170–175, 181, 184, 195–196, 205
Mitchell, Ian, 183
mobile money, 143, 145
Monterrey conference 2002, 73, 76
Montserrat, 59–60
Moore, Michael, 186
Mordaunt, Penny, 214, 216–217
mortality rate *See* infant mortality
M-Pesa, 145
Mullin, Chris, 50, 214, 226–227
multilateral agencies, 149–151, 172, 188
multilateral effectiveness framework (MEFF), 77
Multilateral Organisation Performance Assessment Network, 78
Museveni, Yoweri, 135

Nandy, Lisa, 248–250
national curriculum, 90
National Security Council, 167
nongovernmental organizations (NGOs), 34, 44, 121, 150–151, 185, 236
Northover, Lindsay, 166

INDEX

Obama, Barack, 127
O'Brien, Stephen, 166, 201–202
O'Donnell, Gus, 114, 118
Office for the Coordination of Humanitarian Affairs, 122
official development assistance (ODA), 43, 60, 64, 73, **101**, *125*, 182–183, **182**, 197–198, 215–216, 221–222, **221**, 235, 240, **271–277**
oil prices, 83
Organisation for Economic Co-operation and Development (OECD), 18, 43, 64, 98; Convention on the Bribery of Foreign Public Officials, 81
Osborne, George, 167, 181
Overseas Development Administration, 7–8, 11, 15, 17, 21–23, 44–45, 50, 53, 55, 58, 180, 233, 255–256
Overseas Development and Co-operation Act 1980, 15, 47
Overseas Development Institute, 118, 121–122, 249
overseas development ministers 1964–79, *10*
overseas offices *See* country offices
Oxfam, 133, 217

Pakistan, 102, 192
Palestine, 101
partner countries, **42**, 43–47, 130–132
Patel, Priti, 190, 213–214, 216
Patten, Chris, 165
Paulson, Hank, 105
peacekeeping, 65
performance management, 115–118

Pergau dam, 15–16, 32, 48, 74
polio, 190
population growth, 252
poverty:
  defining, 29; and economic development, 13; goals for, 19–20, 66–69; impacts of, 2; reduction, 13, 22, 39, 43–44, 48, 84, 96, 128, 131, 151–152, 161, 169, 208, 217–218, 224, 237–238, 246, 252–253
poverty line, 2–3, 29, 43, 142, 251
Poverty Reduction and Growth Facility, 71
Powell, Jonathan, 7, 24
Power, Samantha, 240
Prentice, Reginald, 10–11
private enterprise, 79–81, 144–147, 195–198
Private Eye, 147
Private Infrastructure Development Group, 80, 86
Prosperity Fund, 183
Public Service Agreements, 36–38, **36–37**, 115
Publish What You Fund, 177

quality assurance, 178–179

Raab, Dominic, 232, 242
Rapid Social Response Programme, 143
Rawnsley, Andrew, 125
recession, 27
refugees, 64, 182, 235. *See also* asylum seekers
reproductive health care, 189, 237
reputation, 51–52, 118, 241, 247, 259
research activities, 147–149

339

INDEX

resource allocation, 22, 32, 36–38, 40–49, 100–103, 148–149, 174–175, 204
Ricketts, Peter, 167
Ritchie, Hannah, 163
Roser, Max, 163
Rwanda, 30, 153, 165
Rycroft, Matthew, 220–221, 227

Safaricom, 145
Sawers, John, 126
Scott Inquiry, 15
sector specialists, 53, 110–111, 149
Sedwill, Mark, 233
Seely, Bob, 226
self-appraisal, 116
Serious Fraud Office, 62
sexual violence, 139, 217
Shafik, Minouche, 109, 132, 154, 156, 163
Sharif, Shehbaz, 192
Sharma, Alok, 214
Short, Clare:
    appointment and values, 7–9, 17–25; on education, 137–138; humanitarian response, 60; on nongovernmental organizations (NGOs), 150; resignation, 24, 26, 72, 89, 119; as Secretary of State for International Development, 25–26, 30–35, 38–41, 45, 47–51, 55–56, 62, 65–70, 73–81, 87, 90, 104–105, 128, 153, 174, 254. *See also Clare's New World*
Smith, Adam, 75
Smith, Gayle, 240
social protection, 142–144

Somalia, 193
South Asia, 29, 43, 159
Special Drawing Rights, 126–127
Spectator, The, 225, 228
staffing, 52–54, 112–114, 170–171, 239–240
Starmer, Keir, 246–247
Stern, Nick, 124, 127
Stewart, Rory, 214, 217, 247
Sugg, Liz, 214
Sun, The, 7, 24–25, 118, 225
Sunak, Rishi, 228, 236, 245
Sustainable Development Goals (SDGs), 217
Syria, 168, 191, 194–195

Taliban, 95, 121, 235, 242
Tanzanian air traffic control scandal, 62–63
terrorism, 98
Thatcher, Margaret, 11, 13, 21
Thomas, Gareth, 106–107, 117, 123, 140
tied aid, 48, 74–76
Times, The, 118
Trade Mark Southern Africa (TMSA), 175
trade policy, 13, 20, 33–34, 57–58
transparency, 176–177, 236
Treasury, 11, 36–38, 40–42, 44, 80, 102, 167, 181–182, 183–185, 218, 228, 236
Treasury, Parliament and the National Audit Office (NAO), 51–52
Trevelyan, Anne-Marie, 214, 217–218
tropical diseases, 189–190. *See also malaria*

INDEX

Truss, Liz, 237, 242, 245
tuberculosis, 78–79, 139, 190
Tugendhat, Tom, 230

Uganda, 72, 135, 252
Ukraine, 221, 235, 243
United Nations (UN), 11, 149–150;
conference agreements, 18–19;
Millennium Development
Goals (MDGs), 66–69, 72, 84,
86, 95, 99, 115, 126, 132–133,
135, 137–139, 153–154,
161–163, 172, 205–206, 253;
Office for the Coordination of
Humanitarian Affairs, 122
Utstein group, 67–68, 70–72, 76, 128

vaccines, 78–79, 141–142, 188–189,
240. *See also* immunisation
programmes
Vadera, Shriti, 106–107
Vector Control Consortium, 141
Vereker, John, 7–8, 12–13, 21, 24,
35, 41, 47, 50, 55–56, 108
Vodafone, 145
Voluntary Service Overseas (VSO),
151

welfare dependency, 226
welfarism, 142
Wells, Bowen, 34
Wescott, Nick, 229
Whitehall, 56, 109;
environmental policy, 65; immigration and asylum, 63–64;
operating costs and staffing,
112–114; trade policy, 57–58

White Papers, 11, 13, 30–35, 38–40,
66, 74, 81, 96–97, 98–100, 128
Whitty, Chris, 148
Wickstead, Myles, 30
Wieczorek-Zeul, Heidemarie,
68, 73
Wilson, Harold, 10, 20
Winters, Alan, 126, 148
Wolfensohn, Jim, 39, 67
Wolfowitz, Paul, 105
women and girls, 195, 198–200, 216,
223, 237, 243, 255;
education, 135, 191–192, 199,
218, 237; reproductive health
care, 189, 237; rights of, 199.
See also gender equality
Wood, Richard, 10
World Bank, 67–68, 105, 149–150,
221;
Britain's status and representatives, 23, 33, 42; contributions, 149, 184; dollar a day
metric, 29; education initiative, 137–138; indebtedness,
70, 83; poverty line, 2–3;
World Development Indicators, 28
World Development Movement, 15
World Development Reports, 98
World Trade Organization, 38,
58, 99

Young Lives project, 149

Zambia, 134
Zenawi, Meles, 127
Zimbabwe, 85, 176

341